# PRAISE FOR *The Writer's Mentor*

"*The Writer's Mentor* recognizes the vast range of different—and often contradictory—experiences that writers have. Rather than provide one-size-fits-all solutions, Cathleen Rountree asks her readers the right questions to help them develop their own writing discipline."

—ELLEN BASS, AUTHOR OF *MULES OF LOVE* AND *THE COURAGE TO HEAL*

"If you yearn to write, but doubts haunt you, this book can be your ally. Both practical and poetic, it addresses your questions so that they can lead you forward rather than block your way. I wish I had had *The Writer's Mentor* when I started out in the writing life."

—CONNIE ZWEIG, PH.D., AUTHOR OF *MEETING THE SHADOW*
AND *ROMANCING THE SHADOW*

"*The Writer's Mentor* by Cathleen Rountree is an excellent, eminently practical introduction to the craft of writing, offering encouragement, support, and creative answers to many of the questions that preoccupy beginning writers."

—MARY MACKEY, AUTHOR OF *A GRAND PASSION*
AND *THE YEAR THE HORSES CAME*

"In *The Writer's Mentor,* highly creative writer Cathleen Rountree takes you by the hand and leads you into the soul of a writer and nurtures your every step. This book is an intimate journey into the spiritual and psychological world of writing, complete with valuable tips on the craft as well. A must for every writer's bookshelf."

—GAIL MCMEEKIN, AUTHOR OF *THE 12 SECRETS*
*OF HIGHLY CREATIVE WOMEN* AND *THE POWER OF POSITIVE CHOICES*

"This is Cathleen Rountree at her best. She has written a literate, multifaceted, and fascinating guide to the daily challenges that face every writer. Writing is a solitary occupation. Ms. Rountree gives her readers the gift of companionship, inspiration, and the accumulated wisdom of many mentors, each bringing a lifetime of experience. We loved reading this book."

—HAL AND SIDRA STONE, PH.D., AUTHORS OF
*PARTNERING* AND *EMBRACING OUR SELVES*

"*The Writer's Mentor* is a 'canon of solutions' to the innumerable challenges writers face, whether we are writing poetry, fiction, or nonfiction. This candid "writer's midwife" is at once inspiring, unflinchingly practical, and rigorously honest. Rountree has produced a book destined to take its place on the shelves of writers at every stage of their careers."

—ROBERT SWARD, GUGGENHEIM FELLOW
AND AUTHOR OF *ROSICRUCIAN IN THE BASEMENT*

"Cathleen helped move my book proposal from a vague idea to a concrete document that impressed literary agents and publishers. She effectively conveys the nuts-and-bolts of proposal writing with a passion, creativity, and firsthand knowledge of the book business. As an author and the son of a bookseller, I can say with absolute certainty that Cathleen Rountree's advice will propel your writing career years ahead."

—RYAN COONERTY, AUTHOR OF
*ETCHED IN STONE: AMERICA'S ENDURING WORDS*

"Cathleen's book went straight to my heart. Its insights and gentle nudgings help us discover and nurture our creativity. It is inspiring for those of us who wish to express our deepest felt experience. This book is a gem for writers and non-writers alike."

—MARIA MATTIOLI, DIRECTOR OF B.A. PSYCHOLOGY PROGRAM,
JOHN F. KENNEDY UNIVERSITY

"Cathleen Rountree's experience as a writer and with writers comes together brilliantly in this book… personal stories and important questions combine to create an enriching way to explore the writing life."

—JUDY ROSE, DIRECTOR OF HUMANITIES,
UNIVERSITY OF CALIFORNIA SANTA CRUZ, EXTENSION

"Quite an original approach to subduing one's demons and mastering the difficult art of writing! Cathleen Rountree conspires ('breathes with') her readers, leads them down the step-by-step path to successful self-expression, and, 'like a midwife,' supports the birthing process of each individual voice via its most natural and organic process. Her wonderful use of contemporary films to illustrate and invoke the Muse adds power and breadth to an already fascinating story of her own experience of becoming a writer, and then a 'writer's mentor.'"

—VICKI NOBLE, CO-CREATOR OF THE MOTHERPEACE TAROT,
AUTHOR OF *SHAKTI WOMAN* AND *THE DOUBLE GODDESS*

"Cathleen Rountree has the gift for guiding others in translating the lives we can imagine into the lives we actually live. This is a book for writers, artists, and teachers who want to bring greater intention, the wisdom born of self-knowledge, and creativity to our daily lives. Cathleen clearly and carefully guides us to give those aspirations roots, to ground them in the world so that they can blossom where others can share them. Any of us who try to live this way know how challenging it is, and how lonely it can sometimes be. Cathleen offers us a companion in the garden: supportive, gentle, determined, and humorous."

—RANDI GRAY KRISTENSEN, M.F.A., PH.D.,
ADJUNCT PROFESSOR, GEORGE WASHINGTON UNIVERSITY

"Cathleen Rountree is a gifted mentor in every sense of the word. She possesses the dual gifts of being a professional writer herself and also being a talented writer's mentor, which means she is able to articulate the unique challenges of the writing profession and offer creative strategies for facing these challenges. Cathleen Rountree is one of those rare people who can both do and teach, and each of these gifts strengthens the other."

—KATHERINE SPILDE, PH.D., SENIOR RESEARCH ASSOCIATE, HARVARD UNIVERSITY

"*The Writer's Mentor* reveals the courage needed as a writer to face daily solitude, the silent muse, the truncated thought, a resistant vocabulary. But the deepening into one's own soul that writing affords is worth the price of admission. Her reflections on writing reveal that writers often live on the edge or the lip of life's motion. From such a perch they, like she, are able to see more broadly and more deeply what the rest of us only glimpse. The writing life is a way, she reveals, for each of us to discover ourselves through written expression."

—DENNIS PATRICK SLATTERY, PH.D., PROFESSOR, PACIFICA GRADUATE INSTITUTE
AND AUTHOR OF *THE WOUNDED BODY: REMEMBERING THE MARKINGS OF FLESH*

"In her new book, Cathleen Rountree draws on her own experience as well as the wisdom of other writers to illuminate all aspects of the creative process. This refreshing work provides new and seasoned authors alike with their own personal 'writer's mentor.' Rountree's practical, thoughtful guide will inspire writers to approach the blank page with renewed enthusiasm."

—MARK CHIMSKY, EDITOR OF NATIONAL BESTSELLERS

## PRAISE FOR *Cathleen Rountree's Previous Books*

"*On Women Turning 40* has come at a moment in time when, more than ever before, women are actively looking for positive models for acting in fullness—And never has our society needed this fullness as much as now!"

—JUSTINE TOMS, EXECUTIVE DIRECTOR, NEW DIMENSIONS RADIO

"I would have a boxful of these books [*On Women Turning 40*]. I would give them as presents to all the women I know."

—*NEW AGE JOURNAL*

"The women presented in *On Women Turning 50: Celebrating Midlife Discoveries* give an inspiring sample of what women in their fifties really are. . . . They speak with force and honesty about careers, family, sex, and menopause."

—*BLOOMSBURY REVIEW*

"One of the strongest attractions of *On Women Turning 50* is its wealth of lore drawn from the interviews. It contains a motherlode of insight and advice from older sisters, providing clues for successful transitions into the second half of life."

—*WOMEN LIBRARY WORKERS JOURNAL*

"*On Women Turning 60* is an enlightening, entertaining, and inspiring collection of women's voices raised in defiance, not muted in compromise."

—*BOOKLIST*

# THE WRITER'S MENTOR

# THE WRITER'S MENTOR

## A Guide to Putting Passion on Paper

Answers to the Most Frequently Asked Questions about Writing

## Cathleen Rountree

CONARI PRESS
Berkeley, California

Conari Press books are distributed by Publishers Group West.

Cover Illustration and Design: *Stephanie Dalton Cowan*
Book Design: *Lisa Buckley*
Author Photo: *Mike De Boer*

**Library of Congress Cataloging-in-Publication Data**
Rountree, Cathleen.
 The writer's mentor : a guide to putting passion on paper : answers to the most frequently asked questions about writing / Cathleen Rountree.
     p. cm.
Includes bibliographical references and index.
 ISBN 1-57324-570-4
 1. Authorship. 2. Creative writing. I. Title.
 PN147 .R67 2002                                                    2001007518
 808'.02—dc21

Printed in Canada.
02 03 04 TC 10 9 8 7 6 5 4 3 2 1

This book is dedicated to Pat Ward Zimmerman,

lifelong friend and mentor.

In memory of Sienna Rountree.

I am not a writer, except when I write.
—*JUAN CARLOS ONETTI*

If you practice an art faithfully, it will make you wise.
—*WILLIAM SAROYAN*

# The Writer's Mentor Contents

—

# CHAPTER 1

# INTRODUCTION

To live in the world of creation—to get into
it—to frequent it and haunt it—
to think intensely and fruitfully—to woo
combinations and inspirations into being
by a depth and continuity of attention and
meditation—this is the only thing.
—*HENRY JAMES*

If you speak with passion, many of us will
listen. We need stories to live, all of us.
We live by story. Yours enlarges the circle.
—*RICHARD RHODES*

Jean Cocteau, the French poet, novelist, playwright, painter, and filmmaker, once was asked what he would save first if his house caught fire. The surrealist and everyday madman answered, "The fire." What I think he was saying is that in both our professional and our personal lives, what counts is passion—the fire. When I first began thinking about writing *The Writer's Mentor,* this anecdote sprang to life for me because so much about writing has to do with passion: the drive and desire, the love and commitment, the turbulence and torment, the zeal and mania, the choice and resolution.

In a gorgeous essay that won first place in a writing contest in California in 1999, Leslie Cole refers to writing in the third millennium as an "Erotic Act." "The sound of a pen scratching out a thought on rough paper will be a major turn-on. . . . The motion of a pen as it moves across paper will be the new tango, and the curve and fall of a graceful script will be compared to water falling over stones. . . . It will be a map, a choreography of what is wished for."

The term *passion* may denote any feeling or emotion, especially that of a powerful or compelling nature (such as desire, anger, jealousy, devotion, or inspiration). To put passion on paper is first to fully embody an emotion and second to tame it through words. But in its essential form, *passion* means "to suffer," as in the passion or sufferings of Christ on the cross and their subsequent revivification in "passion plays." (A form of playing with passion?) It is in this conjunction of meanings that I refer to "passion."

"Writing is easy," Madeleine L'Engle, the author of more than fifty books of fiction and nonfiction, once told me—herself paraphrasing the famous, now deceased baseball writer Red Smith—"all you have to do is sit down at the typewriter and sweat blood." I have heard similar aphorisms from other writers during many years of interviewing such accomplished writers as Doris Lessing, Isabel Allende, Fay Weldon, Natalie Goldberg, Christopher Lehman-Haupt, Maxine Hong Kingston, Ursula LeGuin, Gloria Steinem, Jean Shinoda Bolen, Colette Dowling, Andrew Sarris, Carolyn Heilbrun, Deena Metzger, Molly Haskell, Oliver Stone, Tess Gallagher, Betty Friedan, Susan Griffin, Marion Woodman, and Riane Eisler. Nevertheless, those of us who are drawn to writing continue to "sweat blood" while creating art. We have a love/hate relationship to writing. We put our passion on paper.

No, good writing does not come easily. It was Nathaniel West who wrote, "Easy reading is damned hard writing." In an interview with John Berendt, the author of *Midnight in the Garden of Good and Evil*, he remembers an occasion thirty years before, when he was sent by *Esquire* magazine to record a conversation between novelists William Styron and James Jones. Styron asked Jones how he felt when each day he sat down to write. "It's like learning how to write all over again!" Styron agreed. And the two proceeded to commiserate about what hard work writing is.

Writing *is* hard work, and it's terrifying, to boot, but if you are compelled to "think intensely and fruitfully" and to express those thoughts in words, it can also be one of the most rewarding ways to engage with yourself and the world. With much effort and good fortune you may reach the juncture in your writing life at which you *must* write; because, if you don't, as Gail Sher describes in *One Continuous Mistake,* "You will feel something terribly important is missing from your life—and nothing, including prayer, meditation, exercise, money or love will make up for it."

Writing takes a single-minded effort. An effort that includes believing in yourself (not in those internal saboteurs: self-doubt and uncertainty); trusting your own instincts (first learning how to *access* those instincts); becoming comfortable with the uncomfortable (the complicated, grueling, solitary, sometimes boring) nature of writing; and making the existential choice to face that insolent blank page every day. No one (except you) has any stake in whether you write or not. It's simply a choice that you make again and again. As Richard Ford has written, "Writing is indeed dark and lonely, but no one really has to do it. . . . You can stop anywhere, anytime, and no one will care or ever know." And the sad truth is that you must be willing to write poorly in order to improve. (And even then there are no guarantees.) "Nothing is art at first," wrote Walter Mosley.

My interest in writing and publishing began when I was thirty-eight years old. For the sake of love, I'd uprooted myself to Los Angeles from Berkeley, where I had lived for nearly twenty years. I'd attended the University of California (receiving degrees in History of Art and Practice of Fine Art, Painting) as a single mother, raised an only child, and owned and operated a restaurant. I found that, away from my familiar lifestyle and friends in Berkeley, I had to re-invent myself for my new life in LA.

Never before had I thought much about age, but suddenly, in Southern California, I felt obsolete and old. During that summer of 1986, I struggled to find people toward whom I felt some affinity. In my quest for role models, I soon discovered that there were countless other women on the same search—a search for identity and creative expression. As it happened, I found many of them through a woman who was to become a close friend and my writing mentor, Deena Metzger, who lived in the mountains northeast of Los Angeles in Topanga Canyon. I began making my weekly treks to Deena's Wednesday evening writers' group. That's where it all began.

From conception to publication, it took me five years to believe in myself enough and to develop the necessary discipline to complete my first book, *On Women Turning 40: Coming into Our Fullness*. I received at least fifteen rejections from publishers, but I persisted because I knew that *On Women Turning 40* was a worthwhile project. The writing of it had become my lifeline to myself and simultaneously to something—thankfully—beyond myself. I became a crusader, and my cause made my life meaningful. During my early forties, while writing that first book, both my father and my maternal grandmother died. The death of two immediate family members brought the gift of an awareness of mortality along with a sense of urgency into my life. I knew that the moment was now—not "later." By the time the forties book was off and running, I was hooked on the writing life. And since then I have written eight books, including the one you are now reading.

During the course of writing this book I went through a long period of grieving for my beloved companion, Sienna, a ten-year-old Springer Spaniel who within two weeks had gone from a robust health and spirit to physically excruciating pain and an all-too-sudden death at high noon on Good Friday. After Sienna's passing, my old demon depression resurfaced with a vengeance, and, in addition, I had one physical ailment after another—from foot surgery and severe back pains to pneumonia. I look back on that year as "lost."

Writing became impossible for me—call it fear of writing, procrastination, resistance—I could not, would not, write. As I missed one deadline after another (June to August to October and finally back to June, again—of the following year), both my agent and my editor supported me as best they could by repeatedly extending the projected due date of my manuscript.

Leslie, my steadfast editor, continued to assure me that the process of writing this book would, like a wayward migrating monarch, find its own course. The creative process does have its own agenda, and what we as writers can do is trust and hold a spirit of gratitude for being able to do this work.

It feels important to share this information with you, the reader because whenever you cannot/will not write—for whatever reason— just know that I and many other writers have been there, too. And as I am writing these words for you, I am also writing them for myself. For every day I face at least one of the questions that organize the chapters of this book. The internal wrestling that takes place when we have to learn "how to write all over again" continues each day.

There *is* a healing power of the pen, to which I can personally attest. And, as scientific proof, the *New York Times* recently published an article about a study done at the State University of New York-Stony Brook. Seventy participants suffering from asthma or arthritis were asked to write about the most stressful experience they had under-gone, such as the death of a loved one, a problem in a relationship, or a serious accident. The results showed that almost half of the writers experienced a lessening of their symptoms for several months after the study took place. But they also found that in order for the relief to continue, writing a minimum of four days a week, fifteen minutes a day, is necessary. Novelist Russell Banks summed up a similar per-sonal experience, when in an interview he said, "Writing in some way saved my life. It brought to my life a kind of order and discipline."

Through my work as a writer's mentor and writing consult-ant—a sort of midwife to other people's creative projects—one of the most important principles I've learned is that writing is a two-person job. The dilemma inherent in the act of writing is that it is an essentially solitary endeavor. And yet what every writer—budding or otherwise—longs for is someone to assuage their loneliness, caress their hand, embrace their psyche, satisfy each of their questions as their fingers jitterbug across a 1940 Royal Deluxe typewriter, pum-mel a computer keyboard, or compose with a gold-embossed Water-man on rose-scented mauve paper.

Short of bringing cappuccino and Godiva chocolates to you personally, it is my goal—as a published author who has extensively interviewed several dozen writers and has had many years' experience as a facilitator of writing groups and as a coach and consultant in my own Writer's Mentor service to other aspiring writers—to offer a comforting voice, an inspiring presence, and an experienced guide during your many hours of setting words on paper.

Friends, colleagues, students, and clients often ask me about my life as a full-time writer: what keeps me hooked after eight books, in spite of the endless hours, the financial struggles, the aloneness engendered by spending most of my waking hours in a room by myself, the uncertainty of knowing whether a publisher will be interested in any one of my proposed book ideas or—if they are—whether the reading public will buy it, and the necessity for self-invention with each new project. *The Writer's Mentor* is my canon of solutions to these many challenges.

The author of *All We Know of Heaven,* Brother Remy Rougeau, a Benedictine monk, said in an interview that "monks and writers lead very similar lives. We spend our best time in retreat from the world, anxious to make something of our rich experiences." It is this deep engagement with the world of ideas and feelings, the "depth and continuity of attention and meditation—this is the only thing" that keeps me coming back to the keyboard, attempting to understand and make sense of myself and the world around me.

And even having a keen familiarity of the economic uncertainty inherent in most writers' lives, I often remember what Clark Gable's character, Gay—in the 1960 film *The Misfits,* written by Arthur Miller—repeated to his drifter cowboy buddies when money got tight: "It beats wages." Yes, that and much, much more.

What would I save first if my house caught fire? Like Jean Cocteau, I would save the fire: my passion for putting words on paper.

∴ ∴

# How to use this book

My wish is that you will use this book in the way that is best suited to your individual needs. Of course, it is your option to read straight through from the introduction to the final chapter or to dip into chapter 5 when you "aren't in the mood to write" or chapter 9 when you find yourself procrastinating or chapter 12 when you begin to wonder what your goals are as a writer. My suggestion is to read quickly through the entire book—front to back—so that you have a feel for the content and style, and then to refer to specific questions as inspiration and/or a guide to help you through rough periods.

Chapters 2 through 12 are arranged in the order that people often approach the writing process:

*Chapter 2:* DIVINE INSPIRATION explores the nature of creativity and offers methods to stir your writer's imagination.

*Chapter 3:* THE WRITING ENVIRONMENT provides suggestions and support for creating the best possible environment to serve and encourage your writing pursuit.

*Chapter 4:* WHEN TO WRITE assesses the practicalities of writing and explores how to integrate the work habits that best suit your lifestyle.

*Chapter 5:* HOW gives examples of several writers' rituals for beginning the writing day and some pointers on what to do about days when you "don't feel like writing."

*Chapter 6:* THE CONTENT OF WRITING offers suggestions for deciding on what you want to write and what form it will take.

*Chapter 7:* WRITING AS A PRACTICE explores how to build your writer's "muscle," how to attain the state of "flow" in your writing, and how the act of putting passion on paper can be a process of self-discovery.

*Chapter 8:* PAGE FRIGHT proposes courage as an alternative to the paralyzing fear that most writers face as they stare at a blank page.

*Chapter 9:* WRITER'S BLOCK AND PROCRASTINATION perceives these seemingly twin tormentors as periods of gestation and incubation and part of your internal creative forces.

*Chapter 10:* THE CRAFT OF WRITING provides concrete methods for improving your descriptive writing through conceptualizing metaphors, developing an instinct for specificity, and sharpening your rewriting and revising skills.

*Chapter 11:* THE LONELINESS OF THE LONG-DISTANCE WRITER explores the physical—and sometimes emotional and spiritual—isolation inherent in the writing life and how to survive it.

*Chapter 12:* THE INNER LIFE OF THE WRITER probes the existential nature of the writing life and confronts issues faced by writers every day, such as commitment, financial expectation, contribution, and goals.

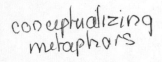
conceptualizing metaphors

The format of *The Writer's Mentor* is question and answer. The questions range from the most basic and practical concerns—How can I find time to write? Where should I write? What should I write? Should I share my writing with others?—to the more abstract, penetrating issues—Where does inspiration come from? What is a writing practice? How do I stay motivated? How do I face the blank page? These nearly sixty questions are those most often asked by my writing clients and students, and by beginning and intermediate writers in general. *The Writer's Mentor* provides an easy reference to these topics, such as when, where, what, why.

germane to
each

Each chapter is composed of several questions germane to that chapter's subject matter. Each question is followed by a quote relevant to the specific topic. The bulk of the text is the answer to the question. The response may be an example from my own writing practice and/or experience, an anecdote about one of my clients, an illustration taken from one of my interviews with a well-known writer, or from interviews and biographies I've read of other writers. For example, I will never forget when I asked Fay Weldon, the popular English novelist, where she gets her ideas for her novels (nearly thirty to date). Fay, who likens the creative process to giving birth, said cheerfully, "It reminds one that there is always more where that came from and there is never any shortage of ideas or the ability to create."

Every question-and-answer ends with the section "The Writer's Mentor Suggests . . . ," which provides practical advice and exercises to assist you in exploring the content of that particular question and answer.

Each chapter concludes with a brief essay on a film about the writing life in general or writers' lives in particular, related to the chapter topic. When I decided to include this feature, I reflected on my own moviegoing history and researched other movies about writing. Eventually, I composed a list of 112 films. The task of deciding which one to use for each chapter was daunting, but the films I have chosen are an assortment of both recent and classic (*Bridget Jones's Diary* and *My Brilliant Career*), American and foreign (*The Muse* and *Il Postino*), known and obscure (*The Shining* and *The Whole Wide World*).

At the end of the book is an extensive list of resources. Here you will find Books on Writing, Reference Works, and Web Sites.

Finally, it is my wish that this book will be a practical guide to dealing with the intellectual, emotional, psychological, spiritual, and even physical aspects of the writing life, and in addition to inspiration, practical advice, and motivation, that you will also find many mentors and many friends. For together all writers are members of a family that eclipses gender and genre and transcends cultures and languages, even as it extends beyond eras. The raison d'être of every writer is to explore, to discover, to experience, to express. We share a passion for putting words on paper, and in the words of that Mistress of Passion herself, the French writer Colette: "We write to taste life twice." May writing bring you challenges, surprises, understanding, and tolerance, just as, most assuredly, it will bring you equal shares of the pleasures and pains of living with passion.

---

# CHAPTER 2

# DIVINE INSPIRATION

## *Meeting the Muse*

Where do ideas come from?

What are some sources of inspiration?

How can I tap into my creativity?

Should I be reading other writers?
Should I try to emulate my favorite writers?

Can dreams inform my writing?

The Writer's Mentor at the Movies: *Shakespeare in Love*

DIVINE INSPIRATION: MEETING THE MUSE explores the world of creativity. In this chapter I distinguish between inspiration and imagination and offer examples of how the creative process functions in the lives of writers such as Joseph Heller, Amy Tan, and Pablo Neruda. The chapter includes practical exercises to increase your readiness for the writing Muse's arrival. You will learn how to track your thought process, purposely enter nonordinary states of awareness, and understand how writing is a 24-hour-a-day process—including dreamtime. Henry Miller, Jorge Luis Borges, and Elmore Leonard describe why reading is crucial to the writing life. And, in an essay on the film *Shakespeare in Love,* I illustrate how the creative process is brought lucently to life.

# Where do Ideas Come From?

> Often when I am very tired, just before
> going to bed, while washing my face and
> brushing my teeth, my mind gets very clear
> . . . and produces a line for the next day's
> work, or some idea way ahead. I don't get
> my best ideas while actually writing.
>
> —*JOSEPH HELLER*

Here, the late Joseph Heller accurately articulates my own experience. I love to walk. It is one of my favored activities for a variety of reasons. Being in nature brings me back to myself, renews and reconstructs me after the many different parts of life leave me fragmented. While walking on the beach and playing with my dog, I am carefree of concern about writing the next chapter or paying the overdue quarterly tax payment or mending the argument I had with my dearest friend. Dante Alighieri, poet of the *Divine Comedy,* believed that the natural impulse of the psyche is to be in motion. There is a direct relationship between the movement of the body and the creative process.

There seems a natural kinship between a relaxed physical and mental state and an unhampered influx of thoughts and images, sensory perceptions, and mental conceptualizations. I find an openness to and a delight in the unexpected juxtapositions and pairings that reveal themselves in free-flowing, unstressed moments.

I don't remember in particular any wondrous idea that has occurred to me while I was brushing my teeth, but in the shower . . . now you're talking. Some of my best ideas for stories, titles of books or articles, and breakthroughs to the other side of writer's block or ennui have come to me under running water—as well as *in* water, while swimming laps. As exciting, even galvanizing, as being intellectually stimulated in the shower can be, it has its drawbacks—such as the possibility of forgetting the fabulous solution that presented itself seemingly indelibly but which by the time I've stepped out of the

*creative process =*
*- a direct relationship
between movement of the
body & creative process*

*- a natural Kinship
between a relaxed
physical & mental state*

*+ an unhampered influx
of thoughts + images*

*- sensory perceptions
mental conceptual-
izations.*

shower and grabbed a towel has evaporated as quickly, and as permanently, as the water down the drain.

That's why I have an accoutrement of pens and compact tablets of paper strategically placed throughout my house. At this moment I can count five, and those are in a rather snug space consisting of an office/studio, a bedroom, a bathroom, and a loftlike arrangement that consolidates kitchen and dining and living rooms. I never have to leave one room for another in order to put my hands on writing paraphernalia.

In bed at night, before going to sleep, I can almost always rely on a gift from my subconscious for the current piece of writing that's resting on my desk. There is something magical, _if mystifying_ (because it is not readily available at one's will), about that hypnagogic state between sleep and awakening. During this state many a quandary for me—both personal and professional—has been effortlessly solved. Is it merely a cultural myth that Albert Einstein dreamt the solution to his theory of relativity?

In Clint Eastwood's 1999 film _Midnight in the Garden of Good and Evil_, John Cusack portrayed a journalist from Manhattan who traveled to Savannah, Georgia, to cover a story for a newspaper. In an amusing scene, when the reporter is getting ready to turn in for the night, he inserts into an audiocassette player a tape of recorded New York City street noise, which he brought along to help him sleep. I wonder if those ambient sounds also somehow generated ideas?

As part of _my doctoral program in Mythological Studies_ and _Depth Psychology_, for three and a half years I have made solitary drives from my home near Santa Cruz in Northern Central California to Santa Barbara, 300 miles south, to attend several days of classes each month. The drive takes anywhere from four and a half to six hours, depending on the stops I make. Over the years these monthly trips have provided exceptional opportunities for me to find solutions to concerns that have become lodged in a limbo of indecision or, worse, a hell of unknowing. Throughout my adult life, driving long distances has provided ideal circumstances for _enforced brainstorming and imaginative meanderings_. And—you guessed it—there are pen and pad of paper ever by my side in the car.

*imaginative meanderings*

*The more I think about the word "idea," the less idea I have what it means. Writers do say things like "That gives me an idea" or "I got the idea for that story when I had food poisoning in a motel in New Jersey."*

*I think this is a kind of shorthand use of "idea" to stand for the complicated, obscure, un-understood process of the conception and formation of what is going to be a story when it is written down.*

—URSULA LEGUIN

Aside from those obvious periods that invoke contemplation, there are numerous other opportunities for generating ideas, such as conversations with close friends or listening to the words of a popular song. My book *50 Ways to Meet Your Lover* was a positive take on Paul Simon's hit tune "50 Ways to Leave Your Lover." And after seeing a documentary on stealing, I was infused with a curiosity about this subject; for two months I researched various aspects of it for a nonfiction book project.

Films have also been consistent sources of inspiration for me, deepening my understanding of character development. For instance, after I had written my first book, *On Women Turning 40,* I taught a film studies class titled "In Full Flower" at the University of California-Santa Cruz, Extension. Through films and discussion we explored issues such as standing at the crossroads of life, sexuality and relationship, independence and interdependence, women and friendship, fear of and resistance to the physical changes of aging and our culture's obsession with youthfulness, and the spiritual awakening that often accompanies midlife development. We viewed foreign as well as American films.

In a scene in *Sunset Boulevard,* directed by Billy Wilder, the aging movie star Norma Desmond (played by the aging movie star Gloria Swanson) tries to seduce her much younger lover Joe Gilles, a Hollywood screenwriter (played by William Holden). Her attempts to engender a more youthful appearance are disheartening, even crushing, to any midlife woman watching the film. And this oppressive feeling is epitomized in Gilles's piercing statement to Desmond: "There's nothing tragic about being fifty—not unless you try to be twenty-five." This utterance inspired me to explore the lives of women in their fifties and the challenges, representations, the fait accompli conditions that are thrust upon women concerning the complexities of growing older.

The German film *Wings of Desire,* by Wim Wenders, posed the notion that perhaps ideas are subtly whispered into our ears by the denizens of disembodied angels who surround us in a transcendent soaring of fairytale possibilities. Could that be true? It's an unlikely but comforting whimsy.

Asking a specific question can also spark good ideas. John Irving and Stephen King often begin new novels with the premise of "What if . . ."? What if "vampires invaded a small New England village?" That question became *Salem's Lot.* What if "a young mother and her son became trapped in their stalled car by a rabid dog"? That became *Cujo.* One evening John Irving and his wife were watching news on television and heard about the first hand transplant in the United States. His wife asked, "What if the donor's widow demands visitation rights with the hand?" In the acknowledgments for *The Fourth Hand,* Irving says, "Every novel I've written has begun with a 'What if. . . .'" In this particular case he was obsessed by his wife's curious question and stayed awake all night, working on it as an idea for a novel. By breakfast he had the title and the sweep of the story.

> We are writers and we never ask one other where we get our ideas; we know we don't know.
> —STEPHEN KING

### The Writer's Mentor Suggests . . .

For a week or longer, consciously make an effort to observe your various activities throughout the day in order to discover the subtle operations of your mind. First of all, ask yourself: Do you have any quiet private time? If not, that may be something you will make an effort to arrange for yourself. Look for the sources of your ideas. Do they appear spontaneously to you when you are brushing your teeth, as they did for Joseph Heller, or do you find, as in my experience, that your mind becomes animated in the shower? Does nature become a partner in providing a magnetic attraction for ideas? Does long-distance—or short-distance—driving ignite your imagination? Do you live in a metropolitan area and simply can't think straight unless you are girdled by a crush of humankind, as was John Cusack's character in *Midnight in the Garden of Good and Evil?* See what works for you.

Think of this exercise as a form of exploring, to find out how you may become a more efficient idea gatherer or idea generator. Keep a running log of all that you chance upon and become aware of. Describe in detail your thought process. When a certain idea came to you, say, to write an essay about neighbor-rage (an extension of road- and sidewalk-rage), was it after a neighborhood dog awakened you— again—at three o'clock in the morning, or when you pulled up to your house and, once again, the next door neighbor's car was blocking your driveway? As expeditiously as possible, when an idea occurs to you, list where you were, what you were doing, how you were feeling. Did the idea come full-blown, or was there a process of development? What prompted the idea? A movie you were watching, an article from this morning's newspaper, a snatch of overheard conversation? (One day while dressing in the locker room of my local gym, I expropriated a fragment of conversation—"Hi Judy," one woman said to another. "I haven't seen you in ages; are you still married?"—for a book I was writing at the time, *The Heart of Marriage: Discovering the Secrets of Enduring Love.* I had been struggling with how to approach the issue of divorce, and I actually used this quote as the lead.)

Eudora Welty said she discovered stories in daily life. "Long before I wrote stories, I listened for stories. Listening for them is something more acute than listening to them."

How does writing about this process affect the shape of the new idea? Does it clarify it, expand it? This exercise is an excellent method of self-study and will be a tool for learning how your mind works and attracts or formulates ideas.

⋅⁚⋅ ⋅⁚⋅

# WHAT ARE SOME SOURCES OF INSPIRATION?

You can't wait for inspiration. You have to
go after it with a club.
—JACK LONDON

All my writings may be considered tasks
imposed from within; their source was
a fateful compulsion. What I wrote
were things that assailed me from within
myself. I permitted the spirit that
moved me to speak out.
—C. G. JUNG

To write is to be moved by spirit. As Carl Jung describes, he was "assailed . . . from within"; he was, as it were, a container or vehicle for what he calls "spirit." In its most fundamental characterization, the term *inspiration* means inhalation or the drawing of air into the lungs. In Greek culture it was thought that inspiration was drawing in the breath of the gods in order to become pregnant with meaning. My *Random House Dictionary of English Usage* includes at least four pertinent definitions of *inspiration:* "an animating action or influence," "something inspired, as a thought," "a result of inspired activity," and "a divine influence directly and immediately exerted upon the mind or soul of a man."

Whether we refer to inspiration as a communication or transmission from the gods, whether we believe it comes from our own individual subconscious or from what Jung calls "the collective unconscious"—an infinite receptacle of all knowledge and experience—most people seem unanimous in their belief that it is a gift that visits itself upon us in moments of grace. Far from calling upon it at will, we wait—and wait—for it to descend into our minds and hearts. Contrarily, the manner of Jack London was to "go after it with a club," an appropriate analogy considering that London, the author of *The Call of the Wild* and *White Fang,* among other novels, was known primarily as an adventure writer. He saw inspiration as an extension of his intrepid pursuit of daring and conquest rather than as a hopeful possibility that may or may not appear on a given occasion.

It is impossible to say where something as elusive and shapeshifting as inspiration comes from. If we knew, we would go there at will whenever we were to begin a day's writing or a new project. As I mentioned earlier, inspiration seems to be a gift that visits itself upon us in moments of grace. What I didn't say is that those moments of grace are, more often than not, preceded by a real willingness to work *and* a long preparation. Ethan Canin, the author of the novel *The Palace Thief,* insists that "you cannot write a novel out of inspiration. There's no substitute for sitting down every day for four hundred days and writing a page."

At a writing workshop with Tom Robbins, I vividly remember his remark in response to a student's question about inspiration: "I'm

*The spirit comes to guide me in my need. . . .*
—GOETHE

always at my desk by ten o'clock in the morning," Robbins said, "so the Muse knows where to find me." He went on to clarify, however, that there are no guarantees. "Sometimes she comes and sometimes she doesn't, but if she does, I want to be there." This pointed remark accurately describes the essentials inherent in any art form: preparation and grace. Apropos of Tom Robbins's statement is a *New Yorker* cartoon by Arnie Levin that shows a man sitting at his computer and a Muse-type figure about the size of Tinkerbell, dressed in classical Greek garments—laurel wreath and all—holding a small harp as she sits in an ornate birdcage, a psychic benefactor/patron/champion of sorts. If only it were that simple!

Pablo Neruda, the beloved Chilean poet, spoke of inspiration in terms of its "animating action or influence" when he said during an interview in the *Paris Review*, "I don't have a schedule, but by preference I write in the morning. . . . I would rather write all day, but frequently the fullness of a thought, of an expression, of something that comes out of myself in a tumultuous way—let's label it with an antiquated term, 'inspiration,'—leaves me satisfied, or exhausted, or calmed, or empty. That is, I can't go on." So the effect of inspiration is sometimes liberating and energizing but may also be enervating. That is, after giving our all to the inspiration that comes through us, we feel spent. Like Jung, Neruda seems also to have understood inspiration as a source that swelled within him.

Another quality of inspiration seems to be its flighty or unreliable quality. A moment of inspiration that brings with it the suggestion for a nonfiction book or a novel or a dissertation will not be enough to sustain the months and possible years of consistently showing up at your desk that will be required for the crafting and completion of a project. So there are those momentous jets of inspiration, and there are, we hope, the daily spurts of juice that keep us going.

### The Writer's Mentor Suggests . . .

It is important to discover your method of sourcing inspiration. Do you "go after it with a club"? Or does it "assail" you from within? When you sit down to write, do you sail along with a breezy impulse,

*If you wait for inspiration, you're not a writer, but a waiter.*
—ANONYMOUS

or do you catatonically stare at a blank page or compulsively revise yesterday's writing? Don't wait until you are moved by inspiration to start clacking away on your keyboard. It could be a very long wait. You may not have a psychological "club" handy as you trek off to Alaska or the South Seas, as did Jack London, but you can avail yourself to stimulating situations.

What are ways that you can purposely enter an altered state of consciousness? Does listening to music relax you enough to be open to your inner voice? Is it important for you to read the *New York Times* or your local newspaper every day in order to get your synapses jumping? Will an early morning run jostle the cobwebs of the mundane from your spirit? While working on a particular literary project for which you are seeking resolution, notice if inspiration seems to be flowing unhindered or differently than it does during those dry periods when you are projectless.

From today's *New York Times* six headline stories inspired my sense of story. They are as follows:

- "Filipino Rebels Claim to Have Beheaded American"
- "Bulgaria Opens School Doors for Gypsy Children"
- "Pursuing a Medical Career, All the Way to Cuba"
- "Guarding Underwater Treasures in the Dry Tortugas"
- "The Frequent Flier and Radiation Risk"
- "42 Arrested during Fracas in the Bronx after Parade"

To me each sentence seems rife with narrative potential. But in a brisk exercise of free association, I'll relate what two of these headlines provoked in me.

"Bulgaria Opens School Doors for Gypsy Children":

- Images of one of my favorite films, *The Time of the Gypsies*, directed by Emir Kusturica
- The music of the Gypsy Kings
- The film and CD of *Latcho Drom*, which traces the roots of the Gypsies from India through the Middle East and Eastern and Southern Europe
- The band of Gypsies in the original 1941 *Wolf Man*, starring Lon Chaney Jr., and their run-in with the werewolf

- Marlene Dietrich as a most unlikely Gypsy in the 1947 movie *Golden Earrings*
- *Bury Me Standing,* a passionate and erudite book by Isabel Fonseca about the Roma culture

Some of the questions that arose for me from the headline: Do the children *want* to attend school? Do their parents? Will they be perceived as second-class citizens? How will this affect their clannish culture? Will Gypsies become an integral part of their country's society, rather than being outcasts? Perhaps a story could track three Gypsy children during their first week of school, highlighting any disparity—or not—between their lives at home and at school and how their respective parents either encourage or denigrate their experiences. The three children are each ten years old. One, Andrzej, brings his violin to class and plays for the other children during recess and lunch time, currying their favor; the second, Django, angry and rebellious, sets a fire in the bathroom; the third, Sutka, has aspirations to leave her parents and live with her sister, who is a secretary in London.

The second headline I've chosen is "The Frequent Flier and Radiation Risk." Here I immediately thought about

- My son, who takes bimonthly transcontinental flights for business purposes
- An imagined story about a flight attendant who is pregnant but continues to fly so that "something" happens to the embryo (à la the dream birth sequence in David Cronenberg's *The Fly*—it's not pretty)
- In Greek myth, Icarus, who flew too close to the sun and crashed when its heat melted the wax that held his wings together. The Icarus myth also reminds me of how John F. Kennedy Jr.—an Icarus of Camelot—died flying too close to the sun of privilege, opulence, and celebrity.

Actively read today's newspaper as if you were a fiction writer. Find at least three ideas for a short story and, as I have done here, use free association to stimulate some possible directions each "story" could adopt.

# How can I tap into my creativity?

> People have talents that are different. Where
> does the creative flow come from—inside
> us, or from a higher power? I don't ask
> questions. I just write it down.
> —*PHYLLIS WHITNEY*

The geography of our own interior is a vast range that lends itself to infinite psychic wanderings. It is a wilderness of the imagination. Everything that we have ever seen, heard, tasted, touched, and felt makes its home in an invisible reservoir called memory. These experiences—all that we have done, all that has been enacted upon us—become the active ingredients in the cauldron that is the imagination. Norman Mailer has said that there is no boundary between experience and imagination. The human mind itself makes the comparisons, the connections, and the adjustments. Getting those comparisons, connections, and adjustments down on paper in the most original and intriguing form and timely manner is our quest. There is a kind of synchronicity evident in the writing process—a dialogue between time and place, thought and emotion, head and heart. Writing is the arena where inner awareness parallels the outer happenings in the world.

It is helpful to remember that within the word *imagination* dwells the root "image." It is as if our imagination, a sort of conceptual repository, is composed of an endless river of visual perceptions. The painter Joan Miró once said, "A big stone on a deserted beach is a motionless thing, but it sets loose great movements in my mind." In other words, the image may be stationary, a mental object, but the imagination is fluid, a river running through the psyche or the unconscious. This is the place from where art comes. Art draws on the memories and emotions of which the unconscious is composed.

*Imagination is
a divine gift.*
—MADELEINE L'ENGLE

In *Becoming a Writer,* Dorothea Brande tells us to come to terms with the unconscious. "The unconscious should not be thought of as a limbo where vague, cloudy, and amorphous notions swim hazily about," she writes. "There is every reason to believe, on the contrary, that it is the great home of form; it is quicker to see types, patterns, purposes, than our intellect can ever be."

Most of us write without ever knowing how this process occurs. We just know that we feel better when we write than when we don't. And it becomes an ongoing process to come to terms with and allow that "enormous and powerful part of your nature," as Brande calls it, "which lies behind the threshold of immediate knowledge." We could also call this imagination.

In an essay in the *New Yorker* about where ideas come from and how the imagination works, the mystery writer John Le Carré writes, "When and where did the novel begin? I always ask myself this same dumb question, and find myself fudging the answer, because there isn't one." He then proceeds to recount an experience that he had in Basel, Switzerland, twenty years before. The story goes that in a beer hall Le Carré met a black-bearded cyclist wearing a beret who referred to himself as a former chemist (or pharmacist) who was now an anarchist because he could no longer be part of the "multis," or multinational pharmaceutical companies. Le Carré writes that he was far more interested in the anarchist part of the man than the pharmacist. "But as a writer I was secretly enjoying one of those frissons of forewarning: one day I'll find a way of writing about you and your *multis* I thought. And fine: today, twenty years later, I've done it."

During those twenty years, of course, Le Carré wrote many other novels, but meanwhile a compartment in his imagination continued to extrapolate on those few latent bits of information gathered in that beer hall twenty years earlier. The creative process works its magic in cabalistic ways: a dream fragment here, a chance meeting there. And before, during, and even after the writing of a piece, discursive elements contribute to the amalgam that becomes a story or essay. How does it happen?

I have found that there is no substitute for simply sitting down and writing. For it is through the process of thinking, seeking clarity,

*I collect lines and snip-
pets of things somebody
might say—things I
overhear, things I see in
the newspaper, things I
think up, dream up,
wake up with in the
middle of the night. I
write a line down in my
notebook. If I can get
enough of those things,
then characters
begin to emerge.*
—RICHARD FORD

and working intently that the implementation of the imagination begins. As Phyllis Whitney says, "Just write it down."

### The Writer's Mentor Suggests . . .

1. Silence seems to be a necessary companion to accessing the imagination because silence leads to both the inner and outer, the cosmos and the unconscious. Sometimes there is only a glimmer of the direction in which we want to go. That glimmer is the bidding of the imagination. It is the call to create. Where one's thought process may be in a muddle, the work itself brings clarity. The chaos and clutter of our fertile imagination begins to take shape as we place one word after another. It is the act of writing, that dialogue between thought and word, which brings answers to the unsolved questions of content and form. Establish periods of silence for yourself and see what emerges.

2. The little known but highly praised English writer Henry Green once claimed that the writer's duty is "to meet as many pedestrian people as possible and to listen to the most pedestrian conversation." For him it was the richness of the felt, heard, and seen moment. Change your environment. Go to a crowded public place—that might be a café, a bar, a gym, the Department of Motor Vehicles or an unemployment office, a race track, a museum, a college campus—the more out of the ordinary for you, the better. And listen. Listen and take notes. Try to get shards of conversations down in writing. Better yet, use a hand-held micro-tape recorder. List at least ten ideas with potential as stories or essays. Listen to how people use language: for instance, few people actually complete their sentences. Listen to their unique inflections and pronunciations. Now take this material home and write a story from it.

3. Create a museum of memories in your journals. Again, go to places that are unfamiliar to you. Take a notebook and fill the "cauldron that is the imagination." Focus on your sensory perceptions—especially what you hear, smell, taste, and feel.

·•· ·•·

# SHOULD I BE READING OTHER WRITERS? SHOULD I TRY TO EMULATE MY FAVORITE WRITERS?

> Read, read, read. Read everything—trash,
> classics, good and bad, and see how they do
> it. Just like a carpenter who works as an
> apprentice and studies the master. Read!
> You'll absorb it. Then write.
>
> —WILLIAM FAULKNER

*You can't write seriously without reading the greats in that peculiar way that writers read, attentive to the particularities of the language, to the technical turns and twists of scenemaking and plot, soaking up numerous narrative strategies and studying various approaches to that cave in the deep woods where the human heart hibernates.*

*—ALAN CHEUSE*

*"They were alive and they spoke to me!* That is the simplest and most eloquent way in which I can refer to those authors who have remained with me over the years." This is how one of my earliest writing mentors, Henry Miller, describes the influence of his favored authors on his own writing. Coincidentally, it was Miller's work that kindled a fire inside me, first for reading and, eventually, for writing. With Miller began my lifelong affair with the written word. That was already the beginning of my writing. There are many aspects of Henry Miller's writing that I was drawn to when I first read *Tropic of Cancer* in 1960, at the age of twelve. Certainly the subject matter aroused my sexual curiosity, but there was much more to Miller than expoundings on his salacious nature. Perhaps primarily was the romance associated with his expatriation, but of equal fascination for me was his absolute enthrallment with language—both English and French—his unflagging attention to detail; his ability to make the spirit of a place (Paris) ring true and come alive on paper; his contagious sense of adventure; his unabashed fervor for the arts; his inimitable way of viewing the world, the baroque, the too-muchness quality of his prose; and his obvious devotion to the act of writing itself. Each of these aspects of Miller's writing had both a profound and lasting effect on my nascent writer's psyche.

On the subject of reading, Jorge Luis Borges says, "I think the happiness of a reader is beyond that of a writer, for a reader need feel no trouble, no anxiety: he is merely out for happiness. And happiness, when you are a reader, is frequent."

That happiness extends to the metaphorical similarity between reading and eating. "Books are food," wrote the English critic Holbrook Jackson, "libraries so many dishes of meat, served out for several palates. . . . We eat them from love or necessity, as other foods, but most from love." Reading for love and necessity best describes my relationship with books. A fellow writer once told me that reading is like breathing to him. As one who had taught herself to read when she was four years old, and since that time has enjoyed the cornucopia of omnivorous reading, I eagerly concurred. It is still difficult to believe, but I once had a writing client who confessed to me that she didn't like to read. I said nothing (although the expression on my face surely spoke for me), but I knew she would not proceed in this craft without that most singular inner companion, the reading fanatic.

For a writer there is a logical progression from reading to imitating, from imitating to emulating, and, eventually, one hopes, from emulating to originality, or at least developing one's unique writing voice and style. Elmore Leonard, a novelist and screenwriter who often uses humor in crime stories such as *Get Shorty*, has spoken of his studying and imitating the work of Ernest Hemingway. He learned quickly, however, that Hemingway's seemingly simple style is misleading. "There's a lot of white space often on his pages. You see the lines of dialogue, the page running vertical rather than horizontal. You say . . . Whoa, that looks easy. I should be able to do that. I know how people talk." But it didn't take long for Leonard to discover that it isn't nearly as easy as it looks. "Because," as he admits, "there's a lot in between the lines that he didn't say." That's where Hemingway's artistry enters the equation. Interestingly, there is a second writer to whom Leonard owes a debt of gratitude. During the 1950s he first read the work of Richard Bissell. Some years later, Leonard, while researching his novel *Killshot*, reread Bissell's writings and realized that, without consciously emulating Bissell and simply

> *I never presume to give advice on writing. I think the best way to learn to write is to read books and stories by good writers. It's a hard thing to preach about. As Thelonius Monk once said, about his field, "Talking about music is like dancing about architecture."*
>
> —MAUREEN DOWD

through the osmosis of reading, Bissell's work had influenced him. William Safire has an acronym for this procedure: GWIGWO— Good Writing In, Good Writing Out.

Still, reading and attempting to emulate our favorite writers can also bring a sense of overwhelming discouragement and inferiority. At some point it can be liberating to relinquish the *New Yorker* fantasy or to admit that one's writing will never be mistaken for Annie Dillard's. For no matter how assiduously Leonard may have tried to *imitate* Hemingway, at heart he knew there was only *one* Hemingway. The task of every writer is to uncover his personal literary fingerprint, to craft her subjective presence on the page.

## The Writer's Mentor Suggests . . .

1.  Read, read, read. Read widely, deeply, and with pleasure. Reflect on those writers who have had the most influence on your own writing. In all probability their resonance for you was due to a combination of shared sensibilities and an appreciation of their writing.

2.  Nicholas Delbanco has written that "to engage in imitation is to begin to understand what originality means." Revisit your favorite writers. As you read their work, make note of which elements of their writing style you would like to possess in your own. Their storytelling ability? Their original use of simile and metaphor? The precision of their language? The poetic nature of their prose? Imitate for practice. Technical excellences can be learned through mirroring. Deconstruct a story, a passage, or a poem word by word, sentence by sentence. Examine it closely. Write a page or a poem in your chosen writer's vein. Now find a cognate segment in your work to use for comparison. What did you learn?

3.  Read *Narrative Design,* by Madison Smart Bell, which teaches one to read *as a writer.* Through example rather than precept, Bell guides the reader through the conscious and unconscious decisions the authors of his sample stories have made in arriving at the finished form of their work.

4. From one of your favorite writers select a paragraph and write it out by hand on paper. Study it. What can you learn? Try to put yourself in the mind of the author when he or she was writing this piece. Imagine the many revisions this paragraph has undergone. Study the language, sentence structure, use (or not) of metaphor, of rhythm. Look at the concision, the distillation, the intense coming together of sound and meaning.

·:· ·:·

# CAN DREAMS INFORM MY WRITING?

> The kind of imagination I use in writing,
> when I try to lose control of consciousness,
> works very much like dreams. The
> subconscious takes over and it's fun. . . . I do
> feel if ever I was looking for a source of
> material, all I would have to do is go back
> to my dreams.
>
> —*AMY TAN*

A recurring dream, or, rather, nightmare, haunted me throughout my childhood. In the manner of a German Expressionist film, something perhaps akin to *The Cabinet of Dr. Caligari,* I am being chased by a man wearing a black coat and hat, which is pulled down over his head. A broad brim shades his face from identification. But his hands, in that exaggerated, nightmarish way, are enormous. White. Spiny. Grasping. Although, as a child, the dream was singular to me, I have since discovered how pervasive this image is in the minds of the collective consciousness. In it was the de rigueur sequence of my running up a broad flight of stairs, falling, and, as the dark figure

*When I write, I follow an image, a piece of music that can't get out of my mind. I let it lead me, like a clue to a mystery to be revealed.*

—E. L. DOCTOROW

grasped for me, regaining my footing and continuing up the stairs until this perpetual suite of events is replayed ad infinitum.

It wasn't until my mid-twenties that I realized the potency of this image when it began to appear in my visual artwork in graduate school. Since then the image has continued to find its way into my writing—both fiction and nonfiction. It has been an interesting journey decoding the meaning of this dream and observing how it changes with the evolution of my life.

The dreamstate continues to provide regular nourishment to my creative as well as psychological life. I find that my dreams are extremely vivid and detailed. And I haven't figured out if that is *because* I write and paint or because the graphic quality of my dreams *makes* me write and paint.

Many writers have revealed that their dreamlife is the occasional source of an idea. Through a series of dreams, John Sayles, the film director and novelist, conceptualized and wrote a screenplay for his film *Brother from Another Planet.* William Styron, the author of *Sophie's Choice,* has allowed that the concept for this novel was the result, if not of a dream, of a kind of waking vision that occurred when he woke up one spring morning in the mid-'70s. He refers to the image as a "lingering vision" and elucidates the progress from the remnant of a dream to a conscious vision that included a memory of a girl he, as a young man, briefly knew. Amy Tan, the popular author of *The Joy Luck Club,* says that when she became stuck in a part of writing the book she took that story problem to bed with her, "along with some other information, and dreamed an ending that turned out to be quite workable and funny."

Before going to sleep at night, one can alert other levels of the unconscious to one's writing needs and intent for the next day. If sought out, the assistance is there, "particularly," Barbara Waters says, "if grasped soon after waking when that cosmic 'choir' still is whispering." Sue Grafton, the author of the series of alphabet mysteries (*A is for Alibi, B is for Burglar,* and so on), believes that when the "analytical self, the left brain, finally releases its grip on us and gets out of the way, the creative side of us, which often surfaces in sleep,

*When I'm writing at my best I'm aware that I'm tapping subconscious sources. . . . There is a kind of interweaving of the dream life.*
—WILLIAM STYRON

comes to the fore and in its own playful and whimsical manner will solve many creative problems." Upon occasion she will write a note to her "left brain" asking for assistance on a certain problem, and it "will often come through in a day or two." I find it comforting to know that I have allies working for me 24/7. These writing deities seem to find special pleasure in revealing the pieces of a particular literary puzzle I may be seeking during the process of writing a book or an essay.

It's impossible to know exactly what goes on in the unconscious during the dream process, but author of *The Invisible Man,* Ralph Ellison, feels that whatever does take place "becomes active in some way in what I do at the typewriter." He acknowledged that he views the entire 24-hour period of each day as an integral part of a writer's life when he said, "What happens during the night feeds back, in some way, into what [the writer] does consciously during the day."

*A frightening dream is wonderful for me because it re-creates all the physiology that I need in describing my private eye heroine Kinsey Millhone in a dangerous situation.*

—SUE GRAFTON

### The Writer's Mentor Suggests . . .

1. Read the anthology *Writer's Dreaming,* by Naomi Epel. It is a galvanizing encounter with various writers discussing their dreams and the connection between their dream lives and the creative writing process. It is not a how-to book. Thankfully, it will not give you a meaning for the yellow lizard who appeared in your dream last week. But it is an absorbing plunge into the souls of some of the best writers working today.

2. The hypnagogic state, that membrane between dreaming and full consciousness, when the left brain is on furlough, is a fertile period for creative notions to propagate. Take advantage of those offerings by writing down the whispers of inspiration that float through you.

3. As in the example of Amy Tan, take your writing problem to bed with you and consciously ask for clarity, guidance, or a specific answer to your quandary. Expect an answer. And give thanks.

# The Writer's Mentor at the Movies
## Shakespeare in Love

What if *Romeo and Juliet* had been called *Romeo and Ethyl, the Pirate's Daughter*? Just doesn't have the same ring, does it? In the rollicking yet ingenious *Shakespeare in Love,* poor Will Shakespeare is so low on inspiration that *Romeo and Ethyl* is the best he can come up with. "It's as if my quill has broken; my inkwell is dry. . . . I cannot love nor write," Will tells his therapist/confessor (who times his sessions with an hourglass) in a crossover of writing and sexual metaphors. Because we have so little actual biographical data on Shakespeare, it seems natural to speculate on the inception of *Romeo and Juliet*. What if . . . ?, the screenwriters (Marc Norman and Tom Stoppard) seem to be asking. What was the catalyst for Shakespeare to make such a leap, conceptually, from his early comedies to the profound emotions of *Romeo and Juliet*?

Young Will (played tempestuously well by Joseph Fiennes) owes a comedy to each of two theatre producers. When one corners him and asks where his play is, Will smiles as he points to his head, "It is locked safely in here." And when will the story be "unlocked," the producer asks suspiciously. "As soon as I find my Muse," Will laments. For Will, the Muse is always Aphrodite.

Enter Viola de Lesseps. As played by a breathtaking Gwyneth Paltrow, we have no trouble believing that Viola, indeed, is a luminous incarnation of both the Muse *and* Aphrodite. But Viola's allure extends far beyond her golden beauty. "I will have poetry in my life and adventure and love," she audaciously tells her nurse after she has auditioned for Shakespeare's as yet partially written new comedy. Of course, during Elizabethan times it was unlawful for women to perform onstage, so Viola must disguise herself as a man—albeit a very beautiful and effeminate one. Will is immediately drawn to her, er, him and, wishing the "actor" to perform in his play, pursues him to his canalside villa. But he is instantly smitten when he soon envisions the radiant Viola. After a few balcony love scenes and the revelation that Viola is already betrothed to another—in a purely business arrangement between the charmless, but titled, Lord Wessex and her father—we get a sense of how *Romeo and Juliet*—and, later, *Twelfth Night*—begin to take form.

It isn't long before Will and Viola are engaging in "poetry, adventure, and love." In between bouts of lovemaking, Will ardently pens a series of Sonnets—"Shall I compare thee . . ."—in Viola's honor, and together they create the dialogue that will become *Romeo and Juliet*. In love, Will's potency—both artistic and sexual—not only has returned but also has far exceeded his previous capacity.

"Can a play show us the very truth and nature of love?" the unwed dowager, Queen Elizabeth, wagers with Lord Wessex. *Romeo and Juliet* answers with a resounding . . . And how! And so does *Shakespeare in Love*. For the nature of "true love" is to be reciprocal; and just as Viola has inflamed Will's imagination, so, too, has he afforded Viola her own creative expression through acting on a stage—even if briefly.

In the final scene, as Will and Viola are set to return to their separate lives—he to his wife and playwriting, she to Lord Wessex and a sail across the Atlantic to (an anachronistic) Virginia and a tobacco plantation—Will swears that for him Viola will never age and will remain as beautiful as she is that day, and he promises to give his lover immortality. She encourages him to write out his passion in a new play. Instantly the playwright begins to unfold the storyline of a character named Viola, who is shipwrecked on an unfriendly island Illyria and, believing her twin brother to be lost at sea, disguises herself in male attire in order to join the retinue of the island's duke....

As Will writes "Twelfth Night" at the top of a sheet of paper, the screen fills with his imaginings of a shipwreck and a lovely, flaxen-haired woman walking, walking toward . . .

———

# CHAPTER 3

# THE WRITING ENVIRONMENT

## *Creating a Sanctuary*

Where should I write? Is it imperative to have "a room of one's own"?

What are the best writers' tools?

What are the best books on writing?
What are the best reference books to have on my desk?

The Writer's Mentor at the Movies: *Celeste*

THE WRITING ENVIRONMENT: CREATING A SANCTUARY offers suggestions and support for creating the best possible environment to serve and encourage your writing pursuit. There are descriptions of the study/office conditions of writers such as Dorothy West, George Plimpton, and Kent Haruf. You will find out about the chosen implements of the trade for several writers and why they chose them. To answer the question about what are the best books on writing, an expansive offering of titles is offered under the headings The Creative Process and Imagination; The Writing Process; Style and Craft; Editing and Rewriting; Journaling/Diaries, Memoir, Autobiography; Poetry; Writing Fiction; Nonfiction Writing; Philosophizing about Writing; Writers on Writing; Interviews with and Essays by Writers; Anthologies; and Getting Published. Some additional suggestions and the best periodicals are also mentioned. The chapter closes with an analysis on a film about the writing habits of the famous author of *Remembrance of Things Past*, Marcel Proust, and his devoted housekeeper, secretary, and friend, Celeste.

# Where should I write? Is it imperative to have "a room of one's own"?

When I was seven, I said to my mother, may
I close my door? And she said, yes, but why
do you want to close your door?
And I said because I want to think.
And when I was eleven, I said to my mother,
may I lock my door? And she said yes, but
why do you want to lock your door?
And I said because I want to write.

—DOROTHY WEST

The famous "a room of one's own" axiom, from a feminist essay by Virginia Woolf, continues to ring as true in the twenty-first century as it did more than seventy years ago, in 1928, when the essay was first delivered in the form of two lectures at Cambridge University. To Woolf, "a room of one's own" was her sanctuary.

Dorothy West, an African American novelist and short story writer who wrote her first short story when she was seven years old and after she'd "close[d her] door," lived until the age of ninety-one. In the summer of 1947, as a respected member of the Harlem Renaissance, she left New York for good, moving to Martha's Vineyard and into the two-bedroom, cedar-shingled cottage in Oak Bluffs that her father, a former slave, had bought years earlier. She lived there the rest of her life, until 1998, and once wrote, "I have lived in various places, but the island is my yearning place. All my life, wherever I have been, abroad, New York, Boston, anywhere, whenever I yearned for home, I yearned for the island." "The island" was her sanctuary.

A photograph of a woman hunkered down, pencil in hand, over what looks like a lined yellow legal pad is secured in the plastic sleeve of the cover of a binder for one of the women's writing groups I facilitate. This repository is full to overflowing with images, notes, pieces of "good writing" by my students and others, essays, writing ideas, and samples. The elderly woman, her hair in Gibson Girl–style, sits at a cluttered circular table. A square gingham tablecloth; a fruit-filled bowl in the shape of a scallop shell; a four-armed candelabra, with candles half-melted; used dishes, paper napkins, and a white ceramic teapot off to one side, perhaps from breakfast that morning; and a row of floral-designed plates floating on the wall above her head tell us this is the woman's dining as well as writing table. The woman is writer Ann Petry. This table is her sanctuary.

The phrase "a room of one's own" seems to make a demand, and yet there is no definite direction in which one is pointed, no guidance, no indication of the size, shape, color, location, contents to which the "room" should adhere. Should there be windows that envisage a bucolic horse pasture, a raging surf, the cement facade of an industrial complex, or the entertaining, if distracting, checkerboard of windowscapes that Alfred Hitchcock's voyeur, Scotty, surveys from his apartment in *Vertigo*? As with all important questions in life, each individual must decide for him- or herself.

Rooms and sanctuaries are wherever you create them. Poet and novelist Sherman Alexie, author of *Indian Killer* and *Smoke Signals*, does much of his writing at 3 A.M. at an International House of Pancakes in Seattle, where he lives. Playwright Arthur Miller has written all of his more recent plays in a 12-by-20-foot cabin adjacent to his house in Roxbury, Connecticut. He calls it "my little synagogue." He admits that he sits there and prays for his writing to go well. Novelist Kent Haruf prefers a coal room in the basement of his house in Illinois. The room is about 6-feet-by-9 and has a single ground-level window through which coal was once shoveled. He says that every time he goes down to work, he feels "as if I'm descending into a sacred place." Eudora Welty said that she straight-pinned pieces of her stories together on the dining room table, as though she were pinning together parts of a dress.

In a literally insightful and beguiling collection of photographs of writers, Jill Krementz' *The Writer's Desk*, the "voyeur" is taken into the most private sanctum of the writer's laboratory: his office, study, studio, library, workplace, retreat. Or, as in the case of Dorothy West,

*Finally, there is no perfection. If you want to write, you have to cut through and write. There is no perfect atmosphere, notebook, pen, or desk, so train yourself to be flexible. Try writing under different circumstances and in different places.*
—NATALIE GOLDBERG

the kitchen table, Toni Morrison's living room couch, Veronica Chamber's kitchen countertop, Saul Bellow's upright draughting table, the back seat of William F. Buckley's custom-built limousine, Kurt Vonnegut's lap, a 2-by-4 laid across the arms of a chair for Ross Macdonald, or Walker Percy's *bed*. In fact, bed is exactly where Colette, Proust, Edith Wharton, and James Joyce wrote masterpieces. The book also shows what surrounds the writers, like sacred talismans: snapshots and portraits, both fine and folk art; cigarettes: lit, spent, and still nestled in packs; an array of pipes; cats, dogs, birds; endless piles of books; clusters and scatters of papers.

These are famous writers, of course. My sanctuary is a simple rectangular room, the second largest of three in my carriage house. There is a sweeping picture window, intentionally curtainless, that offers a view of a darkened sky when I begin to write at five o'clock in the morning and, on clear late afternoons, presents the sultry mixture of magenta and salmon that California sunsets offer. There is also a neighbor's unsightly brown house off to the left, whose view I try to block with a wooden planter box filled with variegated ivy, dracaena, palms, three types of ferns, and a raspberry cyclamen thrown in for color. There is always a fresh bouquet of flowers—preferably scented—because flowers make me happy and encourage me to enter my study, even when I dread doing so. As I am a painter at heart, images are profoundly important to me. There are photographs of me with my best friends: Deanne, Christiane, Katherine, Maurine, Leslie, Linda, Vicki. At least a half dozen of my son, Christian. A few photos I have taken of the many exceptional people I've been fortunate to meet, many of them writers: Doris Lessing, Michael Ondaatje, Isabel Allende, Ursula LeGuin, Betty Friedan, Oliver Stone, Fay Weldon, Gloria Steinem, Ann Richards, Catherine Deneuve. Framed covers of my eight published books in turn frame the large multipaned window—a giant form of tic tac toe. Three postcard images of Freud's study (couch and all), which I visited during my last trip to London, an 18-by-24-inch poster of Buster Keaton editing a movie, and magazine pictures of Sam Shepard, Gore Vidal, Salman Rushdie, Philip Glass, and Susan Sontag are taped to the sliding closet doors. There are several thousand books lining two walls, floor to ceiling, and against one half-wall, hundreds of videos. The walnut double library desk I bought at an antique store eight years ago sits in the center of the room at an angle so that I may take advantage of the open space and also observe the Feng Shui principle of facing the door and therefore welcoming incoming energy rather than blocking it. These items on my desk and on the walls connect me emotionally to memories and to people who are important to me. Oh, did I mention Dios, my nine-month-old English Springer Spaniel? He's here, too. Usually lying within reach of one of my feet, if, indeed, not directly atop them. When I get up it's difficult to walk without stepping on the toys he brings in one by one in the hopes that I will surely find any one of them much more tantalizing than the strange machine that seems to have some mesmerizing power over me. I think it might be impossible to write without him—as it surely was after the unexpected death of my favored Sienna last year. He reminds me that I am loved and that, yes, there is life—and loads of fun to be had—even when I'm not writing.

In a sense, where one writes, that elusive "room of one's own," is more of a concept than a thing. Natalie Goldberg, the writing teacher, is known for her promotion of writing in cafés. That could be a local Peet's Coffee or the Café Deux Maggots in Paris. The novelist Richard Ford believes that the "room" or the "desk" can be any where: "On an airplane or a Greyhound bus, or in a rental car or a rented house." But wherever one chooses to write, he or she will be creating a sanctuary. All that's needed is the intention, the desire to write, and the "talent" to remain there long enough (in terms of hours, weeks, years) to produce work that satisfies you.

*You do not need to leave your room. Remain sitting at your table and listen. Do not even listen, simply wait, be quite still and solitary. The world will freely offer itself to you to be unmasked, it has no choice, it will roll in ecstasy at your feet.*

—FRANZ KAFKA

## The Writer's Mentor Suggests . . .

1. If there is not one room in your home that you can call your "own," select a corner of the living room or the kitchen, the laundry room, or even a small closet—as did Antoine Doinel, the twelve-year-old protagonist and alter ego of the film director

François Truffaut in Truffaut's *400 Blows*—and mark that territory, designate it as your space, your "synagogue" or "sacred place," and request that the other members of your family respect it as such. Try a variety of surroundings until you select one that feels safe to you. (Note: If you find that your family members or roommates do not respect your wish for privacy, there may be other underlying issues that need to be addressed.)

2. As Richard Ford suggested, the "room" or the "desk" can be anywhere. Where is that place for you? Experiment with a number of local cafés, restaurants, clubs, parks, a library, or even a gym, and determine which feels right and works best for you. Dedicated writers can practice their craft almost anywhere, but some places are more conducive than others to "jump-starting" the writing process.

∻ ∻

# What are the best writers' tools?

> I always write with a Ticonderoga #2 pencil.
> I started out with it, and I'll go to that
> Great Bookstore in the sky with one
> of those in my hand.
> —ROBERT LUDLUM

> I write on the typewriter. I don't want to be
> forever bound to this machine, this very old,
> circa 1930, I would say, Royal Typewriter. I
> hate to think what will happen when it
> finally gives out. . . .
> —JOHN ASHBERY

It is said that Tolstoy revised *War and Peace* over five drafts. By hand. Without the use of a typewriter or, obviously, the aid of an iBook. Postmodern life—and art, it would seem—is all about speed, getting faster results, producing more (but not necessarily better) experiences and work. But slowing down also means more time to think, less time to be on automatic. True, the computer makes working faster and easier, but are faster and easier always better? The biographer Robert A. Caro asks the natural question: "Is it really a good thing to write as fast as your fingers can move? I think with my fingers, so I want to slow myself down." This is the perspective of a man who still uses a Smith Corona 210. Of course, it has become exceedingly more difficult to acquire spare parts for his favored tool of choice, and he has taken to cannibalizing the needed components from his collection of *fourteen* other Smith Coronas. This is a man dedicated to his primary writing tool.

On the practical side of this issue is the fact that a typewriter will not "crash," and you cannot lose what you have written because of a power surge or a technical breakdown. But Andy Rooney, of *60 Minutes* fame, reluctantly admits that his writing has improved during the ten years since he began using WordPerfect because "I can now redo things that I wouldn't have taken the time to redo."

On the other hand, William Styron declares that he has never written any prose fiction on a typewriter. He is another author who has "a very comfortable relationship with No. 2 pencils" and yellow legal pads, which, he quickly adds, vary in quality. "I would be almost in deep despair if I found myself on some island on vacation and unable to get yellow sheets." He says he could compose on white sheets, in longhand, "but it would be an added handicap." An inveterate user of an eraser, he bemoans those tablets with poor erasable quality.

The act of writing is surely the most affordable of art forms. If you want to write and you are ready to write, fundamentally, all you really need is pencil or pen and paper. The question to ask yourself is, Do I need the most recent Microsoft upgrade in order to write my book, or am I delaying the writing of my book until I can afford the upgrade? Your answer is in your actions: If you are already writing—

and continue to write—with or without a new laptop or a leather-bound notebook or a marbled, gold-trimmed Waterman fountain pen, then you are not merely using the absence of expensive technology as an avoidance tactic to cover your own fear and dread of composing words—by any means—on a sheet of paper. John Updike said, "The humblest and quietist of weapons [is] a pencil." It is a weapon to use not only on behalf of one's intellectual and ethical convictions about world issues but also as artillery against those inner demons whose full-time career is to keep you from writing.

Desks or other writing receptacles are other tools of importance. A photograph on a wall in my study shows Susan Sontag—with that enigmatic Mona Lisa smile, her direct, dark eyes, a cigarette clasped in her right hand—sitting at a long, wooden table with matching benches on either side that looks well-suited to an English pub. Behind her is an oversized poster with a speeding train and an Olivetti typewriter heading right for the viewer—*la rapidissima*. In Jill Krementz' book of environmental photographs, *The Writer's Desk,* we are privy to the writer at work. We see George Plimpton, in 1995, writing on a typewriter that is placed on a small side table, the size of a TV tray; his twin infant daughters entertain themselves as they roll on the floor directly behind him. Walker Percy, a crucifix overhead, lies atop his double bed, a backrest supporting him against the headboard, working on a portable reading desk. Rita Dove writes standing at a lectern, lit candles before her. Richard Ford sits tilted back in a striped-cushioned swivel chair, a wooden table serving as an ottoman for his long legs; he writes on a simple clipboard. He says that his "desk" is "more of a concept than a thing. . . . Like Emerson's giant, I carry my desk with me." Toni Morrison sits on a velour couch writing in a simple spiral notebook with a pen. William F. Buckley sits in the back seat of his chauffeured limousine, talking on the telephone as he writes; his King Charles Spaniel, a sort of canine muse, hovers over his left shoulder in the back window space. And Kurt Vonnegut, the husband of Krementz, sits in a rolling director's chair, barefoot; his "table" looks to be a huge atlas on which he is completing a crossword puzzle. All of this to illustrate the point that, as Richard Ford says, we carry our desks with us—in our minds.

*I know that I talk about my pens and notebooks the way the master of a seraglio talked about his love slaves.*
—MARY GORDON

*The Writer's Mentor Suggests . . .*

1. Give some consideration to what writing tools you prefer. Are they what you already possess and are using, or are they part of a fantasy that prevents or inhibits you from getting down to actual work? Once writers discover what their favored writing accoutrement are, they tend to be fiercely loyal to them, as is Robert A. Caro to his Smith Corona 210 or William Styron to his No. 2s. Are you being too intransigent or self-indulgent?

2. If you have yet to firmly settle on specific "tools," be willing to explore some different writing implements. If you generally write on a computer, for a week spend part of each writing period using a hand-held writing implement—either a pen or pencil. Write about how this new process feels, how it slows you down or doesn't, how ideas come more quickly or not, how it may affect the content of your writing. Perhaps you feel that writing by hand is more conducive to creating poetry than to writing an essay.

3. Review the week's worth of your "new" writing and compare the style and content with that of your "normal" mode.

4. Buy yourself a micro-cassette recorder and use it. In Woody Allen's *Husbands and Wives,* the character played by Alan Alda uses a micro-recorder to document his ridiculous ideas. Carrying a micro-cassette recorder has become a habit for me since Kate Braverman suggested it to me in a writing course I took with her. Toni Morrison also uses this tool.

⋅:⋅ ⋅:⋅

Wʜᴀᴛ ᴀʀᴇ ᴛʜᴇ ʙᴇsᴛ ʙᴏᴏᴋs ᴏɴ ᴡʀɪᴛɪɴɢ?
Wʜᴀᴛ ᴀʀᴇ ᴛʜᴇ ʙᴇsᴛ ʀᴇғᴇʀᴇɴᴄᴇ ʙᴏᴏᴋs ᴛᴏ
ʜᴀᴠᴇ ᴏɴ ᴍʏ ᴅᴇsᴋ?

> Is there any real writing that has no reading
> behind it? I don't think so.
> —ᴅᴀᴠɪᴅ ʀᴇᴍɴɪᴄᴋ

I would prefer to list all 5,000-plus volumes in my personal library as the "best books on writing." (But, of course, that would be indulgent.) Each tome has taught me something, if not specifically about writing, then about the internal process that happens before, during, and after an act of writing: thinking and understanding. I have divided the books into general categories for easier reference. There are many more books available than are listed here, but these are the ones I know and have personally used. And remember that literary fiction (as distinct from genre fiction: mystery, science fiction, thriller, detective, romance) and poetry are essential reading for any writer.

*The Creative Process and Imagination*   There are many books on this topic. These five have been especially helpful to me. *Creators on Creating,* edited by Frank Barron, Alfonso Montuori, and Anthea Barron, and *The Poet at the Piano,* by Michiko Kakutani, both present creative artists in all media: writers, visual artists, playwrights, filmmakers, musicians, actors, and others. *Narrative Design,* by Madison Smart Bell, teaches one to read as a writer. Through example rather than precept, Bell guides the reader through the conscious and unconscious decisions the authors of his sample stories have made in arriving at the finished form of their work. *Thinking Through Writing,* by Susan R. Horton, is about the fundamentals of the writing process, such as what writing is and what purpose it serves, how you get an idea and how to transform it into words. It is a fascinating study and a rich experiential approach to understanding how the mind works and how thinking and writing are connected. *Creative*

*Characters,* by the Jungian analyst Elisabeth Young-Bruehl, looks at the creative processes of several artists and offers an original approach through psychoanalysis, philosophy, literary criticism, history of science, and biography to support her thesis that creativity is based on a theory of character.

*The Writing Process*    In her book *On Writer's Block,* Victoria Nelson approaches that dreaded writer's companion with fresh insight. She views this complicated human phenomenon as an organic part of the writing process and sees it as a positive element in a writer's or artist's growth. *Finding Your Writer's Voice,* by Thaisa Frank and Dorothy Wall, is about the ways a writer uses his or her sense of humor, irony, point of view, language, dialogue, and other elements to tell a story. *Word Painting,* by Rebecca McClanahan, demonstrates ways to fully utilize one's senses, develop powers of observation, and find the most evocative word, all in the service of developing a captivating descriptive style. In *Writing in Flow,* Susan K. Perry makes use of the concepts developed by Mihaly Csikszentmihalyi and transforms them into practical applications for acquiring and maintaining a "zone" or "writer's high." For those who are confined by fear and anxiety about the act of writing, Ralph Keyes has written *The Courage to Write.* And *Writing with Power,* by Peter Elbow, a professor of writing at Amherst College, offers techniques for "mastering" the writing process, especially the propitious method he calls "freewriting."

*If you read good books, when you write, good books will come out of you.*
—NATALIE GOLDBERG

*Style and Craft*    A style of writing refers to the arrangement of words in a manner that at once best expresses the "voice" or individuality of the writer and the idea and intent in his or her mind. The poet Robert Lowell said that style is "the establishment of a perfect mutual understanding between the worker and his material." Style includes diction, sentence structure and variety, imagery, rhythm, coherence, emphasis, and arrangement of ideas.

*The Art of Styling Sentences,* by Marie L. Waddell, et al., is a must for learning sentence structure, pattern, and combining. *The Deluxe Transitive Vampire* (really) by Karen Elizabeth Gordon, is a delightful way to brush up on your grammar. *Vampire* is the book we should have had in grade school. *Sin and Syntax,* by Constance Hale, is a superb book on crafting effective prose. Hale's chapter on verbs is, alone, worth the price of this softcover. And Strunk and White's *The Elements of Style* remains a direct and concise classic.

*Editing and Rewriting*  Editing and rewriting is a specific skill and one that every writer should develop. To aid that pursuit I can recommend three books, all excellent. *Self-Editing for Fiction Writers,* by Renni Browne and Dave King, is especially successful at illustrating methods of the "show, don't tell" imperative and at improving dialogue mechanics, interior monologue, and stylistic devises. Noah Lukeman's *The First Five Pages* skillfully teaches a writer how to recognize and avoid bad writing and how to improve both form and content. In *A Piece of Work,* edited by Jay Woodruff, five exceptional writers— Tobias Wolff, Joyce Carol Oates, Tess Gallagher, Robert Coles, and Donald Hall—discuss in detail the process of revising their own work from first draft, through various rewrites, and to the final published version.

*Journaling/Diaries, Memoir, Autobiography*  I first began Ira Progoff's Intensive Journal process in the late 1970s. Although I no longer work with this method, his book, *At a Journal Workshop,* still holds a place of honor on my bookshelves. It retains much value for its open-ended, self-integrating Journal Feedback techniques. In *Your Life as Story: Writing the New Autobiography,* Tristine Rainer shows how to combine the arts of storytelling and first-person narrative revelation through memoir or autobiographical writing. James Olney, in *Memory and Narrative: The Weaving of Life—Writing,* traces the history of life-writing from Saint Augustine to Samuel Beckett and illustrates how memory, identity, and narrative are inextricably connected. Two engaging books on diarists throughout history are Thomas Mallon's *A Book of One's Own* and Alexandra Johnson's *The Hidden Writer: Diaries and the Creative Life.* And, finally, the best of them all is Deena Metzger's *Writing for Your Life,* a book that, I can honestly testify, helped save mine.

*Poetry*   There are three books that I recommend as solid and absorbing introductions to the understanding and writing of poetry. *Poem Crazy,* by Susan G. Wooldridge; *How to Read a Poem . . . and Start a Poetry Circle,* by Molly Peacock; and *The Poet's Companion,* by Kim Addonizio and Dorianne Laux. For delving deeper into the soul of poetry, its embodiment of metaphor rather than its structure, refer to two books by George Lakoff and Mark Johnson, *Metaphors We Live By* and *More Than Cool Reason.* And for a cogent multidiscipinary approach to the creation of meaning in language, read Paul Ricoeur's *The Rule of Metaphor.* But the most substantial and significant way to learn about poetry is to read it. Widely and often.

*Writing Fiction*   Two fine books by Josip Novakovich, *Fiction Writer's Workshop* and *Writing Fiction Step by Step,* lead a writer through every step of creating a fictional work. Sources of fiction, character, plot, point of view, setting, beginnings and endings, scene, dialogue, voice, description and word choice, image and metaphor, style, and revisions—all are covered in depth. *Creating Fiction,* edited by Julie Checkoway, offers perspectives and advice on the craft of fiction from many notable writers and teachers of writing. And Rust Hills's *Writing in General and the Short Story in Particular* is also of high caliber. There is a subgenre of fiction called brief fiction, which is also referred to as sudden, micro, flash, or fast fiction. *Micro Fiction,* edited by Jerome Stern; *Flash Fiction,* edited by James Thomas, et al.; and *Sudden Fiction,* in two volumes, edited by Robert Shapard and James Thomas, are all filled with prose writing. *Fast Fiction,* by Roberta Allen, is a "course" in constructing quick fiction.

*Nonfiction Writing*   The best work in this fact-based prose is called creative or literary nonfiction. Many M.F.A. programs in creative writing now include this genre in their curricula. Nonfiction is in the facts. Creative nonfiction is in the telling of those facts. It is literary because it is infused with the stylistic devices of the best fiction and the most lyrical of narrative poetry. It has enduring value, a fidelity to truthfulness, and it assumes the intelligence of the reader. There are several books available on this genre. I have found the following to be particularly salutary.

In *Creative Nonfiction: Researching and Crafting Stories of Real Life*, Philip Gerard has written the quintessential guide to the genre. He accompanies the reader from the inception of an idea for a story through the researching, interviewing, writing, and revising of it. There is even a chapter on how to avoid a libel suit. The second book, which Gerard co-edited with the poet Carolyn Forché, is *Writing Creative Nonfiction*. In this collection of essays, writers of the genre, who also teach writing, talk about what they do and how they do it. The *New Yorker* profiles are stunning examples of creative nonfiction. There is now a collection of them entitled *Life Stories*, edited by David Remnick. *The Essayist at Work*, edited by Lee Gutkind, is another collection of interviews with and essays by several well-known writers in this area of writing. Two collections of essays, *The New Journalism*, edited by Tom Wolfe and E. W. Johnson, and *The Literary Journalists*, edited by Norman Sims, are also of value. A collection of brief creative nonfiction pieces—between one and five pages each— is found in a book titled *In Short*, which is edited by Judith Kitchen and Mary Paumier Jones. This is just the thing for a quick read before beginning a day's writing. And *On Writing Well*, by William Zinsser, is considered "the classic guide to writing nonfiction."

*Philosophizing about Writing*   *Becoming a Writer*, by Dorothea Brande, and *If You Want to Write*, by Brenda Ueland, are two long-standing handbooks on writing that, in a conversational style, deal with the workings of the imagination and the process of the unconscious as they pertain to writing. *The Forest for the Trees*, by Betsy Lerner, is an intelligent and knowledgeable tour through the writer's psyche. If you are an Ambivalent Writer, a Natural-Born Writer, a Wicked Child, a Self-Promoter, or a Neurotic Writer, you will find yourself described in these pages. The second half of Lerner's book offers, from the insider perspective of a former editor and now agent, an authentic tour through the publishing process.

*Writers on Writing*   There are too many of these to list, but the most indispensable are Carolyn Heilbrun's *Writing a Woman's Life;* Annie Dillard's *The Writing Life* and *Living by Fiction; Henry Miller on Writing,* by Henry Miller; *The Art of Writing*, by Lu Chi, the second-century Chinese poet; John Steinbeck's *Working Days* and *Journal of a Novel*, about his work, respectively, on *The Grapes of Wrath* and *East of Eden*; Ursula K. LeGuin's *Steering the Craft* and *Dancing at the Edge of the World* (which every woman writer should read for "The Fisherwoman's Daughter," an essay about what it means to be a woman and a writer); and the contemporary classics *Writing Down the Bones* and *Wild Mind*, by Natalie Goldberg. Thomas Farber's gem *Compared to What?* is a rich blend of meditations on and nonfiction stories about the writing life.

*Interviews with and Essays by Writers*   I am especially drawn to interviews with writers, and there are none better than those culled from the *Paris Review* and gathered in George Plimpton's series "Writers at Work." The series is now up to twelve volumes, including *Women Writers at Work* and *Poets at Work*. Other books of interviews are *Novelists in Interview*, by John Haffenden; *Writing Lives: Conversations Between Women Writers*, edited by Mary Chamberlain; *Passion and Craft*, edited by Bonnie Lyons and Bill Oliver; and two unusual compilations, a revealing selection of interviews by Naomi Epel, *Writers Dreaming*, and, equally unveiling, *Tales from the Couch: Writers on Therapy*, essays edited by Jason Shinder. There is now a plethora of collections of essays by writers discussing their work, but Janet Sternburg's edited two-volume *The Writer on Her Work* is good. Two of my favorite books in this genre are Doris Lessing, *Conversations*, edited by Earl G. Ingersoll, and, the best of all, *The Egotists*, by Italian journalist Oriana Fallaci. Although her selection is not solely of writers, Fallaci's writing in general and her chutzpah in particular make this book essential reading.

*Anthologies*   An essential compendium of quotes is *Advice to Writers*, compiled by Jon Winokur, and another basic anthology of advice is *The Writer's Home Companion*, edited by Joan Bolker. I have bought copies of Susan Shaughnessy's *Walking on Alligators* for at least two dozen friends and clients. My own copy is well worn.

Anthologies of writings from various cultures are significant to my library. *To Live and Write: Selections by Japanese Women Writers,* edited by Yukiko Tanaka; *Black-Eyed Susans/Midnight Birds: Stories by and about Black Women,* edited by Mary Helen Washington; *Black Women Writers at Work,* edited by Claudia Tate; *Writing Women's Worlds: Bedouin Stories,* by Lila Abu-Lughod; *Latina Self-Portraits: Interviews with Contemporary Women Writers,* edited by Juanita Heredia and Bridget A. Kevane; and *Asian American Women Writers (Women Writers of English and Their Works),* edited by Harold Bloom, have all been rewarding excursions into unknown realms for me.

*Getting Published*   One purpose of writing is to share one's work through the publishing of it. It is usually a lengthy and arduous path to that destination. A book that has been with me since I wrote my first proposal many years ago is Michael Larsen's *How to Write a Nonfiction Book Proposal.* I have probably written ten or more proposals using Larsen's method. The beauty of thinking in terms of writing a nonfiction book proposal is that you begin to ask the right questions about your project: What's my purpose for writing this book? Is there a need for another book on this topic? What is my vision or goal for it? What is the "hook" or selling point of the book? Who will read this book? What is the organizing principle or spine of the book? How will my book be different from other books similar to it already on the market? What is the overview of the book? Elizabeth Lyon's *Nonfiction Book Proposals Anybody Can Write* is also excellent and perhaps even more thorough than Larsen's. And *The Shortest Distance Between You and a Published Book,* by Susan Page, is indispensable as a book to guide you through the "seeking-to-be-published" phase of your career.

*Miscellaneous*   Here are a few books in my list that defy the previous categories, at least in terms of books about writing: *The Writer's Desk* by Jill Krementz and *The New Yorker Book of Literary Cartoons.* John Berger has long been a writer whose work I read both for its lyrical prose and intellectual curiosity. *His Ways of Seeing* and *About Looking,* in particular, seem appropriate to include because we experience life through our sense perceptions and the written word becomes an expression of our inner visions.

### The Writer's Mentor Suggests . . .

1. It is a luxury to have an expansive library of one's own, but it is not crucial to the process of writing itself. As you begin to forge your practice of writing, you will move from the state of apprentice to practitioner and in the process, propagate an ever-increasing body of work. While so doing, organically begin to assemble a collection of books into a library. I hope you learn from me: It isn't necessary to personally own every book listed on Amazon.com! Select wisely and prudently.

2. The following are not books on writing per se but are literary necessities, nonetheless. A subscription to the *New Yorker* is crucial. Between the lush profiles and the preeminent fiction, you will learn about people and matters of interest, yes, but you will also learn about good writing—and the cartoons will add both pleasure and a modicum of sanity to your day. Buy this magazine and read it religiously. Other excellent literary periodicals are *Harper's* magazine and the *Atlantic Monthly*. My favorite quarterly journals are *Granta* and *Anteaus*, but there are numerous others from which to choose.

3. The annual anthologies of "The Best American . . ." series are also excellent. I try to at least peruse each new volume of *The Best American Essays* (2001, for instance), *The Best American Fiction*, and *The Best American Poetry*. Inevitably, I discover the work of a new author, who is then added to my growing stable of favorites.

## The Writer's Mentor at the Movies
### *Celeste*

We are fortunate to have the memoir of Celeste Albaret (an uneducated farm girl and not regarded as a writer herself), a record of her nine years of devoted service as housekeeper, cook, secretary, confidante, companion, and surrogate mother to the French writer Marcel Proust. Based on this winsome memoir is the equally entrancing German film *Celeste* (1981), directed by Percy Adlon. It seems odd to have the life of a writer of such flamboyant prose made by a German rather than a French director, but perhaps the spartan setting and inhibited sensibility serve its subject well.

When we meet Celeste, the housekeeper, she is sitting rigidly at a wooden table in a small kitchen. We wonder what she is doing until a voice-over explains that she is waiting for "Monsieur" to ring for his café and croissant. The moments seem barely to proceed as the camera oscillates from the face of the large-handed wall clock to the emotionless face of Celeste and back again. The only sound is a confusion of the exaggerated tick . . . tick of the clock, which subtly becomes what we perceive as the flagging staccato of Celeste's heart. We are shown, actually *placed in*, this claustrophobic environment until we feel its suffocating effects and, like Proust, who suffered from asthma throughout his life, we find ourselves gasping for air.

*Celeste* is one of those rare films to successfully portray with insight, wit, and poignancy the creative and emotional life of an artist. We are shown Proust as he is overcome with the feverish passion for finding words for his thoughts and putting them down on paper. During the last ten years of his life, an increasing invalidism and what previously had been Proust's gradual disengagement from social life became a self-imposed confinement to his bedroom and, like Colette and Truman Capote after him, he wrote exclusively from the sanctuary of his bed. He had ingeniously devised a way to add new sections of writing to those that had already been written: Proust would write on a scrabble of papers, then Celeste, the secretary, would take them and tenderly glue them together in the order he had indicated; she would then fold them in an accordion fashion. Thus, into the cohesive "manuscript" additional annotations could easily be inserted. This is fascinating movie-watching for any writer, especially those of us who were writing during the pre-computer era, when "cut and paste" actually meant with scissors and glue.

However, the film is less successful in its attempt to demonstrate through the camera the workings of Proust's writing style, which is by turns psychological, allegorical, and often stream-of-consciousness. For although we become privy to certain scenes about which he is thinking or even writing, Proust's verbal and literary acumen do not translate well into a visual medium.

Nor does *Celeste* endeavor to recreate that singular moment in literature in which, during a real-life incident, an involuntary childhood memory was revived through the sensory pleasure of tasting tea and a biscuit. In *Remembrance of Things Past,* the biscuit of course metamorphosed into the mnemonic madeleine.

But in *Celeste* we experience the palpable intimacy between this middle-aged homosexual author and his virtual life support, Celeste. Proust shares with her his profuse anxieties about his health, his vitriolic gossip, his genuine concerns and uncertainties about his writing, and, on the rare occasion, his deep affection for her.

Every writer needs a Celeste.

# CHAPTER 4

# WHEN *to* WRITE

## *Assessing the Practicalities of Writing*

What is the best time of day to write?

How long should my periods of writing be?
Should I write by hours or pages?

Is it necessary to have a writing schedule?

Do I need to work with a project timeline or set daily writing goals?

The Writer's Mentor at the Movies: *Henry and June*

WHEN TO WRITE: ASSESSING THE PRACTICALITIES OF WRITING takes on the topic of when to write—morning, afternoon, evening, or late night—and how to decide the time of day that works best for you. It addresses the issues of working with a writing schedule or not, whether to set daily writing goals, and the contest between writing by hours or pages. It explores the work habits of such writers as Joseph Campbell, Aleksander Solzhenitsyn, and Norman Mailer and provides a detailed outline for orchestrating a writing schedule that suits your personal needs.

My commentary on the film *Henry and June* looks at how the writers Anaïs Nin and Henry Miller produced their early works while living in Paris. Although one was secure in her husband's financial and emotional support and the other often destitute and ridiculed, even abandoned, by his wife June, they shared in common a manic devotion for putting passion on paper.

# WHAT IS THE BEST TIME OF DAY TO WRITE?

> I have a very rigorous work schedule. Every
> morning until two in the afternoon. . . .
> —*MARIO VARGAS LLOSA*

> I think the afternoon is a good time to work. . . .
> —*ANTHONY BURGESS*

> I write at night . . . and work until about
> three or four A.M.
> —*JAMES BALDWIN*

I happen to subscribe to the early morning writing schedule, even to the extent proposed by poet W. H. Auden, to "get up very early and get going at once, in fact, work first and wash afterwards." During the writing of certain of my books, some friends and acquaintances will be flabbergasted to learn, I often rose for writing as early as four in the morning in order to enjoy that gorgeous time of calm and quiet that gives my nomadic consciousness more open road, so to speak. Because, along with the burgeoning light of day, comes noise, even, on a more subtle level: the inaudible hum of electrical, telegraphic, and human energies—all those heaters and radios and showers and toasters being turned on simultaneously; the multitudinous telephone calls being placed and answered; the staggering sameness of all those first murmurings—"Good morning"; "Come and eat your breakfast"; "I had the strangest dream . . ."; "Mommy, I don't feel well"—that begin when the world's eye opens. To put it bluntly: The emerging day brings on a cacophony of human activity. Sometimes I feel like Damiel, the angel in *Wings of Desire,* who hears the inner-most thoughts of every person he passes. Not that I'm any angel, by a l-o-n-g shot. But perhaps the aural and kinetic sensitivity is similar between angels and writers.

So, what about you? When is the best time of day for you to write? Do you feel more dynamic in the evening or more productive in the afternoon or more creative in the morning? You probably already have a good sense of your own circadian rhythms. Some folks can barely get themselves out of bed by 10 A.M., let alone encounter a blank sheet of paper, without wanting to jump back into bed and pull the covers over their fuzzy minds. Others can't keep their eyes open anytime after eight o'clock in the evening. (Toni Morrison, the Nobel Laureate, insists that she is "not very bright or very witty or very inventive after the sun goes down.")

Of course, because we are socialized creatures, when we write often depends largely on our age, occupation, living situation, marital status and/or parental responsibilities, and the degree of urgency involved with whatever writing project may be at hand. For example, when Toni Morrison first began writing seriously, she was a single mother—make that a *working* single mother—who wrote in the predawn hours before she heard her first "'Mama"—and that was always around five in the morning. She then got her kids fed and off to school and went to her nine-to-five job as an editor at Random House publishers. Many years later, after her children had left the nest and when for two years she stayed home and wrote, she had to discover anew what her own preferences were, outside of her children's needs and her employment obligations. What time she wanted to go to bed. What time she wanted to eat. What time she wanted to write. Interestingly, she realized that the habit of rising early, which she had formed out of necessity when her children were young, had now become her choice.

### The Writer's Mentor Suggests . . .

1. Plan writing sessions during various times of the day and night. Try every possible permutation of the day: early, mid-, late, morning, afternoon, evening. Sense what feels most comfortable, most productive, most creative.

2. Keep a record of your daily energy levels for a few weeks. Did you find that entire Mondays are "lost" days to you? That even

though you prefer to write between 5 and 8 P.M. your family resents your absence from the collective? That staying up until two in the morning after four cups of coffee felt great at the time but was a disaster the next day at the business office? By keeping track of both your spirited and flagging periods of the day, you will discover which times work best for you.

❧ ❧

# HOW LONG SHOULD MY PERIODS OF WRITING BE? SHOULD I WRITE BY HOURS OR PAGES?

> The goal is not a number of words or hours spent writing. All you need to do is to keep your heart and mind open to the work.
> —WALTER MOSLEY

The question of whether to write for a set amount of time or number of pages during any given writing period fully depends on a writer's needs, disposition, energy level, and life circumstances. Are you working on a deadline? Is that thousand-word article for an online magazine due by next Tuesday? Do you find that you work better if you procrastinate and then allow an adrenaline rush to propel you to complete a term paper for your college class? Or do you pragmatically plan out a schedule of the *days* you will write, the number of *hours* you will write, and the *amount* you will have completed after each day's period of writing? Are you a slow, meticulous writer, who works at the steady pace of a tortoise? Or are you a kinetic hare, with bursts of creative vigor and potency but an inability to sustain this pace for longer than thirty minutes? Do you prefer to rush through a first draft and edit it later, or do you correct and edit as you write? Asking yourself all of these questions will allow you to determine answers to the hours-versus-pages predicament.

As it happens, patterns of writing often change over time and/or with projects. Writers often work on different projects at different speeds and through dissimilar means. During the writing of *The Naked and the Dead,* for example, Norman Mailer was able to maintain a steady pace of seven pages a day. But when it came to writing *Barbary Shore,* he was only able to complete three pages per day. Often the complexity of a topic, one's familiarity with it, and its emotional impact on the creator direct the mode and tempo of writing.

In my own work I have found that setting a specific goal, such as writing until I have completed a chapter, works best for me. Working by hours doesn't seem to be as productive—it's too easy to sit at my desk for, say, two or three hours and, at the end of the writing period, discover that very little has been accomplished—except, perhaps, an online reading of the *New York Times* and responses to several E-mails. Because I am usually working on an external deadline—imposed either from a publisher's or school's structure, I have had to train myself to work in segments of time and to prudently adhere to them. With this very book, in fact, toward the final three months of writing it, I set the goal of completing four questions per week. When I first began this schedule I found that I was spending upward of six or more hours a day on a given question. And then one morning I had only three hours to write before attending a meeting. I made the decision to complete the question in that period of time, as if I actually had to submit it to a magazine editor. To my surprise, I finished it. Since that time I've tried my best to formally set the hours and within them commit to completing a first draft of writing, or the editing of it. It doesn't always work, but generally it does. If I have four hours, I'll use four hours. If I have six hours, I'll use six hours. But with focus, a lot can be produced in a two- or three-hour slot of time.

The most important element here is to develop a form of addiction to your writing, to establish a pleasurable relationship with it. Make writing a place where you can go to experience privacy with yourself.

*I might write four lines or I might write twenty. I subtract and I add until I really hit something I want to do. You don't always whittle down, sometimes you whittle up.*

—GRACE PALEY

*I work until the vein is out. There's something about the way you feel, you know when the well is dry, that you'll have to wait till tomorrow and it'll be full up again.*

—KATHERINE ANNE PORTER

*The Writer's Mentor Suggests . . .*

There are at least four methods of getting your writing done.

1. You can decide on a certain number of hours that you will be at your desk. So you might determine that you have two hours, four days a week, for your writing. So far so good. You may find that this system works well for you and that writing does indeed get done. But instead, what if during that time you talk on the telephone, respond to E-mails, read the *New York Times,* or simply stare out the window? The two hours have passed, but few words were put to paper.

2. You might try to complete a certain volume of writing. This is the "seat of the pants" method in which you sit at your desk until you have finished the allotted amount of writing. Writing doesn't happen unless you train yourself to stay put and concentrate.

3. Using the inspiration technique, you sit until your Muse has sufficiently inspired you with one or two good ideas. With this approach, however, you never know *when* the Muse will make an appearance. If you wait for her to appear and nothing transpires, you will have wasted your time *and* produced nothing. Also, you will be extremely disappointed and may use this as an excuse to enter a funk and feel poorly about yourself as well as about writing. And, frankly, not every day is one of invention.

4. Write by pages. Your goal could be one page to five pages of a rough draft, a journal entry, a poem, or a piece of sudden or flash fiction. The advantage to this method is that you have an incentive to get the writing done expeditiously and without the often accompanying wringing of hands. And it trains you to write faster, to have more conscious access to your creative process.

One of these methods is bound to work for you. Try each of them for a week and see how you feel about your writing and about yourself as a writer. Stick with the method that works best for you, be it by pages or hours.

# Is it necessary to have a writing schedule?

> Now this is very important and can hardly
> be emphasized too strongly: You have decided
> to write at four o'clock, and at four o'clock
> write you must! Teach yourself that
> no excuse of any nature can be offered
> when the moment comes.
>
> —*DOROTHEA BRANDE*

In the documentary about the life of Joseph Campbell, *A Hero's Journey,* Campbell talks to his interviewer about his work schedule, which ran six to seven days a week. First he took the twenty-four hours in a day, subtracted eight hours for sleeping, and divided the remaining sixteen into four equal blocks of time of four hours each: 8 A.M. to 12 P.M., 12 P.M. to 4 P.M., 4 P.M. to 8 P.M., and 8 P.M. to 12 A.M. His day began at eight in the morning with breakfast. By nine o'clock Campbell was at his desk ready to begin a day's work of scholarly research and writing. After three hours, at noon, he broke for an hour lunch period. Back to work by one o'clock, he utilized the next three hours, again, for work. By four o'clock that afternoon he was ready for another hour-long respite, during which he often did his physical exercise for the day (in his youth, Campbell had been an Olympic athlete). The following two chunks of time offered a bit more flexibility. If he and his wife, Jean Erdman, a dancer with Martha Graham, had a social engagement, he would shift his schedule to accommodate it, but, afterward, he would be back to the task at hand until the midnight hour, when the luxury of sleep would offer up its quiet pleasure.

Of course, I might add, this was when Campbell was still a relatively young man. However, even as a man in his late seventies,

Campbell still adhered to a work schedule that, by any standards and at any age, was Herculean. A colleague of mine, who knew Campbell well and occasionally traveled with him to various cities in the world where Campbell was either lecturing or doing research on his beloved mythological studies, once told me that Campbell always took to the road with two suitcases: one for clothes, the second filled with books for study. But, even more impressive, by the time they returned to their lodgings in the evening, and after a full day of work and socializing, Campbell was eager to return to his writing and reading, even if it was quite late at night. My friend, who was perhaps forty years Campbell's junior, shook his head in amazement when he added, "I was exhausted, but Joe was ready, impatient, even, to switch gears and keep going. His energy and ability to focus were remarkable."

Okay, I agree with you, it's unlikely that the average writer will be able to adhere to a schedule this demanding, and, I admit, ever since I first heard this story perhaps ten years ago, I've been trying to devise a similar schedule of my own. Naturally, the difficulty is not with originating the schedule; it's maintaining it.

In early 2001, David Remnick, the editor of *New Yorker* magazine, interviewed Aleksandr Solzhenitsyn at his home in the country outside of Moscow. In his profile of Solzhenitsyn, Remnick comments on the eighty-three-year-old Solzhenitsyn's diminished energy. Apparently, when he was writing *The Gulag Archipelago,* he would make two writing days out of one. Remnick says that Solzhenitsyn would "get up at 1 A.M. and work until nine; take a break and then work again until six, eat dinner, go to bed at 7 P.M., sleep till one, and then start again—all while expecting a knock on the door" from the KGB.

I share these anecdotes not to dishearten you about your own fortitude but as a model, a paradigm of what developing a work schedule and adhering to it might accomplish, as well as to demonstrate that the ingrained positive habits we develop early in our lives and in our work can affect and serve the remainder of a lifetime.

Good work habits include effective planning. And an additional benefit is that an expedient organization of time can help make one's writing far less stressful. A certain methodicalness and routinization

*It's a job. It's not a hobby. . . . You have to sit down and work, to schedule your time and stick to it. Even if it's just for an hour or so each day. . . . If you're going to make writing succeed you have to approach it as a job.*

—ROSELLEN BROWN

is what, in the end, gets those poems, essays, school papers, articles, and books written. It is by structuring your time that you *make*—not *find*—periods to write on a regular basis. Scheduling assures that we will get our writing started, keep up a momentum, and complete our projects.

And, last, a paradox about a scheduled writing plan is that as we thoroughly integrate it into our lives, we will discover that our other activities, which have nothing to do with writing, miraculously become more enjoyable because we have alleviated the gnawing feelings of guilt and regret at not doing what we most wish to do: write.

### The Writer's Mentor Suggests . . .

Begin to plan a schedule for your writing today. Take an 8½-by-11, or larger, piece of paper, or use a weekly schedule from your datebook or personal organizer, or apply the following instructions to a piece of graph paper. If you are using a blank sheet of paper, design a one-week grid. Draw seven equal columns using the length of the paper. At the tops of the columns, list Monday through Sunday. On the width side, draw a line for every hour of the day, beginning sometime between five and seven in the morning (earlier, if it's appropriate). Continue down the grid until you reach nine or ten o'clock at night (later, if need be). Now begin to parcel off blocks of time that signify activities other than writing. For instance, you might work nine to five, so that will absorb a substantial amount of time during the day, Monday through Friday. (In this case, reserving weekends for your writing may be the most practical.) Section off Tuesday and Thursday evenings, when you attend an Italian conversation class, and Friday evening, when you go out to dinner and a movie with your girlfriend or husband. Proceed in this manner until you whittle down to your "free" periods of time. You will now see that Monday and Wednesday evenings are without a pre-arranged activity. Therefore, those can be used for writing, perhaps from seven to nine or even ten. Keep in mind that this schedule may be altered when circumstances in your life change: a move, a marriage, a newborn infant, a divorce, a job change.

# Do I NEED TO WORK WITH A PROJECT TIMELINE OR SET DAILY WRITING GOALS?

> I work . . . just about every day.
> If I sit there like that for two or three years,
> at the end I have a book.
> —*PHILIP ROTH*

Unlike grocery shopping or housecleaning, writing is cumulative. There is an often-repeated maxim among writers, similar to Philip Roth's statement, that goes like this: If you write a page a day, at the end of a year, you will have a 365-page manuscript. Of course, it should go without saying that this method does not guarantee the *quality* of those 365 pages. But in this chapter we are concerned with *accumulating* those pages—we will deal with the content and its caliber elsewhere in this book.

Since the day I placed my first book, *On Women Turning 40*, with a publisher in 1990, it seems that I have been living on deadlines and working within specific timelines for each project. The problem is, I had no concept of what a project timeline was, much less how to fashion one. To date I have written and been fortunate enough to have published eight books. The first few were completed, I often believe, *grace à Dieu*. And, believe me, it's not as if I didn't work my tail off in the process; it's just that I *wasted* so much time out of ignorance. I knew nothing about how to organize my writing time. And it never occurred to me to find a book on the topic that might be helpful to me—if, indeed, any existed.

Slowly, I began to devise schedules and calendars, routines and procedures. They each seemed to provide something sound in terms of structure and direction, but there was never a cohesive plan of action that I could "carry" with me from project to project. By the time I began work on my Ph.D. dissertation, I was teaching regularly through the University of California, Santa Cruz, Extension, and at the UCLA Writer's Program, I was lecturing at a variety of venues, I was presenting papers at various conferences, *and* I was writing a book every year or two. Being back in school full time and beginning to write my dissertation, I knew I needed professional help on getting organized. I researched scores of books and discovered two—among many—on the subject of writing (and *completing*—an important factor!) dissertations, theses, and books. They are *Writing Your Dissertation in Fifteen Minutes a Day: A Guide to Starting, Revising, and Finishing Your Doctoral Thesis,* by Joan Bolker, Ed.D., and *The Clockwork Muse: A Practical Guide to Writing Theses, Dissertations, and Books,* by Eviatar Zerubavel. *The Clockwork Muse* was especially helpful in training me to create practical and workable project timelines. This book rethinks the writing process in terms of time and organization. It offers writers a simple yet comprehensive framework that considers such variables as when to write, for how long, and how often, while keeping a sense of momentum throughout the entire project. And Zerubavel's recommendation for devising an effective timetable for translating the language of text (the number of pages) to the language of time (in calendrical terms) is exceedingly knowledgeable and pragmatic.

### The Writer's Mentor Suggests . . .

1. A project timeline calls for a particular kind of road map. The book mentioned, *The Clockwork Muse,* clearly describes how to divide a project into various constituent segments and how to project for each of those segments its approximate length in pages, the pace at which you reasonably think you can write it, the estimated amount of time you will need for writing it, and a tentative deadline for its completion. (Remember that it is always a good idea to *overestimate* the writing time needed for each section. By doing that you save yourself from the disappointment inherent in underestimating.) By fashioning these

*I started active work on Feb. 19, so it is just a little over two months. At that rate the book should be done by the first of November, but that is allowing for no accidents whatever and it would be an odd year when something drastic did not happen. I am allowing two weeks for accidents and will figure to be done by Christmas.*
—JOHN STEINBECK

elements together on a 2-by-3-foot, four-month planner that is erasable and has a plastic surface, you will be able to depict on this chart every single step of your project over the next several months or years. Being able to visualize your writing plans in such detail certainly helps demystify them. It allows you to monitor the process and makes projecting your progress more predictable and therefore less intimidating.

2. If you have undertaken the creation of the Great American Novel and feel impeded by any external structure or timeframe, you may wish to forego this method and, as Philip Roth described in the opening epigraph, "work . . . just about every day" so that at the end of two or three years you will have a book. This method will work well *if* you actually do get that page a day written. But if not, proceed with the instructions in the preceding exercise.

## The Writer's Mentor at the Movies
### *Henry and June*

The film *Henry and June* is known to be based on a portion of the "unexpurgated" diary of Anaïs Nin, written between 1931 and 1934, which in 1986 was published in book form as *Henry and June*. But it is also seasoned with Henry Miller's autobiographical novel *Tropic of Cancer*—a frank and lively account of an American artist's adventures in Paris during the same years. For many writers and artists—including myself—there is an interest that boarders on obsession about the bohemian expatriates who in the early decades of the twentieth century left American soil in order to find their voices in a free-living and -loving European milieu. From across the Atlantic these writers arrived in waves, the most well known of them being Gertrude Stein and Ezra Pound in the 1910s, F. Scott Fitzgerald and Ernest Hemingway in the 1920s, and that intensely individualistic and rebellious spirit, Henry Miller in 1930.

Although the film is titled *Henry and June,* it could easily have been called *Henry and Anaïs.* It portrays the love triangle that developed between Anaïs Nin, Henry Miller, and Henry's wife June. However, the story also delves into the beginnings of an artistic friendship between Henry Miller and Anaïs Nin that would last throughout their long lives.

When Miller first arrives at the elegantly bourgeois home of Anaïs and her sweet, mild-mannered banker husband, Hugo, we learn that she is struggling to complete her first book on noted novelist D. H. Lawrence and that Henry is working on a sexually explicit book that he can't decide whether to call *Sing the Equator* or *Tropic of Cancer.*

We also learn that Anaïs is erotically adventurous and is looking for the kind of fulfillment that the soon-to-be cuckolded Hugo cannot provide. Thus, two strands of common interest—sex and art—intertwine a virile Henry and a craving Anaïs. Eventually, a third will be Henry's wife, June.

The volcanic release of Anaïs and Henry's literary and sexual energy produced some of the most highly regarded fiction written during this fecund milieu of Paris. And *Henry and June* allows us to be privy to their unfolding. We see how, through a mutual respect, encouragement, and artistic camaraderie, these two writers develop and sustain a practice of writing. As a child Anaïs began writing in her journals as a means of logging her experiences and emotional longings for a father who had abandoned her. As a woman, her daily accounting of facts and feelings had continued, but now she was prime for developing her writing into new forms.

Anaïs and Henry met each other at a crucial point in their personal and professional lives. The film is about the attraction of two hungry minds in search of artistic, intellectual, and sexual liberation. The characters recognize in each other a co-conspirator and kindred spirit. Essentially, *Henry and June* provides a visually lush and noetically stimulating account of two writers who lived through a revolutionary creative period that spawned a variety of culturalisms, especially surrealism, which had infatuated artistic, intellectual, and psychological sensibilities. Henry's financial struggles are accurately depicted, as are his and Anaïs's internal creative wrestlings and uncertainties about the quality of their written work. After their friendship began, Anaïs (and Hugo) afforded Henry economic sustenance—including a typewriter—and even paid for the original French publication of *Tropic of Cancer*.

We see Henry, in the cockroach-infested garret on the Left Bank that he shares with an assortment of bohemian guests, writing throughout the various stages of both the sun's and moon's rising and setting. The wall he faces as he sits at his typewriter is covered with notes to himself about the novel he is writing. An ashtray overflows with cigarette butts as clouds of smoke circle around him like ethereal muses. But we also see the life he lived in atmospheric Paris cafés, cinemas, and on city streets. And the consummate soundtrack of authentic period music, which includes pieces from Satie, Poulenc, and Debussy, and the voice of Josephine Baker, is an additional pleasure. Henry's picaresque friends—pickpockets, magicians, circus performers, contortionists, prostitutes, a lawyer, writers, painters, gypsies, and the happy-go-lucky photographer Brassai, setting up some of his most recognizable tableaux of the demimonde—flit around him like the characters that will celebrate and memorialize them in *Tropic of Cancer*.

For Henry (in his early forties) and Anaïs (in her late twenties) there was no best time of day to write, nor a need to set daily writing goals, nor have a writing schedule. In *Henry and June* we see artists who are consumed by their work. We see them writing in and out of bed, at all hours of the day and night. And reading each other's manuscripts with the same fervor that they eat the delicious soufflés and pot-au-feu served up to them. Their passion for writing is contagious.

We are fortunate to have this visually bringing-to-life of images that had heretofore only been fantasized while reading about them in the novels of Henry Miller and the inexhaustible diaries of Anaïs Nin—who seldom had an unrecorded experience. It is impossible to imagine a film being made from these books when they were first published, partly because for decades the books themselves were banned in the United States and England. *Henry and June* stirred me to revisit the original writings on which it was based. And, aside from provoking a fantasy to time travel back to 1930s Paris, this film imbued me with the desire to go to my desk and put my own words on paper. And for a writer, that is a film worth watching.

# CHAPTER 5

# HOW

## *Getting Started*

How do I get started? What are some helpful pre-writing rituals?

Should I write by hand or on a computer?

I don't have any ideas; where do I begin?
I feel overwhelmed by so many ideas; where do I begin?

What should I do when I'm not in the mood to write?

The Writer's Mentor at the Movies: *Quills*

How: GETTING STARTED offers examples of the commencements devices used by writers Toni Morrison, Don Delillo, and Dame Edith Sitwell, among others, to get started on a day's work. It looks at reasons that writers prefer to write by hand or by computer, what to do when you have too many writing ideas—or none at all, how to deal with all the excuses we make for not writing because we aren't "in the mood," and what the writers Joyce Carol Oates, Peter Matthiessen, and Francis Ford Coppola have to say about it. In this chapter you will learn about the concepts of an idea fund and an image bank and how to "invest" in both of them. And in an analysis of the film *Quills*, I look at the Marquis de Sade, who, even without writing implements, was the quintessential writer who put passion on paper.

# HOW DO I GET STARTED? WHAT ARE SOME HELPFUL PRE-WRITING RITUALS?

> Getting started is partly stalling, stalling by
> way of reading and of listening to music,
> which energizes me and also makes me rest-
> less. Feeling guilty about not writing ... But
> once something is really under way, I don't
> want to do anything else.
>
> —SUSAN SONTAG

Many writers have psychological or quasi-spiritual stratagems they use to help get their writing started each day. Toni Morrison has said that "writers all devise ways to approach that place where they expect to make contact, where they become the conduit, or where they engage in this mysterious process." In an interview with the *Paris Review,* Morrison describes how a writer friend of hers ritually touches something on her desk before she hits her keyboard; Morrison's own observance is to rise in the morning before dawn, make a cup of coffee, and drink it while she watches "the light come." Don DeLillo complains about squandering his writing time by looking out the window or reading random entries in the dictionary. "To break the spell," he looks at a photograph of Jorge Luis Borges that he keeps in his study. Even though DeLillo admits he knows nothing about Borges' writing process, he sees in the photograph a writer "who did not waste time at the window or anywhere else. So I've tried to make him my guide out of lethargy and drift into the other-world of magic, art and divination."

*There isn't any secret. You sit down and you start and that's it.*
—ELMORE LEONARD

These methods of preparing the brain for the concentrated effort of writing and the accompanying ceremonial functions can provide some structure to a shapeless day. Betsy Lerner calls this "developing a successful formula for getting pages written. . . ." According to editor Michael Korda, Jacqueline Susann "wrote on pink paper, and she had apparently not discovered the 'Shift' key on her typewriter (a pink IBM Selectra) [because] she wrote everything in capital letters, like a long telegram. . . ." Gore Vidal has said, "First coffee. Then a bowel movement. Then the Muse joins me." Reputedly, Dame Edith Sitwell liked to lie in an open coffin before beginning her day's work. But, personally, that's where I'd draw the line.

My own favorite practice is to read a bit before I get going. Sometimes it might be an interview with a writer and then a few pages of that writer's work; I may read a poem or two to soak myself in an emotive atmosphere and to get myself thinking verbally, or I might select a book from one of my reading piles and randomly choose a passage to spark my synapses. Some writers swear off reading other writers just before they begin their own work because they don't want to be influenced. But I guess it depends on who's influencing whom: Willa Cather began her sessions by reading passages from the Bible. But, most important, as Susan Sontag said, once you get going with your writing, you don't want to do anything else. So the sooner you start to write, the sooner you leave the predilection of stalling behind you.

### The Writer's Mentor Suggests . . .

The most important thing about writing is, simply, doing it. We all know that, but sometimes having a ritual of your own can ease you into the process, without having to tear your hair out or resort to drink! The following suggestion will get your pen moving and your keys clacking.

One of the easiest ways to go from staring at a blank sheet of paper to becoming engaged with a pageful of words is through the process of "freewriting," which was innovated by the writing instructor Peter Elbow. Freewrite as fast as you can, without worrying about grammar, spelling, or punctuation. If you can't think of anything to say, repeat the last word you wrote, or write, "I can't think of anything to write," over and over again until you do think of something (you will). Write for ten minutes. Think of this exercise as a way of stretching your mind, the way you stretch your limbs before a run. Or as a way of warming up your intellect, the way you warm up your car on a freezing morning. Write for ten minutes and then throw the

*It's very simple, really. You have to go to the typewriter, that's all you have to do. I have a word processor now, and you turn it on and something happens after a while. . . .*

—TERRENCE MCNALLY

pages away. One of the greatest gifts you can give yourself is to use this freewriting warm-up period as an opportunity for play. The purpose is the process, not the product. The function is to relieve your anxiety, not increase it.

If you still have trouble getting started, watch Jack Nicholson in *The Shining* typing the same line over and over again, and if that doesn't get you going . . .

···   ···

# Should I Write by Hand or on a Computer?

> Ever since I had an accident in which I broke a finger and couldn't use the typewriter for a few months, I have followed the custom of my youth and gone back to writing by hand. I discovered when my finger was better and I could type again that my poetry when written by hand was more sensitive; its plastic forms could change more easily. . . . The typewriter separated me from a deeper intimacy with poetry, and my hand brought me closer to that intimacy again.
>
> —PABLO NERUDA

> *I love the word processor. . . . I have to sneak past that internal censor who basically wants me to shut up and be silent, and the best way for me to get something said has been to move real fast. The faster I can write, the more likely I'll get something worth saving down on paper.*
>
> —RUSSELL BANKS

Have you ever had your palm read? It is remarkable that there are so many systems of folk belief and even science that say our entire lives—past, present, and future—can be read like a kind of cartography, a blueprint: in our eyes (iridology), on our feet (polarity therapy), in the shape of our skulls (phrenology), and in our hands (palmistry). "Blood is the body's ink," writes Julia Cameron. "We write our lives in it. The blood remembers what the mind forgets, and when the blood remembers, it tells the hand." Cameron, like

Pablo Neruda, elucidates one of the most compelling reasons for writing by hand.

They are right, for a rhythm evolves when writing by hand. A pulsating cadence springs directly from the beat of your heart and runs its course through the miles of arteries, veins, and capillaries that live in a 5-to-6-foot frame all the way to the edges of its circuitous world: the toes and fingertips. It's like thinking with your fingers.

Personally, I prefer longhand when I am beginning a piece of writing that I know eventually will be revised and rewritten later on my iBook. These are two different creative animals, and each fascinates two distinct and equally vital jurisdictions of consciousness. The one is where inspiration dwells: the extravagance of sensory current, the roaming free of the mind's eye, the tingling provocation of instinct, intuition, gut-level knowing. The other is where the judge and the critic live: in a psychological climate that is prudent and pragmatic, rational, shrewd, concerned with outcome and consequence, and devoted to adjudication.

Of course, this is my own bias. And for the very same reasons I favor writing by hand, other writers prefer the machine—and with good reason. As you read in the first margin quote to this section, Russell Banks has said that, for him, the computer is the most liberating because it is the fastest: "I can sneak up on myself and write things that I would never dare to say or write if I had to write it out longhand or if I had to say it publicly."

Since 1960, when I typed my first term paper (on Ezra Pound) for my eighth-grade teacher, Sister Marian Therese, I have hauled my circa 1940 Royal typewriter—a hand-me-down from my grandmother—around with me through nearly three dozen moves. My first article ever published came off that tireless antique. It still seems nearly as empathic as Dios, my dog. Of course, in this age of technical wizardry, a working sixty-year-old typewriter is an anachronism. But I love it. Even though I rarely use it, I know that after I die, someone will have to decide what to do with this beautiful instrument.

A rewarding aspect of either writing by hand or by typewriter is that the original words survive. Memory and history are tangible on paper, whereas on a computer, changes are made so quickly that

*I grew up with wet clay and a stylus. . . . From the very beginning, I've grabbed onto any technology that would allow me to write faster: a soft pencil instead of a hard pencil, ball point instead of a fountain pen, electric typewriter instead of manual and now, working with light on a screen rather than marks on a page.*

—RUSSELL BANKS

subtleties and accidental moments of brilliance can be lost forever. I try to train my clients to save each version of their rewrites because there will inevitably be something useful that would otherwise be deleted by a swift click on a keyboard and long forgotten.

### The Writer's Mentor Suggests . . .

Whatever your usual mode of writing is, change it for a week. If you are comfortable with writing longhand, switch to a word processor; if the word processor is your normal writing companion, sharpen up a few No. 2 pencils, experiment with various pens—ball point, felt tip, and fountain. Whichever one feels the most like home, begin to write with it. Give yourself enough time to notice the difference. In other words, if you try the new method for one week only, make sure you are actually writing every day. If you only write twice a week, go ahead and give yourself a month for the trial period. Record what the differences are. Does your hand quickly become tired with longhand? Do you feel too removed from your work by the computer? Note any change in mood, impressions, ideas, sensation, intuition. Sneak up on yourself.

-:-　-:-

# I DON'T HAVE ANY IDEAS; WHERE DO I BEGIN?
# I FEEL OVERWHELMED BY SO MANY IDEAS;
# WHERE DO I BEGIN?

> Another reason for writing in your diary is
> to discover that the ideas in you are an inex-
> haustible fountain. "No communications
> and gifts can exhaust genius," said Lavater.
> No human being as long as [she] is living,
> can be exhausted of [her] ever changing,
> ever moving river of ideas.
> —BRENDA UELAND

My agent is a saint. So is my editor. For many reasons, but in particular, both have the patience of Job when dealing with me and my fount of ideas. Just as Athena sprang fully grown from the head of her father, Zeus, so do my ideas. In fact, they often materialize as titles of books. And a copy of the published book—long before it is published—just as likely will present itself squarely in front of my mind's eye. I dutifully write down the concept and make a new file for it, for I never know which idea will swell my enthusiasm the most—or the soonest. This kind of seminal creative environment is excellent for the seeding of ideas, but it rarely sustains them to fruition. Would I prefer to have fewer literary ideas? Not on your life. This Grand Central Station of concepts that dwells in the prima mater of my mind is what gets me up in the morning and keeps me going throughout the day. "How you spend your days is how you spend your life," wrote Annie Dillard. My life is spent as a psychic receptor for and transmitter of ideas.

When it's time to settle into the serial monogamy inherent in writing a book (although, between you and me, I secretly practice biblio-polygamy—I can't help myself), I ask myself several questions. Primarily, Which idea engages me the most? and secondarily, Will it sustain my mental inquisitiveness during the course of the one to five years it will take me to complete it? Two additional questions of a personal nature are, Will the book, in some way, make a contribution? Is the content of the book a direction in which I'd like to take my professional career as a writer, lecturer, instructor, writing consultant, and cultural mythologist? Two practical questions are, Am I qualified to write this book? Do I have or can I acquire the necessary skills to research, interview for, and write it? Then, in the case of nonfiction, I must consider the publishing industry beast. The beast that, although it must be fed on demand, is very impetuous about its diet. Has what I want to write about already been done? Can I do it better, differently, updated? Is there enough of an audience for this topic to justify its existence? Will my agent find a willing and enthusiastic publishing house? Carefully answering these questions allows me to eventually focus on one idea long enough to complete a written proposal that can be shopped around.

*Fortunately, I have to force myself not to write. I get up every morning with a desire to sit down and work. My imagination has been overstimulated all my life by life itself.*

—ISAAC BASHEVIS SINGER

But what if your issue is just the opposite: You feel that you don't have or retain enough ideas? Take heart. As Brenda Ueland says in her quote, "The ideas in you are an inexhaustible fountain." Often people say they "don't have any ideas," when what they should be saying is, "I forget my ideas." The mind is continually drumming up new tableaux for consideration. What we do with them is up to us.

Personally, I have too many files, but then I'm never at a lack for ideas or substantiating support for them. And because I keep them fairly "groomed," I can usually find what I'm looking for—when I know what that is; if I don't, just the process of reviewing the files stirs my creative juices.

But I didn't feel so guilty when I read that Dwight Macdonald, the intellectual journalist, wrote in a letter, "Anal-retentive virtue is rewarded, also packratism." And speaking of his dog-eared files, he describes "the pleasure of a dirty old man voyeuristically tompeeping on his past." I don't carry it quite so far, but I get his gist.

Creativity is a matter of listening to yourself think, of being privy to the conversations that course through your mind, or being awake to the messages delivered to you by nature's psyche. Or, as Dorothea Brande observed, of hitching the unconscious to your writing arm. It's also a matter of training. Be on the lookout for the sources of your ideas: when and where they occur to you, what you were doing, how you were feeling, what you learned. Ascertain what excites you and which sphere of activity, study, or interest you'd like to investigate. Learn to listen, think, and notate quickly enough to outmaneuver the editing process that is always on guard to let us know "what a stupid idea that is." Nothing is stupid. Everything has possibilities.

### The Writer's Mentor Suggests . . .

Whether you have too many ideas or not enough, there are a few ways to keep track of them and to encourage the many ways in which they flow to us.

1.  Analyze circumstances that are most conducive to acquiring ideas and writing about them. Do ideas come to you as a natural

course of life while you are performing your daily tasks, or does it take the stimulation of conversation or a thought-provoking book or movie?

2. Keep an account, or more accurately, a file or archive, to categorize ideas when they arrive unannounced on your mindscape.

3. Think of concepts as a sort of bankable commodity and start an idea fund. What intrigues you? By what images are you surprised? What are some original juxtapositions or metaphoric impressions that occur to you? Write every one of them in your idea fund. You will be surprised at how quickly it fills up. To further assist the process of retrieval, index them by category.

4. When ideas come in a more tangible form, such as in the newspaper or magazines or passages in a book, collect them in a clipping or an image bank.

5. One of the exercises I present to the students in my writing groups is to show them a photograph or an image of some kind and ask them to write a story about it. In a group of twelve, it is remarkable how distinct and completely novel an approach each person takes. Select an intriguing image and write a story about it during a twenty-minute writing period.

❖   ❖

# WHAT SHOULD I DO WHEN I'M NOT IN THE MOOD TO WRITE?

> It's important to write when you are in the
> wrong mood or the weather is wrong. Even
> if you don't succeed you'll be developing a
> muscle that may do it later on.
> —*JOHN ASHBERY*

Sometimes I think we have a need to hold writing as if it were a romantic endeavor: everything has to be just so, just right, before we can sit down and face the page. Mood falls into this category. We readily put provisions on the conditions under which we can put words to paper: If I don't write before six o'clock in the morning, my writing spirit dissipates; I can't write until my study is better organized; my computer is down, and I can't write until it is repaired next week; I can't write when anyone else is in the house.

What would happen if we said, I can only feed my child when I'm not feeling rushed, or I can't leave my house and go to work until it stops raining? I know a young American woman who convinced herself that she could only write her dissertation in Europe. Fortunately for her, she had an inheritance to support her fantasy. The romance outweighs the practicality.

"One must be pitiless about the matter of 'mood,'" said Joyce Carol Oates, the prolific novelist. And she should know. "In a sense, the writing will create the mood. If art is, as I believe it to be, a genuinely transcendental function—a means by which we rise out of limited, parochial states of mind—then it should not matter very much what states we are in."

Peter Matthiessen wrote in *The Snow Leopard,* "The lions never get out of the road of the person who waits until the entire course is clear before taking the first step." So it is with writing. This is the conundrum: There is never a right time, yet it is always the right time. Perhaps the only way to get "in the mood" for writing is to begin to write. Just as the John Ashbery epigraph counsels, "Even if you don't succeed you'll be developing a muscle that may do it later on." A wonderful quality inherent in writing is that it can be transportive. If you are in a regretful, disenchanted, even mournful state of mind, writing can sweep you off your feet and convey you by magic carpet or hot air balloon or Porsche to a new world of your own creation.

If we wait until we are "in the mood" to write, we may never do it. Recently, on the television series *Inside the Actors Studio,* the film director Francis Ford Coppola told the story of getting married when

*Write even when you don't want to, don't much like what you are writing, and aren't writing particularly well.*
—AGATHA CHRISTIE

he was still relatively young, at least professionally speaking. He was struggling financially and trying to give flight to his movie career. He said that it seemed imprudent to get married under those circumstances, and yet he now feels that having that supportive (and dependent) base of family was what propelled him into the world. His advice to others was not to wait until everything was perfect before they did what they really wanted to do, because if they did they might never do anything at all.

This advice holds true for most situations in life, including writing. Don't wait. Make a date with yourself and *write*!

### The Writer's Mentor Suggests . . .

1. Write about why you are not in the mood to write today. In detail, write about what you would rather be doing. Is there a special friend with whom you'd like to have lunch? Which friend? Which restaurant? What is the meal? Would you rather be hiking, biking, sailing, skiing? Write about that. Would you rather be sleeping? Write about your fantasy bed. Is it a canopied European featherbed with a down duvet and hand-made Wedding Band quilt? Or an austere Japanese futon on tatami mats? Bring your imagined sleeping environment alive through your writing.

2. Interview yourself about your relationship with your writing. Actually prepare a list of questions and respond to them in writing.

3. Give yourself the permission to take a guilt-free vacation from writing. Decide in advance how long it will be—one or two days, a week—and honor that decision, guilt free.

There is something intrinsic in the process of writing itself that gets you out of your self-conscious concerns and angst and places you in the world you are creating on paper. That world is of your choosing. Where do you wish to go today?

# The Writer's Mentor at the Movies
## Quills

Every writer's dream is to be so overcome by a passion to express and create that writing itself becomes an obsession. When this happens, concern for anything else—loved ones, external strictures, even physical needs like food and water—is dispelled. While few writers actually attain this state of fecund rapture, the infamous Marquis de Sade was one who did.

Although at times a difficult film to watch, *Quills* is nearly unrivaled in its portrayal of a man whose true devotion to writing is his lifeblood. "My writing is like the beating of my heart," de Sade tells his captor, the conflicted Abbé de Coulmier (played by Joaquin Phoenix), who encourages de Sade to write as "a purgative for [his] corrupted mind."

Quills, directed by Philip Kaufman (*The Unbearable Lightness of Being, The Right Stuff, Henry and June*—see chapter 4) is not a strictly historical biography. The screenplay by Doug Wright was adapted from his 1995 Broadway play of the same title. Here de Sade—brilliantly depicted as a flamboyant pansexual with gleeful élan by Geoffrey Rush—has been imprisoned in Charenton Asylum by the order of the Emperor Napoleon Bonaparte, no less, who views de Sade's writings as "the most abominable book ever engendered by the most depraved imagination." But for de Sade, "art is waiting to be born"—regardless of his circumstances. Ironically, it was this very incarceration in a luxuriously furnished cell that afforded him both the time and privacy needed to produce his pornographic works.

In the film it is the succulent Madeleine (Kate Winslet), a virginal prison laundress, who inspires de Sade, as would a muse, and equally serves as a conspirator by smuggling his scandalous pages—so freshly written that "the ink is still wet," he teasingly rebukes—to a waiting horseman and subsequent printer. Although Madeleine is a member of the lower class, her native intelligence and desire to learn—"Reading is my salvation," she tells the Abbé—make her more than just an attractive body to the marquis.

After de Sade's *Justine* is published, the essentially good Abbé Coulmier is pressured into revoking the marquis' writing privileges. It is at this point that de Sade's character begins to make its slow transformation from sociopathic confidence and spoiled conviviality to an artist's desperation for personal expression. After his quills and paper are removed from his room, de Sade, at mealtime, ingeniously ravages a plump roasted chicken until he tears free the wishbone; and for ink, there is always the decanter of red wine. The sheets upon which he writes are not made of paper but are the linen ones on which he sleeps. Back in business, de Sade hums a tune of pleasure as he sets forth word after word. Madeleine then takes the sheets and copies out the work on paper before they are laundered. It seems like a workable solution until the claret-colored sheets are discovered.

No more wine . . . or bones, for that matter. Sade's room is emptied of all creature comforts, save a mirror and his clothes. The marquis then uses the first "ink" of humankind: blood. After breaking the mirror, like a diabetic he pricks each finger until all ten are raw with wounds and bound up with strips torn from his waistcoat. A mirror shard has served both as needle and writing implement. "Blood is the body's ink." His clothes—jacket, vest, shirt, trousers, socks, even shoes—are now a tableau of literary vignettes. "My writing lives!" he shouts like a thrilled and determined child.

But his ingenuity is unappreciated. When at last it seems as if there is nothing more of which to deprive him, in humiliation de Sade is stripped even of his clothes. The metaphor is powerful: A writer without words is naked.

When it seems that every recourse has been denied him, in a state of mental and emotional anguish, de Sade—an artist possessed—devises a plan to transport brief passages of a new story in a kind of vocal relay of messengers through the walls of the prison, from one inmate to the next, until, at the end of the line, Madeleine transcribes his words. Unfortunately, this scheme results in tragic consequences.

The marquis is then physically tortured and placed in a dungeon. Like an abused animal or an abandoned child, he is left to the squalor of his own feces, which—out of sheer desperation—he uses to write his final words:

The act of writing is a writer's redemption.

The Marquis de Sade was a writer. One may or may not appreciate his controversially lascivious material, but he was a writer who wrote every day for some forty years. And during his lifetime in the late eighteenth and early nineteenth centuries, laptops did not exist. Writers wrote by hand. (Indeed, as for 1,500 years they had written the world's classical literature.) In a sense, the notion of a quill as a writing tool bears a metaphoric loftiness, multifarious permutations of writing and spirituality. A quill is a feather from a winged creature: to write with "wings" is to fly, to soar through imaginative realms, to approach the gods.

# CHAPTER 6

# THE CONTENT

### *of*

# WRITING

## *Knowing What to Write*

Should I write what I know or what I want to learn?

Do I want to write fiction or nonfiction?

What is a genre? How many genres are there?

How do I know if what I'm writing should be an essay or a magazine
article or a short story or a book?

Do we choose topics and book ideas or do they choose us?

Does e-mail correspondence count as writing?

The Writer's Mentor at the Movies: *Almost Famous*

THE CONTENT OF WRITING: KNOWING WHAT TO WRITE endeavors to answer the question of whether to write about what you know or about what you want to learn. The chapter includes a lengthy discussion about genres—what they are and examples of their variety—and how to know into which one a piece of writing might fit. Russell Banks offers his view on the difference in process between writing fiction and nonfiction, and there are examples from Jane Smiley, Beverly Lowry, and my own work about how book ideas can choose us. A five-step plan of action is proposed in the answer to the question of how to determine whether your idea is magazine article material or has the makings of a book. And if you are addicted to e-mail writing, take heart; there is a section on how e-mail correspondence can actually improve your writing. At the close of the chapter I use the film *Almost Famous* to illustrate how, by following his twin passions for music and writing, the character—based upon the adolescent experiences of Cameron Crowe—developed a career as a successful writer and film director.

# Should I write what I know or what I want to learn?

> One of the dumbest things you were ever
> taught was to write what you know. Because
> what you know is usually dull. Remember
> when you first wanted to be a writer? Eight or
> ten years old, reading about thin-lipped heroes
> flying over mysterious vinyl jungles toward
> untold wonders? That's what you wanted to
> write about, about what you didn't know.
>
> —*KEN KESEY*

What you write depends on your purpose for writing. Are you a beginning writer looking for ideas, or are you a seasoned writer tackling your first book? Writing poetry about your first love will entail a very different process from writing a dissertation on the mythology of Hindu goddesses. My book on long-term marriage, *The Heart of Marriage: Discovering the Secrets of Enduring Love,* was part of my own discovery process and exploration into relationships. Even though I had been married once as a very young woman, my husband and I divorced after five years of marriage. And because my parents had divorced when I was only eighteen months old, I felt that I had no model of a long-term, committed, enjoyable marriage. So, in the case of that book, I wrote about what I wanted to learn.

And that is my tendency—to write about what I want to learn. Writing is a way of engaging with the subject matter—first through thought. Writing demands a concentrated process of thinking. And much writing, both fiction and nonfiction, involves research. Research is one of the most enjoyable parts of writing for me. I love to learn. Writing is also a combination of analysis and synthesis, and I enjoy synthesizing newfound material with my personal experience and my own writing style.

It's easy to become engrossed while researching the answers to what I don't know. Information is unearthed in archives and museums, on the Net, at the library, and from experts, and rewards writers with authority and originality. Margaret Atwood and John Irving built careers writing about what they wanted to know.

Nonfiction books are written by someone who either has a wealth of knowledge about a topic—for instance, the nature of parenthood and how it is depicted in the cinema—or who is fascinated by an issue and wishes to pursue the study of it. So there are subjective and objective reasons for writing, even though the seemingly most objective reason must still originate and emerge through the lens of a writer's subjective consciousness.

And, in the words of poet Antonio Muñoz Molina (in a translation by Michael McGaha), "The only thing the writer . . . knows or suspects is that he is being driven toward a territory where his usual norms won't work . . . that he will discover things he couldn't have imagined—inner galleries of his own consciousness, virgin islands of his imagination and his gaze, even his skin."

Fiction can be written from either perspective. How much of Isabel Allende's novel *Of Love and Shadows*—a story about a woman journalist in Chile, written by a woman who was once a journalist in Chile—is autobiographically based? And how much of Stephen King's *The Shining* is predicated on personal experience? (A writer who, up until a near-death experience only a few years ago, declared that he never had writer's block.) One would hope, very little.

Even writing about what you *think* you know—yourself—can be misleading and deceptive. Writing in order to understand yourself better is a noble undertaking and covers both what you know *and* what you would like to learn more about. "The best work that anybody ever writes," said playwright Arthur Miller, "is the work that is on the verge of embarrassing him." Writing about anything—known or unknown—is a way of discovering more about your theme and about yourself.

*Well-meaning people are always going to tell you to "write what you know." That's nonsense. Do that and you'll starve. In this business [sportswriting] you've got to write what they'll pay you to write.*

—HERB GRAFFIS

*Writing teachers invariably tell students, Write about what you know. . . . [But] how do you know what you know until you've written it? Writing is knowing. What did Kafka know? The insurance business? So that kind of advice is foolish, because it presumes that you have to go out to a war to be able to do war. Well, some do and some don't.*

—E. L. DOCTOROW

*Why write if this too easy activity of pushing a pen across paper is not given a certain bull-fighting risk and we do not approve dangerous, agile, and two-horned topics?*

—ORTEGA Y GASSET

Listen calmly and quietly to yourself and to what most stirs you. What is it you are most passionate about? Fascinated by? What quality do you care to expunge from or integrate into your life? What do you tend to read? You might try compiling a list of everything you have read during the past six months or year. Do you see any patterns in genres, content, style, authors? Your reading preferences may hold the key to your conundrum. You might find that romance novels are your life support, or you can't get enough of "how-to" books, or, even though you travel less than you'd like, travel books keep you up at night. You might find that you read only literary fiction of the likes of Michael Ondaatje, Margaret Atwood, Salman Rushdie, Thomas Mann, and Jean Rhys or short stories from the *New Yorker,* the *Atlantic Monthly,* and *Granta.* Perhaps for the past five years you have been secretly writing brief personal essays about your childhood as an Army brat or about all the animals you've cherished and for whom you have been custodian during the course of your life.

Most of the time, what you write will be a mercurial or ambiguous combination of what you think you already know and what you wish to learn. You will encounter many surprises on both counts. But remember: It is easier to write about "something" than about "anything."

---

# Do I want to write fiction or nonfiction?

Good fiction is not preaching. If a writer is
trying hard to convince you of something,
then he or she should stick to nonfiction.

—*TERRY MCMILLAN*

According to *A Handbook to Literature*, narrative (or fiction) writing is drawn from the imagination of the author rather than from history or fact. The term is most frequently associated with novels and short stories. When authors weave fictional episodes about historical characters, epochs, and settings, they make "historical fiction." The *Handbook* goes on to say that the function of fiction is to entertain, to be "interesting," in the phrase of Henry James, but it often serves "to instruct, to edify, to persuade, or to arouse. It is one of the chief devices by which [writers] communicate [their] vision of nature and of reality in concrete terms."

So, then, we might ask, what is nonfiction? Nonfiction is by far the broadest category of written work. Traditionally, it is the branch of literature comprising works of narrative prose dealing with or offering opinions or conjectures based upon facts and reality, including biography, history, and the essay. But to be more precise, Terry Tempest Williams observes, "In a good piece of nonfiction, there has to be a *story*." I like that perspective because, aside from reference books, I think it holds true, especially when we remember how compelling the acts of both telling and hearing stories are in human history. Curiously, the term "nonfiction" came into general use through the cataloging of books in libraries as recently as 1905 and in the past twenty-five to thirty years has expanded exponentially with such categories as personal growth, self-help, lifestyle, spirituality, food, parenting, women's issues, relationships, and health.

"The level of imagination can be very high," Gail Godwin, the novelist, says of her experience about writing her first book of nonfiction, *Heart: A Personal Journey Through Its Myths and Meanings*. "Where do you draw the line between the two kinds of prose?" she asks.

Try: "Henry Blanton turned forty on an April day when the first warm winds of spring crossed the Texas Panhandle and the diamondback rattlers, fresh and venomous from their winter sleep, came slipping out from under the cap rock of the Canadian River breaks."

Or: "The last mediaeval war was fought in Italy in 1943 and 1944. Fortress towns on great promontories which had been battled over since the eighth century had the armies of new kings flung carelessly against them."

Which would you describe as fiction prose, which as nonfiction? Each is especially beautiful writing. The Texas Panhandle description is from a nonfiction essay called "Cowboys," by *New Yorker* writer Jane Kramer, and the Italian fortress town passage is a chapter opening from Michael Ondaatje's exquisitely masterful novel *The English Patient.* But they could just as easily have crossed genres. Good writing, fact or fiction, should stand on its own. And if all, or most, of the elements of good writing are present—attention to language, craftsmanship, a kind of architectural structure, use of metaphor and specificity, a sense of time and place, a defined context, continuity, story, and voice—the piece, if fiction, will offer up a view of reality, or at least an environment (even an unearthly one), that we feel ourselves in or may have already similarly experienced and, if nonfiction, even though filled with a series of facts, can transport us to the wildest reaches of our imaginations. "There's lots of artistry. But you don't make it up," writes the literary journalist John McPhee about nonfiction, whereas in fiction we seek human complexity, not historical veracity.

Russell Banks, the author of thirteen published novels—including *Affliction, The Sweet Hereafter,* and *Cloudsplitter*—believes that "when you write fiction, you enter another world, the fictional world, and when you write nonfiction, you don't. It's a completely different mindset, a different level of intensity. Writing fiction is a little bit like hallucinating or out-of-body travel." Some of the same techniques are used in both but for very different ends. In nonfiction, those techniques are used to build an argument, win a case, make a point. "In fiction," he says, "you're using those techniques to build a fictional alternative world to the one you or the reader lives in."

My own writing has consisted of both nonfiction and fiction writing, and I enjoy the crossover when it happens. All of my published work has been nonfiction, and I look very forward to the day when it may also include a novel or two or three. Most of my Writer's Mentor clients seem to think that their choice of writing is an "or" rather than an "and." One or the other. But I often encourage them to try their hand at both.

*Things that are cheap and tawdry in fiction work beautifully in nonfiction because they are true. That's why you should be careful not to abridge it, because it's the fundamental power you're dealing with. You arrange it and present it. There's lots of artistry. But you don't make it up.*

—JOHN MCPHEE

*The Writer's Mentor Suggests . . .*

If you are working on a nonfiction essay or book, take either a passage or a chapter and while maintaining the veracity of the story and the details, consciously bring fictional elements into it. And, conversely, if it is a short story or novel you are writing, do some research to add an authority of truth. For example, even though James Michener's work (*Hawaii; Alaska; Texas;* among many others) was primarily fiction, he is known to have done massive amounts of research in order to make his stories not only believable but also inhabitable. Assist your reader in participation and immersion in your work. Describe how the chenille blanket feels against your bare legs, how morning sickness casts a pregnant woman into a hyper state of sensory awareness, why the serenade of cicadas in Kyoto during a full moon on the equinox is unforgettable. Researching material for both fiction *and* nonfiction can be fun, exciting, and creative.

❖ ❖

# WHAT IS A GENRE? HOW MANY GENRES ARE THERE?

> Respect the genre you're writing in.
> In an effort to put your own stamp on it,
> don't ignore the established conventions
> of that genre—you'll alienate your core
> audience of loyal buyers.
> —KATHLEEN KRULL

A *genre* is a distinctive type or category of literary composition used to denote specific types of content or categories of books. It originally included forms such as the epic, the tragedy, the comedy, the lyric, and the pastoral. Today a grouping of literature into genres would also include the novel, the short story, and the essay. Despite attempts to systematize the art of literature, such categories must remain somewhat flexible, and there are many cases of hybrid forms, such as the tragicomedy and the prose poem. And, in truth, forms continue to be created through new "crossbreeding," such as Vikram Seth's *The Golden Gate* (a novel written in rhyming verse form).

The word *genre* comes from French, where it means "kind" or "type." This classification implies that there are formal or technical characteristics that exist among the same "kind" of work regardless of time or place or composition, or author or subject matter. Critics frequently regard genre distinctions as useful descriptive devices but rather arbitrary ones.

There is also a variety of genres within the categories of fiction and nonfiction. The current *Writer's Market* lists numerous genres under their Book Publishers Subject Index. Fiction includes, among others, Adventure, Erotica, Experimental, Fantasy, Feminist, Gay/Lesbian, Gothic, Historical, Horror, Humor, Juvenile, Mystery, Occult, Plays, Poetry, Religious, Romance, Science Fiction, Short Story Collections, Spiritual, Sports, Suspense, Western, Young Adult. The following are many of its entries under Nonfiction: Agriculture/Horticulture, Americana, Animals, Anthropology/ Archaeology, Art/Architecture, Astrology/Psychic/New Age, Autobiography, Biography, Business/Economics, Child Guidance/Parenting, Coffeetable Book, Communications, Community/Public Affairs, Computer/Electronic, Consumer Affairs, Contemporary Culture, Cooking/Foods/Nutrition, Counseling/Career Guidance, Crafts, Creative Nonfiction, Educational, Entertainment, Ethnic, Fashion Beauty, Feminism, Film/Cinema/Stage, Gardening, Gay/Lesbian, General Nonfiction, Gift Book, Government/Politics, Health/ Medicine, History, Hobby, Home, House, How-To, Humanities, Humor, Illustrated Book, Labor, Language/Literature, Law, Literary Criticism, Marine Subjects, Memoirs, Military/War, Money/Finance, Music/Dance, Nature/Environment, Philosophy, Photography, Psychology, Real Estate, Recreation, Reference, Regional, Religion, Scholarly, Science/Technology, Self-Help, Sex, Social Sciences, Sociology, Software,

*If the spies intrigue, if the romance blossoms, if the horrors haunt, devoted readers apparently don't notice the quality of the writer's prose or don't care. . . .*

*Literary critics, who tend to judge all writing by the same high standard, may groan at these facts of life; genre readers read on enthusiastically, and genre writers laugh all the way to the bank."*

—RICHARD RHODES

Spiritual, Sports, Technical, Textbook, Travel, True Crime, Women's Issues/Studies, World Affairs, and Young Adult.

   If the subject matter of your project doesn't fit into one of these categories, you may need to rethink it!

### The Writer's Mentor Suggests . . .

1. For a bit of detective work and an excellent piece of research, buy a current copy of the indispensable *Writer's Market.* Copies should also be readily available at any local library. In the Table of Contents, find the section titled "Book Publishers Subject Index." For the sake of exploration, even if you only write or wish to write, say, short stories, examine both the Fiction and Nonfiction Subject listings. Pay attention to what sparks your interest and makes the hair stand up on the nape of your neck, then select one of the publishers listed under that subject heading. For example, under Fiction choose Adventure, and under Adventure select "Bantam 155." On page 155 you will find an entry for Bantam Books, including the company's contact information, their publishing staff, the number of titles per year they publish, the type of work they publish, and, in many cases, a title of a book they recently published. This exercise should not only ignite your curiosity about the many genres available but also give you a practical insight into how to find out who publishes what.

2. Go to several bookstores to see how booksellers categorize their stock. Wander throughout the many sections and see which are of the most interest to you. Study the type and titles of books in these areas of interest. I always give this suggestion to my Writer's Mentor clients when they first tell me about a proposed book project. This is a crucial piece of initial research in order to discern how their book would be distinct from other books already on the shelf. It's sobering for them and often shifts their thinking when they discover what their competition is.

# How do I know if what I'm writing should be an essay or a magazine article or a short story or a book?

> The form chooses you, not the other way
> around. An idea comes and is already
> embodied in a form.
> —MICHAEL FRAYN

In his book *On Writing and Publishing,* Mark Twain describes attempting to start the story of Joan of Arc six times over twelve years and explains why this happened. "There are some books that refuse to be written. They stand their ground year after year and will not be persuaded. It isn't because the book is not there and not worth being written—it is only because the right form for the story does not present itself. There is only one right form for a story, and if you fail to find that form the story will not tell itself. You may try a dozen wrong forms but in each case you will not get very far before you discover that you have not found the right one—and that the story will always stop and decline to go further."

The first challenge is to decide which form fits the story you wish to tell. And, whether fiction or non-fiction, novel or personal essay, poem or memoir, writing is always telling a story—even if it's a how-to about buying a used car. But the second challenge is finding the structure that best suits your writing style and ability. We can't all be a John Updike who seems to write in every form known to literature. If you are used to writing poetry but feel compelled to launch into a novel, why not write a few short stories or literary essays first, to feel out how the novel fits your sensibility? If you are daunted by the length of a novel and the time necessary to write one, why not try working on a few personal essays? If you want to write a book about the historical accuracy of the portrayal of African Americans in the cinema, why not begin with a few articles aimed for publication in some suitable venues?

Think of various literary formats as analogous to distinct modes of dance. If you were a dancer, would you be more comfortable in modern dance or classical ballet, in ballroom or tap, in the tango or interpretive? Writing styles and structures are just as distinct and also just as open to hybridization.

Writing articles and prose pieces for magazines and journals is very different from settling in for a year or two—or longer—to write the Great American Novel or a nonfiction book on the state of divorce in the latter half of the twentieth century. In terms of nonfiction, there are a number of steps to follow before you decide in favor of an article or a full-length book. For instance, my editor has told me that she reads "tons" of book proposals that are great ideas for articles, but often the topic is too specific or trendy or unable to be deeply developed for a book. Books entail planning, and ideas necessitate refining. It isn't enough to have expertise in or bursting enthusiasm for your topic. Planning, organization, and research are prerequisites. This process begins with deeper examination of your idea, of its merits and marketability (study the demographics of your projected reading audience: gender, age, geographical location, social and economic status, lifestyle), and of your writing skill.

## The Writer's Mentor Suggests . . .

1. Read several weeks' or months' worth of issues of the magazines or newspapers for which you think your article idea(s) might be appropriate. This will be a reality check for you. It will also be a means of culling new ideas. You are reading to see if your idea is original or at least has a fresh slant.

2. Go to bookstores and libraries, check *Books in Print,* and surf the Amazon.com book categories to find out what else is already published about your topic, that is either similar or complementary, and how yours would be different.

3. It is important to be aware of popular trends in order to gauge the public's interest in your topic and, equally important, to stay ahead of them. Remember that magazines have a six- to nine-month "lead time" (before an article is actually published), and a book can take anywhere from six months to a year and a half from the time a publisher receives a completed manuscript to the date of publication. Add this frame of time to the length of time in which you can *realistically* finish the writing of your manuscript. Will your topic still have any interest at the time of publication, or is the market already saturated with it? A few years ago, knowing my attachment and utter passion for the canine species, my agent suggested that I write a book about dogs. It seemed like a natural. Within a day I came up with a fun title: *Women Who Love Dogs Too Much.* In less than a month, I had a fine proposal. When my agent shopped it around, there was zip interest. Why? Market saturation. And, indeed, within the next two years it seemed as if scores of books about (in one case, even, *by* a dog; in another, *for*) dogs had been published.

4. Now you have to ask yourself: Is my idea a big idea for a book or only a big idea for a magazine article? Be aware that a book-length idea will have to sustain several hundred manuscript pages. Does your idea have the depth, public interest, and substance to do this? Many of what seem like worthy ideas today will be old news by the time they hit either the magazine rack or the bookstore shelf.

5. And, even more important, will your topic maintain *your* interest? Choose wisely.

❖ ❖

# Do we choose topics and book ideas or do they choose us?

> It is as if the novel was already written, float-
> ing in the air, on a network of electrons.
> I could hear it talking to itself. I sensed
> that if I would but listen, it would come
> through, all ready.
>
> —*A. S. BYATT*

> The material's out there, a calm lake waiting
> for us to dive in.
>
> —*BEVERLY LOWRY*

> Sometimes I believe these books are already
> written and my job is simply to allow them
> to come through me. My job is to get out
> of my own way so that I can let the
> process take care of me.
>
> —*SUE GRAFTON*

> Nor will certain ideas forget me; they keep
> filing away at my lethargy, my complacency.
>
> —*RALPH ELLISON*

Some writers speak to the idea that they do not "possess" their work but are, rather, channels for it, conduits for the inspiration and ideas that already exist in the ethers or on some other plane of consciousness. "I sensed that if I would but listen, it would come through, all ready," said A. S. Byatt. "My job is simply to allow them to come through me," said Sue Grafton. According to Ralph Ellison, "certain ideas" would not forget him. Jane Smiley amplifies, "I decided that my writing was not something possessed by me, that I didn't possess my own works. They simply *were,* they passed through me and I passed through them." Smiley offers the example of her fifth and favorite novel, *The Greenlanders.* In *Writing in Flow,* Smiley discusses how this book—about a factual Norse colony in Greenland in the fourteenth and fifteenth centuries—was "absolutely a vision or communication from somewhere else," from the historically attested characters, she believes. She had the strong feeling that she was "receiving and transmitting it." She said that it was an uncanny and, even, frightening experience. From that time on she no longer felt that she possessed her own work. In this sense, a writer is a sort of midwife of words and stories, allowing them to gestate, "pass through," and see the light of day as they are written on a white page.

A rather graphic and extreme example of this notion that book ideas choose us is Beverly Lowry's compelling and unflinching book *Crossed Over: A Murder, A Memoir*—part memoir of the tragic hit-and-run death of her eighteen-year-old son, Peter, and part biography of Karla Faye Tucker, the murderer on death row in Texas with whom Beverly developed a friendship. In 1992 I met and interviewed Beverly for a book I was writing. She told me that if her son hadn't died, she would "never have made that first trip to visit Karla Faye in prison." In a seamless way, the twin stories are juxtaposed one against the other. It is the way a mother comes to terms with the devastating loss of her own son through the emotional adoption of a young woman. In a sense, because this story could only have been told by Beverly, it chose her, but she also chose it, as she was the one to commit to "diving into the lake". The eventual religious conversion and redemption of Karla Faye was, psychically speaking, Beverly's own.

Robert Penn Warren felt that a writer may, in a way, "stumble" upon a book idea. But he believed that there was a necessary period of preparation, which was the work of "liv[ing] right." In other words, a writer's entire life leads him or her to ideas. "If the work is done the dream will come to the man who's ready for the particular dream; it's not going to come just from dreaming in general."

Books have their own lives: they choose us. They have their own destinies. Every writer is a combination of a particular collection of DNA, childhood experiences, personal preferences, curiosities, dreams, and desires; and the aggregate of these act as a kind of calling card to the world's collective psyche.

Something akin to this happened to me with my first book, *On Women Turning 40*. The book was an idea that "captured" me when I was in my late thirties. Recovering from a long bout with depression, I began seriously to look toward my next decade. Through my own experience and trials I became a ripe vessel for *On Women Turning 40*. There sometimes seems to be a collusion or an unconscious covenant between a writer and her topic. A psychic correspondence. No matter how often—and how severely—my inner critic tried to convince me that I had nothing of interest or importance to add to the world, the idea for the book was relentless. It clamped onto me like the claws of the Cancer crab that is my birth sign. It would have nothing but my full commitment to this budding project. Although I don't pretend to understand it, I continue to be in awe of the mystery of this process.

On my desk, sitting directly in front me, is a tiny silver frame, perhaps 2-by-2½-inches with double glass. Floating inside the frame—like images in the ether—is a picture of a pile of books. The top one is open and has writing on it. This representation is a continual reminder to me that not only does the book I am writing now already exist, but also that there are many more where that one resides.

### The Writer's Mentor Suggests . . .

1. What are some ideas for stories or books that are compelling you? Are they relentless in their pursuit of your attention? Do these ideas seem obvious and already well formed, like "a calm lake waiting for us to dive in," or are they parts of a mystery waiting to be correlated and connected? Whichever, what is needed is the ability to make time to allow and encourage their delivery. Create a space for quiet, a stillness that will enable you to become one with the material that wishes to be transmitted. This can be done through a form of meditation or breathing exercise or, even, during an athletic workout. Listen for the language that emerges. Believe that these words are meant for you and that they will come.

2. After you have created a receptive frame of mind and have one or several ideas at hand (if you are having trouble thinking of ideas, refer to chapter 2: "Divine Inspiration"), develop a list of questions to ask each topic and write down both the questions and the "answers" that come to you. That's right: use your active imagination to engage in a dialogue with the subject. Try to make a definite distinction between your own "voice"—the aware part of yourself—and the unconscious or spontaneous voice that might speak to you in words, sounds, or images. For instance, I am currently thinking about writing a book about the creative Muse and how to use movies to tap into creative inspiration or the "juice" in various artistic media such as art, music, dance, acting, writing, and teaching. So my active imagination dialogue might go something like this:

C (CATHLEEN): I've been thinking a lot about the idea of the Muse, especially since I've been writing this book *(The Writer's Mentor)*. And I'd like to find a way to make a bridge between the creative process and film viewing—how an artist or musician or writer can receive inspiration from films.

I (IMAGINATION): So this is what I'm offering you—a bridge. There are movies on every sort of creative endeavor, and you can categorize them according to disciplines.

C: I like that because I can already think of several films for each art form: writing, painting, acting. But how would the book be structured?

I: At least two ways are possible: according to each individual form or according to a series of concerns that are relevant to every form. For example, how every creative person in every field deals with staying with a project to completion or breaks through a creative block.

C: I can see either of those working okay. What's the first thing I should do in regards to this potential project?

I: Make a list of all the creative art forms that you want to include and associate all the movies you can think of that are in each category. Start with the one that is the most exciting to you and see where that leads you.

I hope you get the general feeling here of what I'm trying to do. It may seem a bit stilted or artificial, but if you stay with it and continue to ask questions, there will be some resolution as to whether the project is one you should pursue. Know that this resolution may not come until after a number of interactions like this one.

⁌: ⁌:

## Does E-MAIL CORRESPONDENCE COUNT AS WRITING?

> E-mail users carry on buoyantly, even uninhibitedly. Writer's block has never been a problem on the Net—far from it. Alone at their computers, tapping away, correspondents report few difficulties getting started, much less continuing.
>
> —*ANNE EISENBERG*

In my home the purpose of a refrigerator is twofold: yes, it preserves food, but, perhaps of equal importance, it is a repository of many years worth of neatly trimmed *New Yorker* cartoons. Dog cartoons are my favorite. One, by cartoonist Peter Steiner, that continues to elicit a smile every time I notice it shows a contented canine sitting in a rolling chair at a desk, his left paw on the keyboard of a computer, looking down at his admiring four-legged buddy and saying, "On the Internet, nobody knows you're a dog" (or, I might add, that you're still in your nightgown at two o'clock in the afternoon).

In a book I wrote a few years ago, *50 Ways to Meet Your Lover,* one of the methods of meeting that I wrote about was through the

Internet and e-mail. Now couples are meeting online with ever more frequency and courting courtesy of e-mail. Well, you can't beat the cost.

Perhaps because of such dalliances, I have found that many clients *use* e-mail as an excuse not to get to their *real* writing. How often have you noticed that you sat down with the intention to get started on a new short story or to rewrite last week's essay, only to realize that three hours have been swallowed in e-mail correspondence? This simply won't do. When e-mail becomes an addiction, it can also become a serious risk. I have a friend who, in order to avoid this trap, refrains from even opening her e-mail until after four o'clock in the afternoon, when she has already spent a substantial number of hours working on her novel or the nonfiction book on which she is currently working.

I generally do that myself, unless there is a message I'm eager to receive or send. I prefer using my quiet early morning hours for my creative writing.

In e-mail correspondence one feels much less self-conscious and limited than when producing a "serious" piece of writing. It offers more room for experimentation in both style and content. Somehow e-mail feels not quite as important or final as does a hand-written letter; it certainly takes less time to compose and send off.

I think a plus of e-mail is that it provides an easy, immediate, inexpensive means of communicating with friends and colleagues who live some distance away or next door. Nearly all of my closest friends live somewhere between 100 and 3,000 miles away, but with e-mail we can "talk" every day. For someone like myself, who lives alone, it has become an integral, even necessary, part of my day. Nonetheless, I also try to maintain a regular, if intermittent, letter correspondence with my friends because there is something irreplaceable about holding in one's hand the same greeting card or personal stationery that a loved one has held in his or hers. The tactile experience remains significant. ; -)

There have even been a few authors who have collected their e-mail correspondence and published it. Many writers feel that their writing style has improved significantly through the freedom that comes with e-mail writing. To them, e-mail seems more closely related to the "natural" voice and then easily transfers over to literary writing.

My copy editor tells me that she has found e-mail to be enormously efficient for tying up the last loose ends in copyediting, especially when the author is in a different time zone. "I can type up my list of questions, paste in the sentences, and send it off at any hour of the day or night. The author can reply at her convenience, and we have a written record of the changes."

In a hilarious piece in the "Shouts and Murmurs" section of a recent *New Yorker*, Noah Baumbach offered an anachronistic sampling of what the inveterate letter writer Vincent van Gogh might have written to his brother Theo if e-mail had existed: "From Vincentvgo@hotmail.com. . . . 'Thank you for the money. With it, I bought a blazing tangerine iMac, which I am e-mailing you on right now'. 'You were right, the Hotmail account was very simple to set up and free, so I can still survive on five francs a day'. 'Whoops, pressed SEND accidentally. Was going to say, *like a star in the azure sky.* By the way, that NPR petition you forwarded me is a hoax'."

## The Writer's Mentor Suggests . . .

1. Take stock of your own relationship with e-mail. Do you find that you abuse it by allowing it to dominate your time at the computer when you could be working on your writing? If this is the case, strike a bargain with yourself that for one week you will complete a certain amount of writing (by pages or hours) before you log on. Make an effort to stay focused on your work at hand while you are engaged in it.

2. You may have not pursued e-mail correspondence because you think that e-mail would be a waste of time—just one more thing to do or message to answer in an already maxed-out schedule filled with telephone calls to be returned, land mail that needs response, annoying faxes awaiting your attention. If so, begin with one or two friends who are already partaking in

the process and let them know that you are eager to take your first steps into this new world. Ask a friend or hire a professional (*everyone* should have a Computer God!) to help you set up an online account if you don't already have one. Start slowly and see how easily you adapt to it.

3. If you already feel that your e-mail use is healthy and balanced, enjoy the efficiency, convenience, and pleasure your relationship with the Internet offers. Use e-mail as a means of liberating yourself from the constraints of your other writing, and let it be a tool in the process of developing your writing style.

## The Writer's Mentor at the Movies
### *Almost Famous*

There are few people who actually know at a young age that they want to be writers—let alone know the subject matter about which they wish to write. By the age of fifteen, however, a precocious Cameron Crowe knew both. In *Almost Famous,* his tender tribute to the rock scene of the early 1970s, Crowe (who wrote and directed his own screenplay) relates an autobiographical tale of his coming-of-age in the midst of sex, drugs, and rock and roll. As the movie opens we see Crowe's alter ego, William Miller (Patrick Fugit), as a very likeable fifteen-year-old nerd who has advanced easily through high school under the protective tutelage of his college English professor mother, Elaine Miller (Frances McDormand), an eccentric woman who quotes Goethe and, even as she drives the sweetly innocent William to rock concerts, somewhat hysterically pleads with him, "Don't take drugs!"

Although 1973 was post–1960s idealism, it was still pre–late '70s punk nihilism. With a desire to create himself as a teenage music journalist, William begins writing music reviews and sending them out to various rock magazines. He is befriended by a real '70s character, Lester Bangs (played by a wily Philip Seymour Hoffman), the brilliant but cynical and sadly isolated music critic. "Call me anytime," he says. "I'm uncool, I'm always home." But Lester mentors William and essentially gives him the break that leads to *Rolling Stone* magazine sending the (unknown to them) schoolboy on the road with the fictional band Sweetwater (in reality it was the Allman Brothers) and to William/Cameron's remarkable entry into the corrupting, decadently excessive world of rock-and-roll and—through responsibility, heart, and a genuine love for the music—his ultimate triumph.

The road tour with Sweetwater in 1973 contributes to William missing much of his senior year and even his graduation, at which, when "William Miller" is called, his mother claps loudly, if a bit forlornly. But what William learns during this rock and roll circus is a confident faith in human decency, not the least his own. He loses his virginity to three groupies in a Tennessee hotel room; he loses his heart to another irresistible groupie, Penny Lane (Kate Hudson), who, in turn, has lost her heart to a well-meaning but amoral (and married) lead guitarist, Russell (Billy Crudup). William's heart may have been broken, but his sense of purpose and a life direction have been firmly established.

"If you practice an art faithfully, it will make you wise," wrote William Saroyan. Part of what makes *Almost Famous* so enjoyable is that now, nearly thirty years after the events depicted in the film took place, we know where Cameron Crowe's writing life has taken him. He is a glowing and enthusiastic illustration of how devotion to an art form—in this case, writing—can lead to personal and professional fulfillment—and, for Crowe, even an Academy Award for Best Screenplay. The moral of the story is, Do what you love, and that love is its own reward.

———

# CHAPTER 7

# WRITING
## *as a*
# PRACTICE

## *Keeping the Focus*

What is a writing practice?

Is it necessary to write every day?

How do I handle the continual interruptions of life while I'm writing?

How do I pick up from where I left off in my writing?

How do I reach a state of flow in writing?

Can writing be a process of self-discovery?

The Writer's Mentor at the Movies: *Bridget Jones's Diary*

WRITING AS A PRACTICE: KEEPING THE FOCUS posits that writing practice is about building a muscle and showing up on the page. The debate about the necessity—or not—to write every day is addressed, as are ample suggestions for dealing with the inevitable daily interruptions of life, which, according to Anne Tyler, actually add to the substance from which we write. The chapter also offers clues from Ernest Hemingway and Tennessee Williams on how to conclude a day's writing in order to promote an effortless resumption the next day. The concept of achieving flow in writing is discussed from the perspectives of the scientist Mihaly Csikszentmihalyi and the psychologist/writer Susan K. Perry. The chapter finally addresses the notion that writing can be a process of self-discovery through self-revelation, and I use the film *Bridget Jones's Diary* as a demonstration of this sentiment.

# WHAT IS A WRITING PRACTICE?

> Through practice you actually do get better.
> You learn to trust your deep self more and not
> give in to your voice that wants to avoid writ-
> ing. . . . Writing practice embraces your whole
> life and doesn't demand any logical form.
> —*NATALIE GOLDBERG*

"How we spend our days is how we spend our lives," Annie Dillard writes in *The Writing Life.* If we spend our days writing, practicing writing, we become a writer. Just as Wynton Marsales practices his trumpet daily, a gymnast daily practices her jumps and rolls, and a Benedictine monk practices his office throughout the day, a writer practices writing. And, as Natalie Goldberg assures us in *Writing Down the Bones,* "you actually do get better."

As a professional writer, I find it sometimes difficult to make time for writing "practice" because I'm so frantic trying to complete some project that has a fast-approaching deadline. Or, more accurately, in my case, make that plural: several projects with several deadlines. Not that I necessarily wish it otherwise, but to practice, one needs time. To me, practice means allowing yourself not to be perfect. It means not having to control everything. There is ample space for spontaneity, for exploration, for a good time. And that time is a river flowing into eternity, word by word. Punctuation doesn't matter. But keeping your hand moving does. Practice offers an occasion, one in which we can challenge ourselves to enter into the unknown and know there are no dead ends or wrong turns because wherever we go is an opportunity to learn something new. Something about the world. Something about ourselves. Something about writing.

It is through writing practice that we learn to trust where we are going and that we will know—every time—how to get there. Practice is the warm-up for writing that review on the new Steven Soderbergh film; it's the finger exercises for writing your first novel based on your hispanic family's early Californian saga; it's the rehearsal for the series of poems you've been contemplating; it's the preliminary to the school essay on the myth of Demeter and Persephone due next week. Essentially, writing practice is about showing up at the page.

In 1986 I visited Natalie Goldberg at her mesa home just outside Taos, New Mexico. I had read her newly published first book, *Writing Down the Bones,* and looked forward to interviewing her for my own first book, *On Women Turning 40.* In the day that I spent with Natalie, she shared her observations on the writing process. It was apparent how closely her sentiments on writing mirrored the philosophy of her fifteen-year-long Zen Buddhist practice. Each "discipline," if you will, is a way of viewing life. No, it is much more engaged than just viewing—it is a means of *living* your life, and that day Natalie was exemplary in both of her primary disciplines. Each requires a commitment if the practitioner is serious about welcoming the boon inherent in them. The effect of each is pervasive in one's thoughts, actions, relationships. As the one, Zen Buddhism, is a spiritual practice, so, too, for Natalie, is the practice of writing.

In *Writing Down the Bones,* Natalie advises us to "think of writing practice as loving arms you come to illogically and incoherently. It's our wild forest where we gather energy before going to prune our garden, write our fine books and novels. It's a continual practice. Don't try to control it. Stay present with whatever comes up, and keep your hand moving."

## The Writer's Mentor Suggests . . .

Remember that what you write during writing practice doesn't have to be perfect. This is the time to let it rip. No one will be grading you or even, necessarily, reading what you write—unless you invite them to do so. *What* you write is also of little import. This may be the opportunity to write a personality sketch for a flamboyant character in your long-dreamed-of novel; fill out a fanciful job application for this character or explore her childhood or your own; describe the year-long process from declination to regeneration of the deciduous maple tree outside your study window; render in words the morning rush hour on the 1 or 9 subway from the Upper West Side of Manhattan down to Wall Street; imagine the previous lives/owners of a particular item: a silver teapot, a red velvet cape, a first edition copy of Darwin's *Origin of the Species* (the innovative film *The Red Violin* is an evocative example of this notion); or simply sit at your desk and set down every word that comes to your mind—even if it is the same word over and over. Writing practice is the warm-up process, the stretching before the long run, the precursory probing, the fortifying of our writing "muscle." All that is necessary is to do it and to "keep your hand moving."

-:-  -:-

# Is it necessary to write every day?

> If you want to be a writer, you have to write
> every day. The consistency, the monotony,
> the certainty, all vagaries and passions are
> covered by this daily reoccurrence.
>
> —WALTER MOSLEY

There are many "schools of thought," multiple approaches and solutions to this question. Gerald Brenan, who was friendly with several members of the Bloomsbury group in the early 1900s and wrote social and political accounts of Spain, felt that it is by sitting down to write every morning that one becomes a writer because "those who do not do this remain amateurs." The American abstract expressionist artist Philip Guston said, "I go to my studio every day because one day I may go and the angel will be there. What if I don't go and the angel came?" This is, perhaps, one of the most important reasons for going to one's desk every day. Another is the idea that habit develops muscle. The poet John Ashbery felt that it is important to write "when you are in the wrong mood or the weather is wrong" because even if nothing happens, "you'll be developing a muscle that may do it later on."

For a decade I was the breed of writer who created only when I was working on deadline and immersed in completing a project. It's just been within the past few years that I have seen the value of facing my computer on a daily basis. Before I began writing professionally, I was a visual artist. I was committed to painting every day and wouldn't have considered doing anything less. I was addicted. It took many years for me to establish a similar kind of intense relationship with my writing, one that necessitated entering each day into the dialogue it offered. The writing—like painting, gardening, music, dance—is always waiting. The words—the paint, the soil and flowers, the notes, the movements—are lingering in a limbo of imagination, loitering in a suspension of dormant dreams. What they require is our consistent presence, a routine attendance. Make writing a habit. Make it a constructive (if often feisty) addiction.

Like the Berlin Wall, reality imposes a blockade between your creative notions and their fulfillment. When inspiration comes, it leaves no room for dawdling or an insignificant dalliance; it is urgent and momentous, fragile. We either acknowledge and honor the gift of the Muse or she flies back into the ether of the collective imagination, where her boon may be lost to us forever as she seeks another. What the fickle whispering Muse requires is a receptive mind, an open heart, and a daily practice. If you want to be a writer, you have to write every day.

On the other hand, you may find resonance with a *New Yorker* cartoon, by Robert Weber, I have on my refrigerator. Two people, a man and a woman, are having drinks at what looks like a cocktail party. The man says to the woman, "I'm a writer, but not, thank heavens, the kind who has to write every day or he gets depressed."

Strive to be the kind of writer who *does* get depressed if she doesn't write every day, or at least senses something missing from her daily routine. But, as Socrates said, "In all things be moderate." Make

*I write for a couple of hours every day, even if I only get a couple of sentences. I put in that time. You do that every day, and inspiration will come along. I don't allow myself not to keep trying. It's not fun, but if you wait until you want to write, you'll never do it.*

—DAVE BARRY

it the ideal to write every day, but do not create anxiety and make yourself crazy if you don't or, for whatever reason, can't. The larger goal is to find that area between discomfort and indolence. The place that makes it possible for you to write on a regular basis.

In a letter to his agent, Audrey Wood, Tennessee Williams wrote, "I work seven days a week, Sunday included. And I don't think it is a violation of the Sabbeth. My only exception is Easter Sunday. It's a habit, an unbreakable habit. I don't know what I'd do if I didn't write. I'd probably go mad."

## The Writer's Mentor Suggests . . .

1. If the thought of writing every day is daunting to you and it becomes a reason *not* to write, try to "sneak up on yourself" by writing three days a week for a month or two until you become comfortable with this schedule. Eventually, add one day at a time until a period of writing evolves into a daily habit.

2. What if you don't have enough ideas to generate day in and day out? There are books that offer numerous topics for writing. There is even a book that includes *daily* suggestions for a year's worth of consecutive writing. Judy Reeves's *A Writer's Book of Days: A Spirited Companion and Lively Muse for the Writing Life* offers suggestions from the common, "October 7, You're in a café . . . ," to the profound, "January 4, A year after your death . . ." (after a poem by Czeslaw Milosz).

3. Select, at random, a sentence from this morning's newspaper and write a paragraph or two about it. Or, again at random, choose a line from a book of poetry and use it as a means of exploring a period in your own life that the line of poetry or a word in it evokes for you.

4. Write about whatever you choose. But write.

5. Consult your journal. Notice those questions you most often ask yourself and the topics you refer to again and again.

# How do I handle the continual interruptions of life while i'm writing?

> Generally material circumstances are against
> [writing]. Dogs will bark; people will inter-
> rupt; money must be made; health will
> break down. Further, accentuating all these
> difficulties and making them harder to bear
> is the world's notorious indifference. It does
> not ask people to write poems and novels
> and histories; it does not need them.
>
> —VIRGINIA WOOLF

The writing life deserves—and demands—a growing ability to concentrate fully. But when it seems that the purpose of everyone and everything in our environment is to distract us, how do we learn to become and stay focused? Each writer needs to develop a method (or methods) for minimizing the occasions for interruption and distraction. The goal is to keep the mental momentum during your writing period. This doesn't mean that you can't leave your desk to get up every once in a while for a drink of water, to go to the bathroom, or to stretch your body. But it is necessary to establish a certain continuity of concentration. You want to therefore make a serious effort to preclude your getting involved in anything that might pull your attention in an altogether different mental direction while you are trying to write.

Maya Angelou takes the preservation of her time to the extreme. She keeps a hotel room in every city she has ever lived in: "I rent a hotel room for a few months, leave my home at six and try to be at work by 6:30 . . . I stay until 12:30 or 1:30 in the afternoon, and then I go home. . . ."

*I suspect I sit at entirely the wrong desk. It is so crowded with distractions that there's hardly room to set a small pad amongst them and get to work. . . . I have often wondered if I swept it all clear—Saint Jerome in his cell—would I do better—churn out the odd masterpiece?*

—GEORGE PLIMPTON

*I've spent so long erecting partitions around the part of me that writes—learning how to close the door on it when ordinary life intervenes, how to close the door on ordinary life when it's time to start writing again—that I'm not sure I could fit the two parts of me back together now.*

—ANNE TYLER

Life is also complicated. Writers have every imaginable permutation of various responsibilities. My only child is now an independent adult who lives in a different city from me. But I recently succumbed to the call of motherhood in another way and brought home a seven-week-old Springer Spaniel puppy. A male puppy. Overnight my writing periods went from blissfully long and uninterrupted to a staccato of dashed words. The torrent of memories of what it's like to have a child in the house have inundated me. And my writer's (and mother's) heart goes out to every person who has household or familial or financial or health or professional imperatives that require constant attention. And who doesn't? I remember seeing an environmental photograph of George Plimpton from the mid-1990s in which he is sitting in profile at his typewriter. Directly behind him, lying on an animal-skin rug, with nursing bottles, are a pair of twins—his. George, the father, is doing his duty, as George, the writer, tries to do his by "stealing" moments for his literary work. The solution is clear: Every writer needs a division of labor—two of him- or herself.

An Anne Tyler essay, "Still Just Writing," is a litany of daily—hourly—interruptions to her writing time. House painting, visits to the vet, the children's spring vacation, grocery buying, scrubbing the bathrooms, visits from the washing machine repairman, the tree trimmer, the meter reader, Jehovah's Witnesses, a death in her extended family, buying a dress for the funeral, her daughter's gymnastic practice and meets, dental appointments, gardening, taking the car to the garage for repairs. . . . This is all written with good humor, of course. She then goes on to reveal that when, as a woman/wife/mother, she has a moment of self-pity, she thinks of her husband, "who is also a man/husband/father," and how, as a full-time child psychiatrist with its many peripheral duties, he still finds time to write novels. She concludes that since she's had children, she's "grown richer and deeper. They may have slowed down my writing for a while, but when I did write, I had more of a self to speak from."

Having said this, there are also many interruptions that, rather than being used as excuses to impede the writing process, can and should be avoided. There are times for saying "No," guiltlessly, to any obligations that aren't absolutely necessary.

### The Writer's Mentor Suggests . . .

1. Distinguish between interruptions that are acts of God—there is no way you can prevent them and not much you can do about them—and those that are in some way the result of your own actions. There are often roadblocks that we establish quite unconsciously.

2. Set clear priorities. Develop your own guidelines as to what circumstances you will allow to divert you from your writing. Learn the difference between what's flexible and what isn't— what you can change, and what you can't—and don't waste your energy struggling with what you can't change.

3. Work on self-discipline. Writing doesn't happen unless you apply the "butt to the chair" philosophy. You need to train yourself to stay put and concentrate. You may have only two hours to write on any given day, but two focused hours can produce more than five distracted ones. Whatever it is that diverts your attention, note it, stay seated, and refocus.

4. Get and stay organized. The time you waste is your own. It is time that could have been spent writing. Arrange your writing environment to suit your needs. Keep your writing paraphernalia orderly and in place.

5. Make no excuses. There will be days when you might allow the slightest interruption to take you away from your writing. Don't do it; be vigilant. Part of writing is being a warrior. Protect your writing as if it were a sacred act. Because it is.

6. Set boundaries and ask for help. I don't just mean praying for "good writing," but make sure you let your husband, girlfriend, son, mother, friend know when you write and that it is private time during which you are *not to be disturbed*, period.

7. *Do not answer the phone* while you are writing! This is crucial. The telephone is arguably the greatest modern enemy of privacy. Nothing can break your concentration like the telephone. Get a message center to which you can have your calls forwarded, turn the sound off on your answering machine, or get Caller ID.

∴ ∴

# How do I pick up from where I left off in my writing?

> I need an hour alone before dinner, with a
> drink, to go over what I've done that day. . . .
> I spend this hour taking things out and put-
> ting other things in. Then I start the next
> day by redoing all of what I did the day
> before, following these evening notes.
>
> —*JOAN DIDION*

The process of writing this book has taught me many things. One of them is how to begin each session of writing without fear and dread, how to face a blank page day after day with enthusiasm and curiosity for what will be delivered to me through the vehicle of my own psyche.

The concept for this book began with the title *The Writer's Mentor,* which is the eponymous name for my business as a writing consultant. In only one day I listed more than 120 subjects I considered necessary to the project. Slowly, and with the assistance of my steadfast editor, I began to whittle those topics down and organize them into their appropriate chapters. This provided a blueprint of what I needed to produce. True, the order in which I tackled each essay was still flexible, but I had something to consult when I made the decision of which chapter to write. Having this structure helped me enormously and provided a kind of security. It also lent itself to a mental momentum that is crucial when trying to complete a manuscript.

The formidable American playwright Tennessee Williams usually had two or three pieces of writing going at one time, and each day he would decide which one he was most keen on and go to town on it. Williams admitted to an inclination toward "excesses" during those infamous periods when he drank while writing. The following day he found that the "extravagance" of the work necessitated severe blue-pencil editing, and then he would sit down and begin a fresh day's writing.

Whatever one can do to encourage and establish a writing momentum will be advantageous. Some of the techniques I have learned for picking up from where I left off in my previous day's work are the following:

- I try to establish a clear sense of what my next day's work will be, how much I would like to complete and the length of my writing period. When I'm trying to complete a first draft, my preference is to move into a fresh piece of writing each day, rather than to begin by editing yesterday's work, but sometimes when a chapter takes longer than I anticipated, my task is already laid out for me, and editing it is. Ernest Hemingway made a rule for himself never to end one sheet and start a new one except in the middle of an incomplete sentence. This tack could be useful at the end of a writing day as well.
- A consistency in how often I write has been important. I've found that it's best to have even a short period of one hour for writing each day. It's surprising how much can get done when you know you have to be at a meeting in an hour and a half.

When too many days pass without my returning to the manuscript, it is more difficult to recapture the flow or mental momentum that was hard won. Sometimes, however, it simply isn't possible to write every day, and I accept that, even though my mind continues to "work" with ideas.

- Some people, like myself, prefer to have long stretches of time, say, six to eight hours. But even if there isn't time to *write* you can find a few minutes to *plan*. A few minutes of advance planning have saved me countless hours of wasted time on those days when I met the page without a strategy and felt a bit lost as to how to proceed. This advance planning is similar to writing your schedule for the week and for each day in your daybook. It works for appointments, and it works for writing as well.

- To prevent myself from having to spend too much time warming up the next day, I have learned to stop the "creative" part of my writing *before* the end of a session in order to allow some time to actively prepare for the next day's writing. There is a soothing quality to this approach because not only do I feel a sense of accomplishment for *this* day's work, but I have quelled my anxiety about the *following* day's plan of action as well. This way, in a manner of speaking, I stay ahead of the game.

- And on those days when I don't have either the time to arrange my next session in advance or the inspiration to create a new chapter, I know there is always plenty of editing and rewriting to do. In his Work Schedule List of Commandments, Henry Miller writes "5. When you can't *create* you can *work*."

- Finally, if all else fails and you still have difficulty picking up where you left off in your writing, you can always resort to freewriting. So much time is wasted in *not* writing when we wonder and worry, have repeated "false" starts, or just stare out the window and wish we were doing something (anything) else. Place one word after the next in as rapid succession as possible. Pay no attention to style, or even content, for that matter. Just get your hand moving. Chances are this exercise will carry you on to the next entry of your project.

*The Writer's Mentor Suggests . . .*

1. Try leaving something incomplete from your day's writing, whether it is a piece you spend several hours on or a new chapter for which you lay down the first sentence. Print out your

segment. When you sit down the next day, you will immediately launch into a new day's work. You may only be able to correct your spelling or revise a paragraph or simply reread the previous day's writing, but the continuity from day to day will help generate and solidify an entrenched habit and sustain an interest in your poem, novel, or essay for another twenty-four hours. If you quit while the going's good, you're more inclined to rush back the next day.

2. An alternative to that method is to surge forward without reviewing yesterday's work. You will have to decide which method works better for you and stick with it.

3. For at least a week, begin your writing periods with a ten-minute period of freewriting. This is like a stream-of-consciousness blitz. Do not be concerned with spelling, grammar, or even content. What you write doesn't need to "make sense." The object of this exercise is to get beyond what Peter Elbow refers to as "the root psychological or existential difficulty in writing: finding words in your head and putting them down on paper."

4. Read Peter Elbow's book *Writing with Power*.

·:· ·:·

# How do I reach a state of flow in writing?

> There's a zone I aspire to. Finding it is
> another question. . . . You want to control
> the flow of impulses, images, words, faces,
> ideas. But there's a higher place, a secret
> aspiration. You want to let go. You want to
> lose yourself in language, become a carrier
> or messenger. The best moments involve a
> loss of control. It's a kind of rapture.
> —*DON DELILLO*

Those periods of ecstatic flow, when time stands still, when there *is* no time, are better than the powers of Scheherazade for writers, or for anyone involved in a creative practice. These spans of transcendence are equal to the most satisfying remembrances I have of lovemaking, long-distance running or swimming, painting, walking on the beach with my dog, or many other mind-altering experiences I have had. Being in flow (or entering the zone, as athletes refer to this state) is when one's truest and wealthiest work steadily cascades forth seemingly without effort. There is a confluence of head, heart, and hand as ideas and language mingle freely with memories, images, emotions, intelligence, and intention. The stilling of the internal chatter becomes a relief, the focus a form of prayer.

Being in flow is what happens when one minute you have no idea how you will maneuver that maze of confusion that is the next chapter and the next moment it would appear that the chapter has written itself—sometimes rather well. Being in flow is allowing a transmission to occur. In flow you sanction yourself as a vessel for divine inspiration. Your creative currency becomes a navigable river. The call to create is satisfied. Here is the only place where you feel lost and simultaneously found.

We have all heard about the bliss of flow. But how to reach it remains the question. Mihaly Csikszentmihalyi has written extensively about the phenomenon of flow. In *Flow: The Psychology of Optimal Experience,* he writes of finding that flow "provided a sense of discovery, a creative feeling of transporting the person into a new reality. It pushed the person to higher levels of performance, and led to previously undreamed-of states of consciousness. In short, it transformed the self by making it more complex." For the writer, flow helps establish a writing fluency, a harmonic dance of images and emotions through words.

In consciously trying to follow my own process of flow, I have identified certain givens. It helps to know that I will have an uninterrupted period of time for writing. This encourages a kind of emotional and physical relaxation because for three or four hours—or however long I have planned to take for my writing period—there is

*I think I write much better if I'm flowing. . . . At first it's a bit jagged, awkward, but then there's a point where there's a click and you suddenly become quite fluent. . . . I don't write well when I'm sitting there sweating about every single phrase.*
—DORIS LESSING

nothing else that will need my consideration. This fosters a certain sense of freedom. I regard this time as sacrosanct and take certain measures to ensure that it is inviolable by man, dog, or child: diverting my telephone messages to a message center, taking my dog out for a walk *before* I begin, and making a bargain with myself that I will remain at my desk until I complete whatever amount it is that I have decided to complete. Having a topic in mind or a proposed intention is useful. Quiet is crucial. If the neighborhood gardeners are polluting the air with those blasted leaf blowers, I'll put my earplugs in place. (They really do work.) Having my dog (now ready for a nap after his romp) close to me—often his head lying securely upon my foot—is a hugely important part of my writing ritual. And the practice I have developed of paying attention to the work at hand steadily serves me.

The final aspect that seems inherent to encouraging this most enjoyable psychological state from which creative expression emerges is the knowledge that it is the writing itself that brings the answers to my questions and provides the clarity and direction in my work that I seek. It took me years to fully understand and trust this simple but profound truth. In the writing is the resolution. Knowing this provides the *temenos* or sacred circle for flow. In the end, though, flow is a mystery far beyond human comprehension, a place where spirit evolves and art is born. And after all the hours of a working day are added up, the truth is that fewer of them than I care to admit were subsumed by flow.

*I show up at my desk at nine o'clock every morning, and I think part of the issue of flow is presenting yourself for the task. I think your internal process needs to be geared to the fact that you will show up for work at a certain time every day.*

—SUE GRAFTON

## The Writer's Mentor Suggests . . .

1. Think back over your life experiences and pinpoint those occasions on which you found yourself in or coming out of the state of flow—this could be in your creative life, during exercise, or even in the process of daydreaming. Make a list of the particular circumstances. Write down exactly what was the procedure. Consciously attempt to replicate them at will. Transfer this approach to your writing.

2. In her book, *Writing in Flow,* Susan K. Perry analyzes flow in the writing process and defines what it is. Through years of extensive research, which included questionnaires to seventy-six poets and fiction writers, many well known, Perry devised a systematic study to observe and comprehend the process of flow. Her book is filled with practical applications for acquiring and maintaining a sense of flow in your own work. It is a worthy and useful investment. And highly recommended.

-:-  -:-

# Can writing be a process of self-discovery?

To write is, above all else, to construct a life.

—*DEENA METZGER*

My life has been saved by art twice. Once by painting and again by writing. That is to say that in the struggle between my personal demons and my will to live, the demons had me down for the count. I was thirty-eight when I made the descent to the interior world of clinical depression. It took a combination of psychotherapy, supportive friends, long, solitary walks in the Santa Monica mountains, and writing to reconnect me with a purpose for living. Although it is difficult to separate these contributors to my salvation, the writing played a catalytic role in my recovery. I think it is because as a creative person I find it difficult, if not impossible, to function without access to my creative *daimon* or energy. I lose psychological and emotional potency, and everything in my life becomes oppressive.

One day, at the nadir of this period of depression, during a Friday afternoon on November 11, around five o'clock, after months of immobility, the phrase "I am caught in a web of misery" circled maddeningly in my mind. It hounded me like my own shadow. There was nothing to do but get out of bed and write it down. The very act, it would seem, opened a watershed of images. The outpouring continued for eight hours. All that had been confined within me was emancipated in a flood of poems. Were any of the poems eventually published? Yes, but that was not their primary purpose. "What is the source of our first suffering? It lies in the fact that we hesitated to speak. It was born in the moment when we accumulated silent things within us," wrote Gaston Bachelard, the French philosopher and writer. The poems returned the voice that had been lost.

So was writing a form of self-discovery? It was for me, and it continues to be. Writing offers the opportunity to construct and deconstruct one's life simultaneously, to examine and change it.

Can writing save your life? It did mine. We tell stories to save our lives.

After that interval I went on to write *On Women Turning 40* and subsequently published seven additional books within a ten-year span of time. Even though none of these books has been *about* me, each has offered a process of self-discovery through self-revelation. It seems impossible *not* to learn about yourself as you learn about the world.

*You can use your own books in the same way you use anybody's books . . . to inform your life about the person who inhabits it. I think the reason you write, after all, is to inform your own life with a book that is made out of the subconscious materials of that life.*

—RUSSELL BANKS

### The Writer's Mentor Suggests . . .

1. For those wishing to take the plunge into the depths of your psyche, the ultimate companion is Deena Metzger's *Writing for Your Life: A Guide and Companion to the Inner Worlds.* I worked both privately and in a women's writing group with Deena, and during the period that I mention above, the experience was profound in terms of providing a cauldron for the turmoil of anxiety, fear, and deep unhappiness that stewed inside me. *Writing for Your Life* is filled with writing exercises and illustrative examples from many of Deena's students who worked with her during the writing of that book. But, most important, it is the sense of humanity and soul guidance that Deena's writing imparts and the connection the reader feels with the struggles both she

and her students have undergone. The book is rich with many true stories of personal descent to a mythic underworld, to a dark night of the soul. What the reader comes away with is the reassuring knowledge that she or he is not alone on their journey.

2. Keeping a journal is not only a tool for your writing but also an implement for self-reflection. It belongs to you; it is a private repository and, therefore, may be privy to any dreams, desires, free associations, native emotions, or unpolished prose that emerge from your inner territory. In addition to this medium of personal writing, a journal can also be that central place where you stash those ideas and phrases that fly through your head, bypassing the calyx of memory, unless they are chronicled. Your journal is not only your bank (of ideas), it includes your safety deposit box (of emotional currency).

## The Writer's Mentor at the Movies
### Bridget Jones's Diary

If you were to ask her, the fictional Bridget Jones—with Renee Zellweger forever associated in our minds as her embodiment—might say that her diary is her writing practice and that it serves as a means for her self-discovery. I wouldn't be surprised to learn that after the release of *Bridget Jones's Diary* the sale of diaries and journals had positively soared.

Aside from the fact that Bridget partly uses her diary in the service of what feminists have been fighting against for decades—a woman's obsession with her weight and an irrational preoccupation with men—you do get the sense that her diary is, if not her best friend, certainly one of them. It is in her diary that she can be exactly who she is without feeling embarrassment or disgust and, most important, without feeling judged. Because words release emotions, it is in her diary that she is at liberty to explore—and develop—an inner life.

It is to her diary that Bridget promises to adopt the usual self-improvement regime, confesses her habit of guzzling too much Chardonnay, slavishly notates her daily caloric intake, makes catty observations about her co-workers at the publishing house, and unabashedly remarks on her fantasies about her sexy but irascible and duplicitous boss Daniel Cleaver (as played by an unusually Mephistophelean Hugh Grant). Let's face it, few human friends would tolerate listening to a girlfriend's compulsive daily tally of her weight, especially if it were an enviable 120 pounds! How might the friend respond? "Get over yourself!" comes to mind. What saves *Bridget Jones's Diary* from being annoying is that Zellweger's Bridget never settles into a cloying self-pity; she remains entertaining even when in a deep funk and entirely endearing and utterly real in all her personal revelations.

Clearly there is a connection between the mixture of insouciance, wit, and candor that the inner Bridget displays in her diary and the disarmingly openhearted charm, implacable integrity, and enchanted unworldliness that infuse her persona and her actions out in the world, whether she is bumbling a welcoming speech on behalf of Salman Rushdie delivered at a book-launching party or apologizing to Daniel for her dowdy oversized knickers (that no fashion-conscious adolescent would be caught dead in, let alone a thirtysomething woman on her first date with her boss). Call it practice. The more she is herself in her diary, the more she can be herself in public. For Bridget, writing becomes a process of not *recording* what she wants to say but *discovering* what she wants to say.

The variation on the self-indulgent Cinderella myth is, of course, irresistible to many women—of any age. Take a single woman on a Friday evening, spellbound by a juicy fantasy of Prince Charming or Mr. Right. Give her a midrange bottle of white wine, add one television set, throw in an oversized terrycloth robe and a pair of white cotton socks—a comfortable couch with extra pillows is a must, a dog, even a cat, would be nice—and what single woman in her twenties, thirties, forties, fifties (how far up the decade ladder should I go?) doesn't relate to Bridget's situation? Perhaps all she needs is a diary "of one's own."

# CHAPTER 8

# PAGE FRIGHT

## *Overcoming the Fear of Writing*

How can I overcome my fear of writing?

What should I do when I'm staring at a blank page?

When I write, the words come painfully slowly. What can I do?

I have trouble writing under pressure. How can I overcome that?

How do I overcome discouragement?

The Writer's Mentor at the Movies: *The Shining*

PAGE FRIGHT. OVERCOMING THE FEAR OF WRITING proposes solutions to this universal condition that manifests itself through painfully slow writing or no writing at all. If you are "afraid" to write, you are not alone. Even Gabriel García Marquez says he fears the page, and Cynthia Ozick defines writing as essentially an act of courage. As an alternative to staring at a blank page, this chapter mixes media and shows how a tried and true technique for bypassing the existential void of an empty canvas can be transferred from painting to writing. Professional writers continually deal with the harsh reality of writing under pressure in order to meet deadlines, and a practical approach to judiciously appropriating your time is explored, as is the root cause of discouragement and its rehabilitation. Undoubtedly, the most well-known film about the topic of page fright is Stanley Kubrick's film *The Shining*, based on a novel by Stephen King, where we see a failed writer who's going off the deep end. On further review, I wonder if page fright is the true culprit here or merely a manifestation of a deeper angst?

# How can I overcome my fear of writing?

> I have known writers over the years, enormously talented, who are so self-conscious about it, who are so terrified of ever writing a bad sentence, that they can't write anything at all. I think a certain fearlessness in the face of your own ineptitude is a useful tool.
>
> —MICHAEL CUNNINGHAM

What do we fear when we are engulfed by page fright? We may be afraid of

criticism
having nothing to say
having nothing original, unique, interesting to say
not having an original, unique, interesting way of saying it
saying it wrong
not being good enough
being too good
exposing ourselves
alienating others
disappointing, hurting, infuriating others
incurring resentment, jealousy, envy in others
saying too much or not saying enough
boredom with ourselves and our writing
commitment to a task
incompletion
accomplishment

*It is scary to write and scary to make that commitment. Writing can go badly and does.*
—ANNE LAMOTT

*And so I remained for several days desiring to write and afraid to begin.*
—DANTE ALIGHIERI

. . . not necessarily in that order—and, mind you, this is only a partial list. These fears absorb so much of our consciousness it's a wonder anything at all ever gets written. Yet, we rarely discuss our fears with others, and we live in shame, thinking that they are unique to us.

It is my contention that the fear of writing is an integral part of writing. As writer after writer has attested, it is not the *absence* of fear that we should aspire to but, in the words of Mark Twain, "the *mastery* of fear." In other words, we're stuck with it and we need to learn to work with it. In his practical and positive book *The Courage to Write,* the author and writing instructor Ralph Keyes substantiates that "trying to deny, avoid, numb, or eradicate the fear of writing is neither possible nor desirable." He states that anxiety is not only an inevitable part of the writing process but also a *necessary* part. "If you're not scared," Keyes insists, "you're not writing."

Cynthia Ozick, the novelist and essayist, once wrote that if she had to say what writing is, she would have to define it essentially "as an act of courage. . . . I have to talk myself into bravery with every sentence, sometimes every syllable." So what we must shift is not necessarily our fear, which is where, as writers, we live, but our courage, which is an existential choice. This is a way of seeing fear less as an adversary than as a constant companion, albeit an often annoying and frustrating one. It was Søren Kierkegaard, the forefather of Existentialism, who said, "To dare is to lose one's footing temporarily; to not dare is to lose one's life."

*All my life, I've been frightened at the moment I sit down to write.*

—GABRIEL GARCÍA MARQUEZ

### The Writer's Mentor Suggests . . .

1. Perhaps the most common source of fear in a writer is overwhelm. I have learned in my own work, and I frequently share with my clients, that when overwhelm sets in, taking baby steps is best. Divide your task into a number of smaller tasks, make them manageable, and then focus on only one at a time. You must proceed like a carriage horse in Central Park outfitted with blinders so as not to be distracted by the pleasurable seduction of fresh-cut grass or startled by the towering double-decker tour bus.

2. I will often "trick" myself into sitting down at my desk ninety minutes before I must be dressed and out of the house for a meeting. It never fails: I become so engaged with the work (which quickly becomes play) in front of me that I nearly have to pry myself from my laptop and jump into a cold shower. It's like saying good-bye to a lover before you've been fully satisfied.

I'm usually a bit late for my meeting, but I'm in such good spirits that we both forgive my tardiness. H. G. Wells once suggested, "If you are in difficulties with a book, try the element of surprise: attack it at an hour when it isn't expecting it."

❖ · ❖

# What should I do when I am staring at a blank page?

I used to spend the morning procrastinating and worrying, then plunge into the manuscript in a frenzy of anxiety around 3:00 P.M. when it looked as though I might not get anything done. . . . The fact is that blank pages inspire me with terror. What will I put on them? Will it be good enough? . . . I suspect most writers are like this.

—MARGARET ATWOOD

*I suffer as always from the fear of putting down the first line. It is amazing the terrors, the magics, the prayers, the straightening shyness that assails me.*

—JOHN STEINBECK

Taped on a closet door in my study are several photographs and images clipped from magazines. One displays a black Underwood manual typewriter placed on a bed that is covered by a gold-colored down comforter. Sitting in front of it is a shivering short-haired blond Chihuahua weighing in at possibly three pounds. It has a black button of a nose, soulful eyes reflecting the camera flash, plaintive ears, and a "deer caught in the headlights" expression on its face. Sometimes that's how I feel when I am staring at a blank page.

There is only one alternative to staring at a blank page, and that is to write. There, I've said it. And I'll say it again: There is only one alternative to staring at a blank page, and that is to write—*if* you want to be a writer. A writer writes. After we've walked the dog, cleaned the house, made those five "can't wait" telephone calls, clipped our toenails, read today's *New York Times,* the blank page or screen is still waiting to be imprinted upon and to help us tell a story.

I began painting with oil paints when I was twelve years old. Until I entered the Practice of Fine Art Department at the University of California, Berkeley, when I was twenty-five, I never had the least trouble facing a blank canvas. But by the time a grade became attached to my painting, I suddenly found that an unadulterated dread confronted me with every stark 4-foot-by-5-foot gessoed canvas. One night, when the existential "void" seemed just too much to bear, almost in a fit of despair I took several brushes, dipped each one into separate jars of medium-thinned paint, and waded into the "nothingness." Aside from the physical and emotional relief this "action painting" provided me, it also gave me a place to start, to experiment, to make mistakes, to make thrilling discoveries. I later learned that many artists make use of this "putting marks on canvas" procedure and that there is a word for it: underpainting.

Unfortunately, I spent years prostrate before a blank page until I thought to translate that same approach of underpainting to "underwriting." It is dispiriting when our fear so easily overrides the sense of play and enjoyment that brought us to a particular form of personal expression in the first place. There's plenty of time for doubt and judgment and browbeating later, during revising and rewriting. But first there has to be something to revise and rewrite.

One method that works every time for me—when I remember to do it—is that of noting down each idea relevant to the topic about which I'm writing at any given time. It's only when I try to corral my thoughts and truncate them into some preconceived order that I get into trouble with the blank page.

Come to think of it, there are really two alternatives to staring at a blank page: One is to take up the dare that the page represents; the other is, simply, to give up writing altogether. Which do you choose?

*There is a deep inner resistance to writing.*
—DOROTHEA BRANDE

### The Writer's Mentor Suggests . . .

1.  In line with the method of noting down each idea relevant to the topic about which you are writing, do the following technique

on your own and see what happens. It may take a few tries before you become comfortable with it, but I can almost guarantee that it will work. As an example, following, you will find a list of words and phrases that I listed—with alacrity—during the process of writing this section. Some, you will notice, have been incorporated, others not. They are presented here in the order they transpired, misspellings, typos, and all.

only one alternative
books on ideas; don't know what to right
painting at 12 was easy; what happened?
too afraid; see FEAR
it has become too serious, lost a sense of play & enjoyment
    there's time for seriousness later during rewrite
include this list of notes/thoughts in the chap. as example??
first thought, best thought—Ginsberg
write anything
what to do?
Alternative: stop writing—makes 2 alternatives, not one
Suggests . . . mindmaping
ALWAYS write down idea—or its gone—poof
better to have more ideas to choose from that none.
words fill up a page
use a more interesting font—play w/ fonts
this is good; do more chapters using this/a method that relates
    to content
writing frres the psyche
picture of chiuahua next to typewriter: big eyes filled with
    FEAR: blank page
alternative—dont write
underpainting/writing

2. If your mind seems to freeze up during this exercise, try writing down words at random, not necessarily related to your topic at hand. Or jot down words by placing them arbitrarily on your paper or screen (although, obviously, this is quicker by hand on

paper). The Beat and Buddhist poet, Allen Ginsberg, is noted for his saying: "First thought, best thought."

3. The system of Mind Mapping is also extremely helpful for this purpose. Mind Mapping, or "radiant thinking," was originated by Tony Buzan. He has written several books on the subject; the one I'm familiar with is *The Mind Map Book*. This is a helpful and nonthreatening way to allow your ideas to expand and lead directly—and indirectly—to building concepts and written material. In this system you begin with a topic, say, an essay on the fear of writing or staring at a blank page. This phrase is placed in the middle of a page. From that core concept, lines are radiated out to other secondarily related ideas, and other lines are radiated out from those to tertiarily related ideas, and so on.

Now try this method on your core concept.

⁖   ⁖

# WHEN I WRITE, THE WORDS COME PAINFULLY SLOWLY. WHAT CAN I DO?

> When you write, you lay out a line of words.
> The line of words is a miner's pick, a wood-
> carver's gouge, a surgeon's probe. You wield
> it, and it digs a path you follow. . . . You
> make the path boldly and follow it fearfully.
> You go where the path leads.
> —*ANNIE DILLARD*

Perhaps it is on that stellar day, when we inelegantly manipulate our first crayon and comprehend the magical red or green or purple impress it can make on a white wall or on the pages of the book our mother happens to be reading, when we first feel that to write is our

God-given gift—no, it is an absolute right. It is our *right* to write. Later we learn the elements of a mystifying hieroglyphic alphabet and how clumps of these isolated shapes can convey meaning, communicate thoughts and ideas. We begin to put one letter after another, much like we did with our feet when we began taking our first steps. Soon we aren't content with simple words; we study sentences and their structure. Before long we are writing that first minimemoir about how we learned to swim at summer camp or how our Golden Retriever, Chamois, died on our birthday or how a new little brother, Brett, materialized (from our mother's stomach?) during Easter vacation.

It is after we have made the decision to "be a writer" that the true effort and diligence it takes to *write* becomes shockingly apparent to us. When the agonizing self-consciousness consumes us. Why doesn't it come easily, we wonder, flow like water or wine instead of molasses? Of course, there are writers who seem capable of setting words down on paper like a dexterous layer of tiles in the Alhambra: the prolific John Updike and Stephen King come to mind. But for most of us the journey of a thousand sentences begins with one word . . . and another . . . and then another, ad infinitum.

When in 1997 I met Madeleine L'Engle, the seventy-eight-year-old author of numerous books, including *A Wrinkle in Time* and *A Wind in the Door,* to interview her for my book *On Women Turning 70: Honoring the Voices of Wisdom,* I asked what advice she might have for beginning writers. "When you write, don't think. Write," said the woman who writes daily in her journal and works at her computer nearly every day. And then Madeleine threw a curve ball. "Writing is easy," she deadpanned. "You just sit and wait for the drops of blood to form on your forehead." No problem. But, she laughed, "It's also the most fun I know." The truth for most writers lies somewhere between the Fourteen Stations of the Cross and ecstasy.

"When you write, you lay out a line of words." Writing is a craft. It builds on words. Sometimes these words come swiftly, but more often than not they meander, they are duplicitous, they can be perfidious. But during the process you should befriend them, and in the end, you must love them; because as a writer you are nothing without them. You will do well to cultivate both humility and courage when it comes to your writing because all art necessitates much sacrifice. Writing assumes deftness of thought and dexterity of imagination. It also demands a willingness to be lost, to be missing in action, and a tolerance (that eventually becomes an enjoyment) for utilizing an hour or more to solicit specificity, to find the word that impeccably describes an object, place, person, or activity. It is said that Dylan Thomas would spend upward of an entire morning or afternoon immersed in Roget's *Thesaurus,* in search of that elusive flawless expression. For him "painfully slow" was intoxicatingly exquisite.

"You go where the path leads." And word by word you have built a poem or a story, an essay, or even, in time, a book. It is the words that become your tool. And as you slowly, even painstakingly, refine and distill them, they will take you on a journey that is far more than "fun"; it is salvation.

## The Writer's Mentor Suggests . . .

1. Imagine that you are being detained in a prison, even solitary confinement, on a false charge, you are stranded on a desert island, or you are a penniless homeless person. In any of these scenarios you are without the means to write: you have neither writing instrument nor receptacle. But, as fate would have it, you are inflamed with ideas for exposé articles or short stories. What would you do? Take a few minutes in an active imagination exercise to really feel the despair of someone in these circumstances. Then, with writing tools in hand, write from the conditions of one of these situations for thirty minutes. Write as quickly as you can; you only have thirty minutes.

2. In twenty words, precisely describe one object that is either on your desk or that you can see from wherever you are sitting. Again, take thirty minutes, but this time limit yourself to only twenty words.

# I HAVE TROUBLE WRITING UNDER PRESSURE. HOW CAN I OVERCOME THAT?

> 7 June. Bad. Wrote nothing today.
> Tomorrow no time.
> —*FRANZ KAFKA*

At times the pressure to complete a piece of writing, whether it be for a publisher, editor, agent, magazine, e-zine, newspaper, professor, writing group, writing partner, or one's self, can be what heaves one into the throes of writer's block. There are primarily two directions a writer can take in her stance to meeting a deadline: approach it decisively and, if not with enthusiasm, at least with trepidation of the consequences of allowing a deadline to remain unmet, or become paralyzed and filled with self-loathing at not meeting your agreement. (Sometimes, between the two, it seems easier and more familiar just to feel completely miserable, albeit far less satisfying.) In either case, however, the moment of reckoning continues to loom over your every action, preventing you from enjoying anything at all.

One thing that can incapacitate a writer is the inability to see where what she is writing is going, to see the broader picture of the connections she is trying to make. As always with writing, the best—and ultimately the simplest—approach to any uncertainty or reticence is to write. Get going. Get excited about the work. Feel how fortunate you are to have the opportunity and the time to marshal your thoughts on paper. Energy releases clarity. Clarity releases energy. Concentration is what's needed. Meeting a deadline releases nervous energy. Let it work for you instead of just giving you a headache or heart palpitations.

As I write this essay, I am facing several deadlines. This very manuscript is due for delivery—yes, just like a baby—in one month. That alone would be enough pressure for most writers. But. I also have a full-time course load in my Ph.D. program, and I have two papers due within the same time frame. Okay. That's doable. But. I also have the rewritten draft of my dissertation concept paper due in exactly one month, when I make a presentation before the dissertation committee. There is also my teaching load at UCLA and UC-Santa Cruz, Extensions and consulting on clients' projects. Something's got to give.

When friends shake their heads and say, "I don't know how you do it," I respond in all honesty that I don't either. Being single and having my adult son living successfully on his own helps immensely. Now, I'm not sharing my circumstances with you ruefully, but from a place of resolution: to pragmatically push on for one month, with both my person and profession intact. For, finally, the point comes when it's just easier to do the work than complain about it, and the one true thing I know about myself is that I do work better and harder under pressure.

It is said that the great Russian writer Fyodor Dostoyevsky labored through the entire 500-page manuscript for *The Gambler* as he simultaneously completed the equally long *Crime and Punishment*. An added impetus was the threat from his Dickensian publisher that, unless punctually completed, he would lose the rights to *all* of his previous work. He dictated one book in the morning and the other in the afternoon. The stenographer soon became his second wife.

Dostoyevsky's trials make my schedule less daunting and my mood less melancholic. In the end, when I ask myself what I would rather be doing with my life other than writing, the answer inevitably is, Nothing.

As always, in the face of overwhelm, the most expedient plan of action is to compartmentalize your tasks into manageable increments, that is, one step at a time. If you have a plethora of projects demanding your attention, organize them according to what is most pressing, which could be defined by magnitude, degree of difficulty, or due date. The important thing is to break the workload down into daily components and focus only on that day's effort. Exercise 1, in The Writer's Mentor Suggests . . . following, offers further guidance.

*There is in the air about a man a kind of congealed jealousy. Only let him say he will do something and that whole mechanism goes to work to stop him.*

—JOHN STEINBECK

### The Writer's Mentor Suggests . . .

1. The outer-world demand of deadlines placed on the inner-world process of conceptualizing and organizing one's thoughts

can seem artificial, but in truth that combination is probably how 99.9 percent of work in the world gets accomplished. The best approach to the pressure of a deadline is to apportion your time judiciously. Begin at the end. Calculate how much time you have until your project is due and divide the time up into blocks of days, weeks, months. Calculate time for both a first draft and two or three revisions. It is best if you can get that first rough draft down on paper as quickly as possible before you begin the revision process.

2. If you are still having trouble getting down to business, ask yourself if your resistance has to do primarily with the external constraint or condition placed upon you or if there is a more insidious rationale behind it. If it is the former, you might make an effort to extend the deadline; if the latter, look hard and long at your subject matter, for therein may lie the resolution. Are you conflicted in some way either about the material or about yourself as a writer? In order to discover the answer to this question, spend some time either in meditation or in another form of self-communication. You *will* receive an answer. The next question is, What will you do with the answer?

∵ ∴

# How do i overcome discouragement?

> If you want to write, you can. Fear stops
> most people from writing, not lack of talent,
> whatever that is. Who am I? What right have
> I to speak? Who will listen to me if I do? You
> are a human being with a unique story to
> tell, and you have every right.
>
> —*RICHARD RHODES*

Unmet expectations and aspirations for writing can be discouraging. But don't allow discouragement to stop you from doing what you wish to do: write. One of the many "selves" a writer carries within her is a cheerleader or an inner support team. Writing itself is difficult enough, but it seems that writers are haunted by uncertainties and are very easily discouraged. One does well to toughen the "skin" of one's writing vulnerabilities.

Diane Ackerman, the poet and author of *A Natural History of the Senses,* says that the best advice on writing she ever received was to "invent your confidence." This is excellent counsel—we are the only ones who can do that for ourselves. Have you ever noticed during those periods of life when you feel that nothing you do is working out—even if everyone you know cheers you on, trying to convince you of your talent, beauty, or worth—the only influence that can change your attitude is you? This doesn't mean that we don't need all the support we can get from family, friends, and colleagues, just that if we don't work to build or "invent" an inner confidence, it simply will not magically appear. You are your own greatest resource.

Sometimes discouragement can take you in a new positive direction. In 1935, after reading James Laughlin's poetry, Ezra Pound told him, "You're never going to be any good as a poet. Why don't you take up something useful?" Laughlin took the advice and founded the New Directions publishing house, which would go on to publish many of the twentieth century's most distinguished writers, including Pound, Tennessee Williams, Henry Miller, Dylan Thomas, and Vladimir Nabokov. And in the midst of this, Laughlin continued to write poetry.

Writing is the act of finding words in your head and arranging and rearranging them on a blank piece of paper. To create something from nothing is a psychological quandary. To create something from nothing is enough to make you insecure at best and, at worst, mentally paralyzed. Choosing to write is an existential act. To write is to plunge into the face of nothing, down its throat, into its entrails, and come out the other "end" into the satisfaction of having done something, having written words, any words, in any order. To invent one's

*Writing a novel is a very hard thing to do because it covers so long a space of time, and if you get discouraged it is not a bad sign, but a good one. If you think you are not doing well, you are thinking the way real novelists do.*

—MAXWELL PERKINS, IN A LETTER TO NANCY HALE

*I would never encourage anyone to be a writer. It's too hard.*

—EUDORA WELTY

confidence is to continue to write. It is to say no to the myriad of voices that try to convince us to stop writing and to say yes to the solitary utterance that says, You *can.* You *will.* You *do.*

### The Writer's Mentor Suggests . . .

1. Keeping a journal can have many benefits. One is that when you read back through it you concretely see the various emotional ebbs and flows inherent in the writing life. You will read passages similar to the one Virginia Woolf wrote in her journal: "despair at the badness of the book; can't think how I ever could write such stuff—and with such excitement: that's yesterday: today I think it good again. A note, by way of advising other Virginias with other books that this is the way of the thing: up down up down—and Lord know the truth." If you have kept journals over any length of time beyond three months—the longer, the better, here—randomly reread passages that relate to your writing life. Keeping a journal is the most concrete way to remember how your relationship is continually jostling between despair and deep satisfaction.

2. As always, the best advice is to write. Just write. For in the writing comes the suspension of judgment, which is the root cause of discouragement in the first place. Write.

## The Writer's Mentor at the Movies
### *The Shining*

To the question, What are some alternatives to staring at a blank page? I suggest that there is only one alternative, and that is to write—if you want to be a writer. Earlier in this chapter I suggested that you try writing down words at random, not necessarily having anything to do with your topic at hand. Someone who takes this idea to the ultimate extreme is Jack Torrance in *The Shining*, Stanley Kubrick's cinematic version of the Stephen King novel.

Jack (played by Jack Nicholson at his maniacal best) already seems on the brink and exhibits an edgy irritation with both his wife, Wendy (Shelley Duvall), and his son, Danny, as they drive to their new winter job as caretakers of an isolated mountain resort, the Overlook Hotel, in the Colorado Rocky Mountains. There are hints of past problems (and portents of future ones): Jack may have been fired from his teaching position; he definitely has had a drinking problem; his relationship with his wife appears lethargic; because Danny clearly fears his father, we suspect Jack of physically abusing him; and, in addition, Jack has illusions of writing the Great American Novel. None of these bode well. But, perhaps, exorcising his demons on paper is exactly what Jack needs.

Under strict orders to remain quiet and stay clear of Jack when he is "working" in his enviable cathedral-like study—the lodge's cavernous wood-paneled, picture-windowed lobby—we see Wendy and Danny virtually walking around on tiptoe to appease him. There are sounds of a clacking typewriter, and Wendy thinks that all is going splendidly with Jack's writing, until he begins to sleep through most days, remains in his robe and pajamas, stops shaving, and surpasses his level of perpetual cantankerousness—all signs of depression and probably cabin fever, if not downright page fright.

Of course, because this is a Stephen King story, there must be an element of horror in the plot, but here we are only concerned with a far more gruesome nightmare that haunts many scribes—that of a failed writer who's going off the deep end.

The story offers us vague possibilities. Are there really ghosts in room 237? Are Danny's visions of the past or the future? Is Jack a reincarnation of an axe murderer? Is all this happening in Jack's imagination—and if only he could write it down it would disappear? Is the whining Wendy enough to push Jack (or anyone else for that matter) over the edge? Are Jack's financial and familial responsibilities driving him to the brink? Or is page fright the true culprit here, the roadway to madness?

Before Jack does his Ed McMahon imitation in the devilishly funny, yet hair-raising, "Heeere's Johnny!" scene, Wendy stealthily has made her way over to his now-silent typewriter (while he is probably looking for a weapon with which to murder her). It would appear that Jack has actually completed a manuscript of several hundred pages, until she looks more closely and in disbelief sees that he has repeatedly written, ad infinitum, the children's verse "All work and no play make Jack a dull boy."

So, like I said before, if your mind freezes up, write down words at random that may not necessarily have anything to do with your topic at hand. I guess "All work and no play make Jack a dull boy" is as good a place as any to begin.

# CHAPTER 9

# WRITER'S BLOCK

## *and*

# PROCRASTINATION

## *Freeing the Writer Within*

How do I deal with writer's block or being "stuck"?

How can I silence my inner critic/censor/editor?

I have a tendency to procrastinate. What should I do?

How do I deal with my self-doubts?

The Writer's Mentor at the Movies: *The Muse*

WRITER'S BLOCK AND PROCRASTINATION: FREEING THE WRITER WITHIN puts forth a progressive look at the causes of writer's block and procrastination and offers a new way to think about them: namely, that they oblige you to suspend your plans and reconsider the nature of your relationship to your internal creative forces. Several writers describe their approaches to these periods of gestation and incubation. This chapter offers a model for a one-day workshop that will help you either "blast through" a block or dialogue with it. It also assists you in identifying an internal navigator as a means of differentiating between the voice of a censoring critic and that of an encouraging interior guide and presents advice on how to pacify self-doubt. The film I discuss in this chapter is *The Muse,* which is a brilliant example of how willing we are to place the power of creative invention on to anyone or anything outside of ourselves.

# HOW DO I DEAL WITH WRITER'S BLOCK OR BEING "STUCK"?

> Sometimes when I'm stuck I go to an office
> building, ride the elevator and stare at
> the lawyers, stock brokers, and accountants
> in their power suits. Just the thought of
> having to wear pantyhose all day and work
> in a building where I can't open the
> windows usually makes me grateful
> to come home and write.
>
> —*MARGO KAUFMAN*

Recently, a new and progressive attitude toward writer's block has been developing. Viewed less as a fearsome detriment, a creative block, as some evidence suggests, may be an artist's or writer's ally. It is almost sacrilegious to say this because creative people have relied on the myth of the "block" for decades, if not centuries. But what, exactly, does "writer's block" mean? Traditionally, we see it as a temporary or chronic inability to put words on paper. And—always—joined at the hip of writer's block, like a Siamese twin, are feelings of anger, helplessness, and, often, despair in the one who is besieged by it.

*Without resistance you can do nothing.*

—JEAN COCTEAU

In the most intelligent and compassionate analysis of writer's block I have yet encountered, Victoria Nelson's *On Writer's Block: A New Approach to Creativity,* Nelson states that a creative block is "not a bad thing in itself. Properly interpreted, a block is the best thing that can happen to a writer. Resistance is a vital regulator of the creative process because it obliges us to suspend our plans and reconsider the nature of our relation to the creative forces inside us, forces that are truly gifts—ours by virtue of grace and not possession." It is her contention that we use writer's block as a way of protecting ourselves from ourselves. This makes a great deal of sense when we consider the kind of grief a writer undergoes—often self-inflicted.

In my own writing process, as well as in those of my clients, I have found that blocks usually are the outcome of a confluence of factors: fear of criticism or that our writing isn't good enough; the complexity of a particular project, or the absence of a significant one; the lack of sufficient time and/or a suitable environment or favorable circumstances for writing; a tendency in one's (this includes most writers) personality to either procrastinate or to blame oneself for being imperfect; and asking oneself too early the inappropriate, if sobering, questions: Will I be able to sell this book to a publisher? and Is there an audience for this book? Any given writer, at any given time, may fall prey to one or more or all of these challenges.

The psychologist Rollo May described the process of "active listening." He noted that when the conscious mind is "silent," it is often because the unconscious is activated. He recommended adopting a positive, trusting attitude toward those periods of "waiting" as one's mind oscillates between the known and the unknown; he describes this process as "a waiting for the birthing process to begin to move in its own organic time. It is necessary that the [writer] have this sense of timing, that he or she respect these periods of receptivity as part of the mystery of creativity and creation."

*A writer should value his blockages. That means he's starting to scale down, to get close.*
—ROBERT PIRSIG

### The Writer's Mentor Suggests . . .

1. Some writers have various techniques for busting through writer's block. Madeleine L'Engle once told me that when she gets "stuck" she swims or walks or does something else she enjoys that is physical. I also have found that method of working through a block quite helpful. Just getting the body moving often seems to uncongeal those clotted brain cells and liberate an inactive psyche. Irving Stone admitted that pulling weeds is "the best therapy there is for writer's block." Dominick Dunne advises keeping a journal and pouring out those feelings of frustration and anger that you have toward yourself. He suggests describing whatever it is that you are *wanting* to write in your journal—without pressure. Take his advice: "Write about it. Believe me, it will start to come, right there in your journal."

2. But there are also writers who prescribe to Rollo May's method. Toni Morrison is one who is no longer bothered by writer's

block, although she concedes that there is such a thing and it should be respected. Her counsel is, "You shouldn't write through it. It's blocked because it ought to be blocked, because you haven't got it right now." Even though Joyce Carol Oates does not "think that writer's block exists really," she does suggest that when a period of "silence" engulfs you, perhaps it is because you are trying to do something "prematurely, it just won't come." Sometimes you simply must wait until this period of incubation has reached maturity and your subject matter is ready to be birthed.

3. If being active in pursuit of the elusive word, either through some physical activity, weed pulling, or journal writing, doesn't bring you satisfaction and your patience with waiting has worn thin, you might try *New Yorker* contributor Ken Auletta's recommendation: "Turn on any Puccini opera."

❧ ❧

# How can I silence my inner critic/censor/editor?

> Love your material. Nothing frightens the
> inner critic more than the writer who loves
> her work. The writer who is enamored
> of her material forgets all about censoring
> herself. She doesn't stop to wonder if her
> book is any good, or who will publish it,
> or what people will think.
> —*ALLEGRA GOODMAN*

The critic who dwells inside seems to represent a perceived external authority. Ask yourself this question: Who does the critic actually represent? A parent? An ex-husband? A literary critic? A fantasy publisher? Perhaps we have placed our written work in the minds—and opinions—of future readers, readers who may never exist. "What will they think?" can become the mantra that keeps us from pressing forward, ever deeper into the internal heart of our own matter.

In *Inventing the Truth: The Art and Craft of Memoir,* the book's editor, William Zinsser, describes writing—and not writing—his first memoir. "I was half paralyzed by the awareness that my parents and my sisters were looking over my shoulder, if not actually perched there, and would read whatever version of their life came out of my typewriter. . . . Since then, reading the memoirs of other writers, I've always wondered how many passengers were along on the ride, subtly altering the ride."

It is the fear of "What will people think?" that the inner critic or specter uses to paralyze us. That and "But it isn't perfect. You must make it perfect. And if you can't make it perfect, don't bother writing at all." The only way out of this trap is to concentrate on your writing: selecting words, stringing phrases together, forming sentences, rewriting, and so on. There are enough paid critics, marketing strategists, and publicists to evaluate your work. And they will. You don't have to do it for them.

Make an effort to differentiate between the voice of the censoring critic and the utterance of an encouraging guide or shepherd. Some internal navigator may be offering you an invitation through an incentive to propel yourself into a new direction, to explore completely new material. When it comes to your writing—as in life—it is crucial to listen, to trust, and to follow any impulse or instinct or intuition that occurs to you. Go where your passion and curiosity lead you, and you will be following your inner voice or guide.

And when you truly "love your material" you will be absorbed by the plot or character development, the metaphor, vocabulary, voice, and humor as they materialize beneath your fingertips. As Allegra Goodman wrote, you will "write in a trance, losing track of time, hearing only [your] characters in [your] head."

1. Look for ways to outsmart, pacify, or coexist with your inner critic. Try writing at what Virginia Woolf called a "rapid haphazard gallop" so he can't keep up with you. To catch him off guard, write at unexpected times, like while waiting for your three-minute soft-boiled egg to cook, or in improbable locations, like waiting in the carpool for the kids.

2. If you simply can't get around your censor, try writing a letter to your closest friend telling her in detail what your story or essay is about. If you are afraid your best friend will judge your writing or its content, create a reciprocal safe haven with a writer friend with whom you have an agreement *not* to judge each other's work. Writing *about* the story or essay will be less threatening than actually *writing* it.

3. In an essay titled "The Watcher at the Gates," Gail Godwin advises getting to know your critic or "watcher." Find out what this inhibitor looks like by drawing a picture of him or her. Turn this critic into an enabler, a helpful, positive, sharp-eyed editor. As a final attempt at peaceful coexistence, you might write him a letter. Godwin's went like this: "Dear Watcher, What is it you're so afraid I'll do?" She says she held his pen for him, and he replied "instantly with a candor that has kept me from truly despising him. 'Fail,' he wrote back."

❖ ❖

I HAVE A TENDENCY TO PROCRASTINATE. WHAT SHOULD I DO?

> Never do today what you can
> Put off till tomorrow.
> —*WILLIAM BRIGHTY RANDS*

Are you a procrastinator? Whether your task is to draft a fifteen-page academic paper on "Tristan und Isolde" for a graduate course or commence work on a novel that you've been thinking about for two years, do you wait until the last conceivable moment to launch the mission at hand? For, to be sure, every assignment, chore, or responsibility carries with it the aura of the impossible. Does the effort needed to wash last night's dishes seem indistinguishable from packing for a three-week trek? No matter what the objective at hand—be it personal or occupational—is your foremost consideration to see how long you can postpone the inevitable?

Stan Freberg, the satirist, composer, and advertising writer, spoke to the issue of procrastination when he once remarked during an interview, "My wife says, 'Did it ever occur to you that if you started this a month ago you'd be finished by now?' But I can't change my mental clock—the emergency part of my brain [he makes a siren sound] doesn't kick in until twenty-four hours before something is due."

Does this sound familiar? If so, then you, also, are probably a procrastinator.

Through a lifetime, each individual develops a way of steering through the flea market of the world, a means of surviving that allows them to barter an innate shyness in exchange for confidence or convert an overbearing parent into a valued confidante or swap a chronic low-level energy (a.k.a. depression) with unprecedented vitality. Over the decades I have discovered that my method of conversion from limbo, apathy, or (let's just say it) immobility to accomplishment is adrenaline addiction. Whereas a good many writers may work in a methodical, orderly manner, I thrive on flying by the seat of my pants. And there is nothing like an impending deadline to activate one's adrenaline, although it seems to me that often it may be *because* of one's procrastination that we actually end up accomplishing as much as we do. There is a lot to be said for periods of gestation and incubation.

Another procrastinator may be a gambler by nature. His bet is that he can complete the portfolio review in a week, when it takes every other investor a two weeks or more to do the same job.

*The best advice on writing I've ever received: Finish.*
—PETER MAYLE

Then there is the prima donna. "Why should I have to spend time doing research for the novel I'm writing? I already know everything I need to know. Next year I'll start the novel."

And in the meantime, procrastination provides a convenient way for us as writers to hate ourselves. It arouses all the ambivalence that we feel about ourselves as writers.

So how to subvert the natural procrastinator's inclination toward postponement? When a friend of mine who lives in Santa Fe was writing her Ph.D. dissertation last year, she went through weeks during which she simply could not get herself motivated to write. The deadline for delivering the dissertation was only three months away. And every distraction, from a visiting daughter to an ailing mother to an inoperative car, exacerbated her resistance. She meant to write every day, but the days scattered in a fluster of very real responsibilities. In a despairing telephone call, she asked if I might come for a visit and offer my support as her personal writer's mentor. Loving both my friend and Santa Fe, I arrived less than a week later at the Albuquerque Airport. By Thursday evening I had read what she had written so far, and by Saturday morning, after a guided meditation, she was writing full throttle.

Next, The Writer's Mentor Suggests . . . describes the method I used with her. It's one I highly recommend.

## The Writer's Mentor Suggests . . .

What follows is a technique adapted from Eric Maisel's helpful book, *Living the Writer's Life*.

Decide to give yourself a One-Day Writing Workshop. If you choose to invite another writer friend or friends, you may do so, but be very clear that this is a *work* day, which will include little, if any, social interaction. Up to a week before the appointed day, select any day of the week during which you will be "free" of all professional and/or familial obligations, at least for a nine-hour period. If your own home is not conducive to this kind of venture, either arrange to use a friend's home or office or check into a hotel for the day. It is crucial that you create this environment for yourself.

When the morning of your writing workshop begins, have a healthful but not too filling breakfast. Now turn all the phones off or forward your calls. Take fifteen to twenty minutes to visualize yourself at your desk writing, see yourself encased in a large transparent bubble in which you are calm and quiet and alone with your writing paraphernalia (and your earplugs!). Imagine yourself writing uninterrupted for several hours, only leaving your chair for bathroom and refreshment breaks.

After you see yourself securely settled in your mental image, write a statement of purpose for your day's efforts. Are you beginning a project, finishing one up, or breathing fresh life into a half-completed endeavor? Whichever, commit to writing what you realistically want to complete during your day of production. Divide the day into morning and afternoon sessions divided by an hour for lunch—you should have something already prepared—with a half-hour break in each session. During your lunch and your afternoon break reread your writing and decide where you want to go next. To an entirely different chapter, a rewrite? See this review period not as an opportunity for self-criticism but as a glance at a map to see if you are going in the right direction or need to turn at the next corner.

This daylong process has helped many of my clients, just as it did for my friend in Santa Fe, to re-invest themselves in their writing project. It can also work for you.

~:· ·:~

# How do i deal with my self-doubts?

> I am discomforted by the knowledge that I don't
> know how to write the books that I have not
> yet written. But that discomfort has an excite-
> ment about it, and it is the necessary antecedent
> of one of the best kinds of happiness.
> —*WENDELL BERRY*

It seems natural for writers to shift back and forth between periods of self-aggrandizement and feelings of worthlessness. This kind of ambivalence is continually fluctuating between the writer and the person—we dare to distinguish the two. If the writer in you feels without value, that emotion will also bleed into your attitude about yourself as a human being, and vice versa. Most writers recognize their dual or multiple natures. Admitting that it is part of one's existence is one part; learning to deal with it every day is the other.

Dorothea Brande, in her brilliant yet sensible book, *Becoming a Writer*—which was first published in 1934 and still sells well—takes for granted that the writer works from both her conscious and unconscious aspects and says, "It is possible to train both sides of the character to work in harmony, and the first step in that education is to consider that you must teach yourself not as though you were one person, but two."

But self-doubt in writing, as in life, can be insidious. It can smother inspiration. It can block each step in the direction of a creative urge. Self-doubt seems to be the basis of nearly every writer's modus operandi. But there is a second aspect to self-doubt that isn't so stultifying. It is valuable to remember that it's your self-doubt that keeps you working and struggling to improve. It is a means to, if not perfection, then at least polish. It doesn't tolerate complacency or laziness, although, God knows, there may be plenty of moments of indecision and even inertia to get through.

There is an importance to building optimism in your life as well as in your creative life. If you don't believe in yourself, how can you expect an agent, editor, book buyer, and reader to? In a letter to his agent, Audrey Wood, Tennessee Williams admitted that he had lived behind "the mobile fortress of a deep and tranquil pessimism" for so long that he felt "*almost* impregnable."

*You will never be satisfied with what you do.*
—FAY WELDON

Doing one thing, taking one action toward your goal, can be an immediate means of pacifying self-doubt. If your intent is to write a short story, commit to writing for thirty minutes three or four times a week. Or begin to do some research that is connected to this project. There's no need to overload yourself with obligation. That often only adds to a feeling of overwhelm and impossibility. Dallying is fine, delaying is not. I firmly believe that the act of writing itself will carry you along on a flight of curiosity and into a cocoon of palliation/catharsis, where being lost (or found) is the process of writing itself.

## The Writer's Mentor Suggests . . .

One of the best ways to deal with your self-doubt is to make a commitment. A commitment changes your focus from yourself and your self-doubt onto your work. There is an appropriate quote that I give to my writing clients when the need arises. It is often attributed to Goethe because the final two lines are his, but it is actually from *The Scottish Himalayan Expedition* by W. H. Murray.

> Until one is committed, there is hesitancy, the chance to draw back, always ineffectiveness. Concerning all acts of initiative, there is one elementary truth, the ignorance of which kills countless ideas and endless plans:
>
> The moment you definitely commit yourself, then Providence moves too. All sorts of things occur to help you that would never otherwise have occurred. A whole stream of events issues from the decision, raising in your favor all manner of unforeseen incidents and meetings and material assistance, which you could never have dreamed would come your way.
>
> Whatever you can do or dream you can, begin it.
>
> Boldness has genius, power, and magic to it.

Make a commitment to your goal. In her helpful, no-nonsense book, *The Shortest Distance Between You and a Published Book,* author Susan Page discusses two types of commitment: intention-style commitment and burning commitment. Only you know which kind is yours. Make the choice, and see the many "incidents and meetings and material assistance" that find their way to you.

## The Writer's Mentor at the Movies
### *The Muse*

Imagine, if you will, a world in which every writer had—like a personal trainer, personal coach, personal assistant, personal chef—a personal Muse. No more writer's block or procrastination. No sabotaging self-doubts. No sadistic inner critic. This writer's fantasy is brought to life in the movies by Albert Brooks's character in *The Muse*.

Steven Phillips (Brooks) has just been honored with a humanitarian award. Driving home from the black-tie ceremony, his daughter asks, "What's a humanitarian?" "It's someone who's never won an Oscar," replies Steven in classic Brooks deadpan. We quickly learn that Steven, a once-successful screenwriter, is slipping from his niche in the Hollywood food chain. His scripts don't sell, he can't write, and, worse, he has no inspiration. In Hollywood-speak, he is "losing his edge"—and no one, from his producer and agent to his best friend, will let him forget it.

What to do?

When Steven goes to seek the advice of his wildly successful writer friend, Jack (Jeff Bridges), at his Bel-Air home, he notices a mysterious (and gorgeous) woman furtively slipping into a taxi. Is Jack having an affair? he wonders. Steven bares his soul to Jack and, as an aside, asks about the mystery woman. After a bit of "Oh, I really can't say" shenanigans, he swears Steven to secrecy and tells him that Sarah (played by a diva herself, Sharon Stone) is a Muse and has been singularly responsible for all of his recent success. As Steven is desperate enough to believe anything, he implores Jack to speak to Sarah on his behalf.

But everything comes with a price. *The Muse* is a bit like a reverse *Picture of Dorian Gray*, by Oscar Wilde. At least Gray—in a bargain with the Devil—maintained his youth (even if his portrait is ravaged with age). Steven becomes contractually involved with a greedy succubus, a vampiric materialist. In Steven's bargain with Sarah he must satisfy her outlandish demands: a $1,700-a-day room at the Four Seasons, a Waldorf salad from Spago's at 3 A.M., a limousine and driver, a gift from Tiffany's. And when all that isn't enough, Sarah begins to encroach upon her "client's" home and family. Steven jokes that she's like "the Muse who came to dinner" (a take-off on *The Man Who Came to Dinner*, the Moss Hart-George S. Kaufman

Broadway play, and eventual film, about a bitter radio celebrity on a lecture tour who breaks his hip and must stay in a quiet suburban home for the winter—driving the residents crazy).

Whenever Steven has doubts about Sarah's muse-ability, he is privy to some well-known movie artists having a tête-à-tête with her. One day it's James Cameron (the director of *The Titanic*), who leaves her bungalow muttering about Sarah's advice: "No water . . . stay away from water . . . forget about water. . . ." On another day there is "Marty" Scorsese, who tells Steven that Sarah has advised him to do a remake of *Raging Bull,* only this time using "a real thin guy." Steven grumbles to himself that the next thing she'll have Scorsese do is a remake of *Taxi Driver* with all women.

But one day it seems as if Sarah might actually be worth her weight in gold. She tells Steven that they need to go to the Long Beach Aquarium. How did she think of that? he wants to know. She saw an advertisement in the newspaper and "dreamt" about it. Steven is certain this is it—the moment of inspiration he has been wait-ing—and paying—for. As he and "the Muse" make their rounds of the aquarium, Steven is suddenly hit with a notion for a story that takes place at—where else?—an aquarium. How about "Jim Carrey inherits an aquarium?" he beams. Not to be eclipsed, Sarah says that yes, she was very pleased with *The Truman Show*. "You were respon-sible for *that*?" he gasps. And as they're leaving they run into Rob Reiner, who fawns over Sarah and says, "Thank you for *The Ameri-can President*," as he removes his Rolex watch and hands it to her.

Steven immediately writes the screenplay and gives it to his agent, who sends it to Paramount Studios. But he is incredulous when he discovers that Universal Studios already has the exact same script in production—with none other than Rob Reiner as the screenwriter/director. "The Muse stole my ideas!" Steven shrieks at his wife (who also has been "inspired" by Sarah to start a very suc-cessful cookie company—with the patronage of Wolfgang Puck of Spago fame).

So the supposed daughter of Zeus, one of nine sisters—"All the women in my family are muses"—turns out to be . . . But then you will find out for yourself when you watch the movie.

You may wonder why I didn't place this film in chapter 2, "Divine Inspiration: Meeting the Muse," rather than using it to illustrate a chapter about writer's block and self-doubts. Think about it. As much as we would like there to be an answer outside of ourselves, a divine Muse to transfer a faithful current of inspiration, like Steven and Jack and James and "Marty" and Wolfgang, we are essentially left to our own contrivances. Every writer must become his or her own Muse. Who breaks through writer's block? Ultimately, we do. Who silences the inner critic? We do. Who conciliates any self-doubts? We do. Who frees the writer within? . . .

# CHAPTER 10

# THE CRAFT
*of*
# WRITING

## *Finding Your Style and Voice*

What is a writer's "style"?

What is the "voice" of a writer?

How important are words and language?

How can I improve my descriptive writing?

Why is it necessary to rewrite and revise?

The Writer's Mentor at the Movies: *Il Postino*

THE CRAFT OF WRITING: FINDING YOUR STYLE AND VOICE defines and distinguishes among "style," "voice," and "craft." It demonstrates writing as an alchemical process, a method of vocalizing your nervous system, and testifies that writing is a visceral expression, a way the body has of communicating with the mind. The chapter explores writing as architecture with words, how a writer builds a poem or story like a carpenter builds a house. Nouns are muscular, verbs kinetic, adjectives sensorial. You learn ways to improve your descriptive writing: one, a map for conceptualizing metaphors by finding improbable juxtapositions between incongruent images, another for developing an instinct for specificity. In the concluding question about rewriting and revising, the premise is that rewriting is the soul of writing. And, with that assumption in mind, a detailed plan for revision is included.

The film *Il Postino* is a fictional account of a summer that the Chilean poet Pablo Neruda spent on an Italian island. Here he befriends a simple postman while educating him in the art of falling in love and confirming that everything in poetry—as well as life—is a metaphor.

# What is a Writer's "style"?

Even in the works of the greatest master we
find moments when the organic sequence fails
and a skillful join must be made, so that the
parts appear as a completely welded whole.
—*PETER ILICH TCHAIKOVSKY*

When I was in my early twenties, raising a small baby and tending an organic garden, I worked in a variety of crafts—pottery, leatherwork, knitting and crocheting, and others—that I sold at weekly arts and crafts fairs. These forms are called "crafts" because there is a certain skill necessary to their production, but until an artisan becomes proficient in the craft of their making, the results may be lovely pots but without the distinctive quality that comes from the mark of style. Mine remained crafts because I did not stick with them long enough to transform them into art through a developed style of my own. Why do we instantly recognize a van Gogh painting or a Mozart piano concerto or a passage by Hemingway? Like an individual's fingerprint, a particular writer's creative work bears a form of unique patterns, rhythms, and attributes, which we call "style." Whether in painting, music, or writing, style is a distinctive manner of expression. And the style of all great artists is inimitable.

Writing is architecture with words. To craft prose or poetry, one begins to "build" it, like a carpenter builds a house. That house might be a crackerjack suburb prefab or a Frank Lloyd Wright visual and structural delight. Anyone can hammer a nail, but it takes practice to hammer a nail with consistent precision—without hitting a thumb. As such, charming poems can be written by a five-year-old, but they cannot contain the singular quality or polish of an Emily Dickinson or a Pablo Neruda, each of whom wrote with a distinct style. And, as a case in point, at a time by which Doris Lessing was thoroughly established as a great writer, she published two novels under a pseudonym. When the first one was published, four or five publishers and editors, both European and American, recognized Lessing's style. And some reviewers even likened the work to "early Doris Lessing."

You can never become a great, or even good, poet or prose writer without developing a style. Developing a writing style takes intention and commitment, a consistent practice and passion. It is imperative to familiarize yourself with developing the craft of writing through your attention to language and its sounds, narrative sentence structure and syntax, grammar, point of view, character development, imagery and metaphor, and revision. While craft is the bones of writing, style is the flesh.

It's important to distinguish between "style" and "voice." Style has to do with sentence structure—a blend of diction, grammar, choice of tense—but more to do with the "feel" and intention behind the structure—the author's philosophy or narrative comments. It is an artistic issue perhaps even more than one of grammar, a matter of fitting the style to the content: Proust's ornate elegance to nineteenth- and early twentieth-century Paris. Voice, on the other hand, has to do with the tone of narration—brazen, irritating, pretentious, sentimental, earnest, formal, sarcastic. You strengthen your voice by fine-tuning your prose to convey precisely and clearly what you want to say. Use words that are expressive, to the point, and evocative. Read your writing aloud to yourself so you can, in the words of Josip Novakovich, "feel in your throat what you've written. If your words taste right, keep them. Your physical voice will tell you where your writing voice has struck a false note and where it has hit the right pitch."

You want your style to complement the story you are trying to tell. It's impossible to imagine the baroque Proust writing in the spare style of Hemingway, and vice versa. Or, to use an extreme example, envision Jacqueline Susann's *Valley of the Dolls* written in the style of Tolstoy's *Anna Karenina*. It is necessary to develop your style according to your mode of writing. In other words, are you writing a mystery novel that has the "feel" of a florid romance novel? Is the style in which you are writing detracting from the story? Is it more about the writing itself (*how* you are saying something) than about *what* you are saying?

*Don't think about style, because your true style you already have. All you need to think about is writing clearly so that you can communicate your story. You'll be surprised at how much style your stories have, how naturally your true voice emerges.*
—ORSON SCOTT CARD

Ernest Hemingway said that the best rules about writing he ever learned were from the *Kansas City Star,* where he worked as a reporter:

- Use short sentences.
- Use short first paragraphs.
- Use vigorous English.
- Be positive, not negative.
- Eliminate every superfluous word.
- Avoid the use of adjectives, especially such extravagant ones as *splendid, gorgeous, grand, magnificent.*

Hemingway developed these "rules" into a masterful style. It's up to each individual writer to develop his or her own unique style.

## The Writer's Mentor Suggests . . .

1. As you write, continue to learn about style in writing by taking classes, reading books, analyzing books and articles that you read for their lessons in style, and sharing your questions and ideas with other writers. You can never learn too much. Experiment with a variety of forms or genres, from short story to poetry, from memoir to literary nonfiction, and focus on the style germane to each one.

2. An excellent exercise for testing the appropriateness of your writing style is to tell the story aloud and notice where the differences are. It probably seems more relaxed, less restricted. Let go of your "style" for a moment and tell your story in the most straightforward way possible.

3. Try writing a piece in the opposite of your usual style. If you have been writing academic papers for three years, say, with overly long, convoluted sentences and obtuse language, make an effort to write in a more minimalist style with shorter sentences and more common vocabulary. If your writing is very crisp and direct, write in the James Joyce style of stream of consciousness.

# What is the "Voice" of a Writer?

The best advice on writing I've ever
received is from Henry Miller's *On Writing:*
You have to write a million words before
you find your voice as a writer.

— *PATRICK MCGRATH*

Writing is an alchemical process. It is a method of "vocalizing" your nervous system. It's a direct link to the visceral, a way that the body has of communicating with your mind. At least it should be. The words *juice* and *electricity* have a direct application to "voice." Writing that contains voice has more than a flourishing excitement; it has a deep resonance that you feel in your body. It rings true. Voice in writing implies words that capture the sound of an individual on the page. Writing with voice has been breathed into—it is alive.

People speak of a particular piece of writing as having an identifiable authenticity. Think of Hemingway's prose, or Faulkner's, or Gertrude Stein's poetic prose. If you read a passage from, say, *The Old Man and the Sea* or *Light in August* or *The Autobiography of Alice B. Toklas* without the title or author's name associated with it, chances are you would instantly recognize the author and perhaps even the specific book. The quality that is unmistakably identifiable as each of theirs is voice. There is a certain quality in the character, the personality, the soul of a writer that energetically flows into their writing. It is natural and unavoidable. But each of the brilliant writers I mentioned probably wrote "a million words" before their "true" voice was established and recognizable, for it rarely, if ever, appears full-blown in a beginning writer. Bad writing is almost inevitable before good writing can emerge.

Often an individual's writing may have some appeal, it may be saying something true and original, it may be logical and fluent, but it is lacking in some undefinable way. It lacks a spirit or energy; it doesn't resonate to you. It seems dead, mechanical, faceless, lacking in texture. It has no voice.

So where does this voice reside, and how can you access it? First of all, you have to be able to recognize it when you see it written or when you first hear it in your internal monologue. Authentic voice is almost always those strange thoughts or phrases that don't seem rational or grammatically correct. One day I was even more in love with my Springer Spaniel, Sienna, than normal, and I said aloud to him, "If you were a man, I'd marry you." It was funny, at first, but then the truth of that statement began to settle in. At the time I was writing my book *The Heart of Marriage,* and from that silly, off-the-cuff remark I eventually wrote a chapter about Sienna titled "If Only Men Were Dogs, or Why I'd Marry My Dog If He Asked." This was my voice. It was true because it issued from my center, from my authentic and lifelong love of dogs. That chapter contrasts my gratifying relationship with Sienna and a previous toxic relationship with an ex-lover. It is humorous, original, specific. It is alive and electric because of its resonance and fidelity to *me* the writer. It is this truth to which a reader responds.

Some of my favorite contemporary writers are Russell Banks, Michael Ondaatje, Martin Amis, and Anne Carson. Not only are they skilled, even perfected craftsmen, but they also have highly developed writing voices. Their writing bears substance, not only in content but in feeling tone as well. On an emotional level I experience a deep and powerful resonance to their work because I sense that each writer has an authentic, even profound relationship to the words he or she is writing. It is this relationship to *what* we write more than *how* we write it that gives voice to writing. In *A Way Out,* poet Robert Frost writes that "all that can save [sentences] is the speaking tone of voice somehow entangled in the words and fastened to the page for the ear of the imagination."

## The Writer's Mentor Suggests . . .

1. Invoke your voice in different ways, through different moods:
 -> Write when you are furious with your girlfriend.

- Write when you are alone in the house on a stormy night.
- Write when you have just been notified that you are pregnant or have just purchased an airline ticket for that long-desired excursion to Bali.
- Write when you are remembering your beloved dog or cat who died last year.
- Write when . . .

    Do you notice any differences in the voices? What are the similarities? Use your memory bank of sensory experiences as a repository of potential story material. Write about that which is important to you, that encourages your voice to express itself, to "sing."

2. Study the work of two of your favorite writers. Try to discern exactly what makes each of their writing voices distinct from all others. Is it their particular use of language, their phrasing, rhythm, humor or pathos, power, resonance, energy, authority? Do you find some of these qualities in your own work? Your growth and development as a writer is the path to attaining voice in your writing. Relinquish your fear of bad writing, for an excessive amount of bad writing is the first step to potential excellence.


⁑ ⁑


# How important are words and language?

> In the beginning was the Word, . . . and the
> word was God.
>
> —*JOHN 1:1*


> Words are to be taken seriously. I try to take
> seriously acts of language. Words set things in
> motion. I've seen them doing it. Words conjure.
> I try not to be careless about what I utter, write,
> sing. I'm careful about what I give voice to.
>
> —*TONI CADE BAMBARA*

The first form of oral communication between humans must have been a series of at first simple, then progressively complex, reverberating grumbles and murmurs. Philosophers of all contemporary schools seem to concur about one thing: humans became human not by the use of tools but by the word. "It is not walking upright and using a stick to dig for food or strike a blow that makes a human being," writes Nadine Gordimer, "it is speech. And neither intelligent apes nor dolphins whispering marvels in the ocean share with us the ability to transform this direct communication into the written word, which sets up an endless chain of communication and commune between peoples and generations who will never meet."

A word has a life and a history. It is the skin of a living thought and therefore gives form to the ineffable. The earliest form of the written word was not a word at all but images—of people, animals, and everyday objects. These are called "pictograms," and the oldest date from around 20,000 (there is increasing evidence that it may be 30,000 or more) years ago. To read pictograms, one didn't need to know how to speak the same language as the person who wrote the pictograms; they merely needed to recognize the symbols. To record and exchange more complex information, societies developed "ideograms," symbols that represent abstract ideas.

*The limits of my language mean the limits of my world.*
—LUDWIG
WITTGENSTEIN

Five thousand years ago, the Egyptians also developed a form of writing with pictures that came to be called "hieroglyphs," from the Greek words meaning "sacred carvings," because it was used in temples, tombs, and other state monuments.

At about the same time as the people in the countries around the eastern Mediterranean were developing hieroglyphs and cuneiform script, 4,000 years ago, the Chinese were creating a writing system all their own, which consisted of an intricate combination of pictograms, ideograms, and signs or symbols that indicate sound. Pictures became words, words developed into language. Their purpose was to impart information through telling a story. "Language is not merely a means of telling a story," says Tom Robbins, "language *is* the story."

Since that first image or symbol was cast on a cave wall, more than 4,000 distinct languages, systems of human communication, have developed. Throughout this history of words there has been a comprehension of the magic and sacredness, sometimes profanity, inherent in them. Words have power. And the ability to write them carries a kind of conjuration. "Words are pure creations of the human psyche," writes Michael Ventura. "Every single word is full of secrets, full of associations. . . . Every single word leads to the same destination: your soul."

It is my contention that if one does not love words—*love* them—one should not pursue a life in writing. But then the Pulitzer Prize–winning poet Marianne Moore had a different perspective when she offered in way of advice to a beginning poet's question of what to do if, as a poet, one hates words. "That may be very auspicious," she enigmatically replied. "Words are a very great trap." Hers, however, is the only such viewpoint I have come across, and I suspect it was said somewhat tongue-in-cheek.

In her autobiography, Caitlin Thomas wrote that while in the process of writing a poem, her husband, Dylan Thomas, would confine himself to his writing cottage for an entire day scouting through his thesaurus in quest of that consummate word, as if it were the Holy Grail itself.

Could it be that writers are really looking for a god when they write?

Loving words seems synonymous with appreciating dictionaries and other books about words—and owning a lot of them. A 2,059-paged *Unabridged Edition of the Random House Dictionary of the English Language* (which includes "concise" French, German, Italian, and Spanish dictionaries) permanently resides on the upper righthand corner of my desk. Even closer is a fifth edition of *Roget's International Thesaurus.* Out of sentimental value I still have my first thesaurus, dated 1961, the year I entered the seventh grade. This was given to me by my Aunt June, who later bought me a set of *Encyclopedia Britannica,* which, regrettably, is no longer in my possession. But there is also a third, perhaps superfluous, thesaurus on the reference shelf, this one an Oxford American edition. Two dictionaries of etymology (*Oxford* and *Barnhart*) a dictionary of "problem" words,

*Language: the one tool that enables us to grasp hold of our lives and transcend our fate by understanding it.*

—MOLLY HASKELL

*Poetry is the human soul entire, squeezed like a lemon or a lime, drop by drop, into atomic words.*

—LANGSTON HUGHES

another of foreign words, a *Fowler's,* and an indispensable *Random House Word Menu* are crowded together with various "desk" encyclopedias and the mammoth *Random House Encyclopedia.* My copy of the compact OED, too large for a bookshelf, sits on the floor, rarely referenced, I'm sorry to admit, now that my vision is no longer 20/10.

And, according the respect due them, these books are all hardcover.

Looking up words as I'm reading or writing adds to the delight of each. Finding accuracy and a multiplicity of meaning in one's choice of words is a singular pleasure, for as Dylan Thomas demonstrated, "There is always one right word."

### The Writer's Mentor Suggests . . .

1. Make lists of words, in a notebook for that purpose, that you come across during your reading and are unusual, unknown, or worth pilfering. Add another section for phrases. Add another for sentences. The point is not to plagiarize but to learn. In photos of Henry Miller at his writing desk during his bohemian years in Paris, there are sheets of paper scrawled with lists of words. The heading plainly reads "Words to use."

2. I subscribe to two online vocabulary-building lists. Every day my E-mail messages bring the DailyWordz@lists.dailycast.com, which offers a word and asks for a synonym. Scrolling down the page, the reader finds a correct answer and definition as well as a close second and how it distinctly differs. The second list is linguaphile@wordsmith.org, which gives several meanings of a word along with its etymology and an example of how it was used in a published article. As often as time permits I place these words on an index card with the synonym and/or meaning on the opposite side. Once a week or so, I will review and quiz myself with the cards. These efforts will both improve and increase your vocabulary.

*That is what I mean when I call myself a writer. I construct sentences. There's a rhythm I hear that drives me through a sentence. And the words typed on a white page have a sculptural quality. They form odd correspondences. They match up not just through meaning but through sound and look.*

—DON DELILLO

# How can i improve my descriptive writing?

Find what gave you emotion; what the
action was that gave you excitement. Then
write it down making it clear so that the reader
can see it too. Prose is architecture, not interior decoration, and the Baroque is over.
—ERNEST HEMINGWAY

It has been said that God is in the details. What is it about certain passages of writing that vault off the page with a kind of athletic vigor? It is undoubtedly a startling use of imagery and specificity. The nouns are muscular, the verbs kinetic, the adjectives sensorial, and the juxtapositions among the three are electrifying. There are three imperatives to creating fresh descriptive prose: an awakened set of senses, an instinct for specificity, and an uncanny ability to conceptualize metaphoric images and fabricate quirky word combinations ("Not everyone lives in olive skin"). I'd rather read a sentence I don't understand than one I've read a hundred times before. Whether writing fiction or non-, these imperatives are substantial allies to any writer.

In writing, as in life, there are six senses. To fully exist in the sensory world is to transcend the Cartesian paradigm of the mind/body split and dissolve the barriers between the inner and the outer, the good and the bad—to breathe into the both/and. A goal in writing is to fully engage the senses: to *be* the eighty-year-old oak tree, not just see it; to *be* the Belgian dark chocolate, not just taste it; to *be* the Vivaldi flute concerto, not just hear it; to *be* the ivory gardenia blossom, not just smell it; to *be* the plush rabbit's fur, not just feel it; to *acknowledge* the intuitive and imaginative realm, not deny it. Depth psychology assumes that the internal world is reflected in the external world, and vice versa. And so does writing.

Writers are various combinations of psychologists, historians, detectives, biographers, and scientists. Finding the soul of your poetry or prose often depends on the details and specificity that you use in your writing. When I was in my early twenties I worked at the first fully stocked cheese shop in San Francisco. There were nearly 400 varieties. Every day I added to my list of cheeses such exotic names as Gjetost, Caerphilly, Appenzeller, Mimolette, Pont l'Eveque, Boursault, and Bucheron. I also learned to distinguish the taste of one from another. Gjetost was dense and had a vaguely caramelized flavor, Caerphilly was flaky and salty, Boursault was smooth and buttery.

In my thirties I had a good-sized organic herb garden. Again, specificity was important. An herb was not simply an herb, it was oregano or hyssop or coriander. In fact, thyme was not simply thyme; it was basil lemon thyme or caraway thyme, English silver thyme or variegated thyme. Each specific herb conjured memories of childhood (sweet cicely, licorice) or biblical stories (burning bush, feverroot, horehound, angelica) or the first trip to Provence (lavender, basil, thyme). Just as calling someone by their given name is more personable, calling things by their specific names gives them dignity and uniqueness; it brings you in closer contact with them. It is also more interesting and colorful to read.

Turn your writing into a visual art. Do what painters do, only "paint" with words, metaphors, and similes. Turn your words into pictures. Writing is an act of magic, of sorcery, even: through words images are born.

## The Writer's Mentor Suggests . . .

1. The best direction on how to improve descriptive writing came from Allen Ginsberg during the course of a workshop I once took with him. He used a similar exercise to jumpstart a state of open-minded receptivity for making improbable, even wild juxtapositions between incongruent images, such as:

   The walls were painted a whitish yellow, the color of old teeth. A snail's shell is home; a woman's is her purse.

He smirked like a petulant skunk.

Divide an 8½-by-11-inch sheet of paper into four columns lengthwise. In the first column, list an array of concrete nouns; in the second, dynamic verbs; in the third, sensory adjectives; in the fourth, more nouns. This is a way of surprising yourself through freely associating disparate images. It might look something like this:

| | | | |
|---|---|---|---|
| cathedral | choke | newborn | sky |
| firescape | fight | red | Cadillac |
| gravel | ricochet | diminutive | muscle |
| tongue | worship | embroidered | actress |
| darkness | vanish | drunken | salmon |
| Tangier | smell | wet | opera |

Now randomly connect one word from each of the four columns and create simple sentences, such as the following. Don't worry about how much "sense" they make. Just get your synapses snapping.

The drunken tongue worshiped the salmon.
Her embroidered darkness vanished at the opera.
His newborn Cadillac smelled like Tangier.
The gravel choked the diminutive actress.
The cathedral fought the red sky.
The man's wet muscles ricocheted off the firescape.

These phrases and sentences are not necessarily the final version—although I very much like "embroidered darkness" and "newborn Cadillac"—but they offer a good place to begin a story or poem. The nonsense of the exercise should get you going in a playful spirit, and it tricks the mind into making metaphoric leaps. This exercise actually works on all three levels that I mentioned: it works with the senses (the drunken tongue, the embroidered darkness), it contributes specificity (the diminutive actress, the wet muscles), and it produces metaphoric leaps (newborn Cadillac smelled like Tangier) and fabricates quirky word combinations (embroidered darkness, muscles ricocheted, the cathedral fought).

2. If you haven't yet, read Diane Ackerman's vivid book *A Natural History of the Senses.* It is a luxurious and delicious mapping of sensory perception.

∻ ∻

# WHY IS IT NECESSARY TO REWRITE AND REVISE?

> Write freely and as rapidly as possible
> and throw the whole thing on paper. Never
> correct or rewrite until the whole thing is
> down. Rewrit [ing] in process is usually found
> to be an excuse for not going on.
> —*JOHN STEINBECK*

As a sort of talisman, for years I kept the rigorously edited copy of my first published essay pinned to the wall beside my desk. A recapping of my essential experiences during the two years I lived in Topanga Canyon, which is east of Malibu, I wrote the piece for a Los Angeles weekly newspaper. It is in no way an impressive piece of writing, but it was the first time I had been taken—and taken myself—seriously as a writer. And it was the first time I saw my writing in print. This edited story/essay also serves as a continual reminder that writing is rewriting, or as Walter Mosley once said, "Nothing we create is art at first."

An interesting feature of this manuscript is that it was typed on my 1940 Royal Deluxe—the one I mentioned earlier in this book. That is significant because even though I had just recently purchased my first computer, I still felt more comfortable working on the Royal. Now, after so many years of working nearly exclusively on a series of upgraded computers and laptops, I grasp just how much is lost— without even realizing it—when working on a computer. For so much of the editing and rethinking process takes place right in the machine, before it is ever printed out and touched by the human hand. Using the computer may be faster, but is it any better? There is much to be said in favor of an unhurried, deliberate, even (dare I say?) leisurely pace of writing. Underlining new material and adding it to the text, while the deletions are kept but crossed out, allows you to see, from draft to draft, exactly what has been added and deleted.

Writers have various methods of rewriting and revising. The poet Tess Gallagher, whom I interviewed for my book on marriage, told me that writing by hand in the morning helps her "move into the mood of the writing"; the afternoons are used for typing and revising her work. Tobias Wolff, the author of the childhood memoir *This Boy's Life,* has said in interviews that he doesn't keep drafts because he finds the early versions "embarrassing" and, anyway, that it is "impossible to identify different drafts because it's all one, with this new machine we've got." Donald Hall, a poet, has said that "at the beginning I search for characteristic diction and characteristic cadence, for the defining words and tone. I *listen* for it. When I get something like it, I refine it, and during the rest of the drafts I keep on refining it. My first drafts show me fumbling toward it." And the prolific Joyce Carol Oates has said this about rewriting: "I am inclined to think that as I grow older I will become infatuated with the art of revision. . . . I am in favor of intelligent, even fastidious revision, which is, or certainly should be, an art in itself."

In truth, I now view editing as the most fun (second only to the periodic surprises that lasso my attention during a first draft) part of writing. The hardest work has been done: you've faced the blank page, assembled your thoughts, "got the whole thing," as Steinbeck suggested, "on paper." The process reminds me of prospecting for precious stones. The laborious part is scouting out the cave, excavating the vein, and extracting the raw gemstones; the finesse and nuance comes with the lapidary. So, too, in writing: you scout for a topic, excavate your soulscape, and extract your psyche in words; finesse and nuance are developed in the editing.

Think of your rewriting and revising stage as exploring a foreign country—your mind. Work on two levels: the global and the

*I turn sentences around. That's my life. I write a sentence and then I turn it around. Then I look at it and I turn it around again. Then I have lunch. Then I come back in and write another sentence. Then I have tea and turn the new sentence around. . . .*

—PHILIP ROTH

*Cut out all the exclamation marks. An exclamation mark is like laughing at your own joke.*

—F. SCOTT FITZGERALD

*Short paragraphs put air around what you write and make it look inviting, whereas one long chunk of type can discourage the reader from even starting to read.*

—WILLIAM ZINSSER

local. The global revision is the overall structure or architecture of the piece: Have you clearly stated what you meant to say, is the character development believable, does the plot of the story or the seam of the essay hold? The local is the small-scale, line-by-line, chapter-by-chapter revision: you work on getting the wording of a sentence or scene right.

A good overall handbook for editing is *Merriam-Webster's Manual for Writers and Editors.* An excellent and more personable guide to the elements of good writing is Noah Lukeman's *The First Five Pages,* in which he writes, "There is no such thing as a great writer; there are only great re-writers." The following is my basic guide to a step-by-step process of editing and rewriting for either fiction or nonfiction work:

1. Begin with an overview of the content.
   What is your message or thesis?
   Are you stating it clearly and completely?
   Is it coherent?
   Is it written in an engaging fashion?

2. Review the style and craft.
   Is the vocabulary accurate, varied, and of interest?
   Are there any clichés?
   Are you telling the story or "showing" it?
   Does the tone reflect the content?
   Is there a unique and defined voice?
   Is the point of view consistent?
   Is any dialogue realistic or hard to follow?
   Are any characters "drawn" to their best potential?
   Is the style alive with images and metaphors?
   Is the language evocative and descriptive?
   Is the pacing even?

3. Review the grammar.
   Agreement of subject and verb, correct case of pronouns, correct and/or overuse of adjectives and adverbs, correct verb tense

4. Check consistency and accuracy.

Use of abbreviations, capitalization style, quotations, and spelling

5. Review the punctuation.
Apostrophes, colons, commas, dashes, exclamation points, hyphens, parentheses, periods, question marks, quotation marks, semi-colons

Alberto Moravia likened the process of writing to that of painting: working from layer to layer. "The first draft," he said, "is quite crude, far from being perfect, by no means finished. . . . After that I rewrite it many times—applying as many layers as I feel to be necessary."

## The Writer's Mentor Suggests . . .

1. Rewrite and revise a piece of your writing using steps 1 through 5. Leave the work for a week, then rewrite and revise again. Repeat this procedure a minimum of four times. Unlike Tobias Wolff, be sure to keep each draft. After you have completed at least these five rewrites, compare and contrast them. What did you learn about your work by going through this process?

2. Rather than simply inserting your changes into the page on your screen, I think it is important and helpful to completely retype each section, whether it be a stanza of poetry or a paragraph or chapter of prose. Doing this will force you to rethink as you type—something you can never do too much of during the rewrite stage—and continue to make active decisions about each sentence.

## The Writer's Mentor at the Movies
### Il Postino

"What is a metaphor?" Mario, the eponymous postman of *Il Postino*, asks the visiting poet and political activist Pablo Neruda. Thus begins an unlikely friendship between the humble Mario and the worldly Neruda, who, in 1952, has been exiled from his beloved Chile and

*Punctuation, one is taught, has a point: to keep law and order. Punctuation marks are the road signs placed along the highway of our communications—to control speeds, provide directions and prevent head-on collisions.*

—PICO IYER

granted asylum by the Italian government in the diminutive but beautiful village of Isla Negra.

We see Mario living with his stoic fisherman father in a bleak shack, resigned to his uneventful and colorless life. But when he is hired to bicycle to a mysterious poet's remote hilltop home to deliver what appears to be primarily love letters from adoring women, all this changes. As the shy postman becomes bolder he engages the poet with his guileless, self-deprecating charms. Mario wants to know what poetry is and why women seem so drawn to poets—at least to Neruda—and possibly how he himself might become a poet because "I could make women fall for me."

And when Mario first lays eyes on the beauteous Beatrice, the local tavern maid, poetry, as it did for Dante, truly comes alive for him. He implores Neruda to write a poem for him in her honor. But Neruda engenders Mario to "try and walk slowly along the shore as far as the bay, and look around you" and vows that the metaphors most certainly will come to him. The film is saying that to be a poet is to spend hours in solitude, staring into space, thinking and observing all that encompasses your senses, seeing comparisons, making connections, personifying nature and inanimate objects.

In a touching scene between the two men at the beach, Neruda recites his new poem about the sea hammering out its name against the shore and rocks. Mario says that the poem's rhythm almost made him seasick, "like a boat tossing around on your words." Neruda is pleased with the analogy and tells him that he has invented a metaphor. Mario modestly tells him that it "doesn't count" because he didn't "mean to." But the poet declares that "images arise spontaneously." It is a lovely exchange. And at that moment, Mario comprehends that "the whole world is a metaphor for something else."

What Mario comes to learn is that poetry is not solely about the juxtaposition of words. Poetry is a way of life. Neruda has encouraged his protégé to see the natural delights that surround him, to understand that nature itself—like love—is pure poetry. That he who sees the poetry in life is a poet. "Better than any explanation," the poet tells the postman, "is the feeling that poetry can reveal to a nature open enough to understand it."

Mario subtly begins to seduce Beatrice with select poems from the master. But when he unself-consciously informs Neruda of his method, Neruda gently chides him to write his own poetry. Mario defends his action with the logical retort, "Poetry doesn't belong to those who write it, but to those who need it." In a magnanimous gesture the poet offers Mario a gorgeous leather-bound notebook tooled with an engraving of what looks like the three Graces. Later, at Beatrice's bistro, directly in front of her, Neruda (who has become the town celebrity) conspicuously signs the notebook "To Mario, My good friend and comrade." Now Mario's winning of Beatrice is secured.

In this fairytale, Mario's life has been forever changed by his brief but meaningful friendship with a generous poet and the enriching powers of words and language.

---

# CHAPTER 11

# THE LONELINESS
### *of the*
# LONG-DISTANCE WRITER

## *Writing as a Solitary Experience*

How do I manage the loneliness of the writing life?

How can I stay motivated to write?

Is it important to do other activities in addition to my writing?

How do I deal with failure in and success with my writing?

The Writer's Mentor at the Movies: *The Whole Wide World*

THE LONELINESS OF THE LONG-DISTANCE WRITER: WRITING AS A SOLITARY EXPERIENCE explores the physical—and sometimes emotional and spiritual—isolation inherent to the writing life and how one can survive it, establish a balance, and, we hope, thrive. This chapter encourages the reader to closely examine why he or she wants to write and/or be a writer. Knowing the source of this motivation is the difference between one who continues to pursue the writing life and another who recognizes that it is not for him. Here you will also learn why it is important to pursue activities other than writing that stimulate your interests, curiosity, and creativity and "feed" your soul. The last question in this chapter addresses the successes and failures that are experienced in the writing life and offers suggestions for managing both. The film examined is *The Whole Wide World,* which is a visceral, incisive examination of the loneliness and the obsessive nature of the writing life. It is the story of Robert E. Howard, the author of *Conan the Barbarian,* as told by Novalyne Price, the woman whom, it would appear, was the only love in the brief life of this eccentric but talented writer.

# How do i manage the loneliness of the writing life?

> The solitude of writing is . . . quite frighten-
> ing. It's close sometimes to madness, one
> just disappears for a day and loses touch.
> —*NADINE GORDIMER*

Writing is a solitary act. The solitary insularity of the writing life is an existential given. If you think you want to write, to be a writer, perhaps the most important question to ask yourself is, Do I enjoy my own company? The second question is, Do I enjoy my own company enough to spend several hours a day in solitude? For even if you are in a café filled with patrons, you will be lost in the private world of your inventive mind. Some writers take naturally to laboring in isolation, others suffer it out of necessity in the service of communication. There is an implied spiritual quality to what Tobias Wolff calls "monkish solitude."

About the necessity of solitude Edmund White has said that writing depends upon a "fairly quiet life, whereas I am a sociable person. I think every writer goes back and forth on this question; it's a constant struggle to find the right balance between solitude and society and I don't think anyone ever does."

As a child I was raised by a working single mother. At the very earliest age, beginning around four or five, I was left on my own at home when she was at work as a Pacific Bell telephone operator. I now understand that as long as I was home and my mother knew how to reach me, she felt that I was "safe." We always had animals for my companionship and "protection"—dogs, a cat, bird, turtle, some combination of, or, not infrequently, all. But, thankfully, my mother kept on hand a myriad of art and craft supplies to occupy my time and attention during this (as yet unbeknownst to me) auspicious "confinement." In addition to these provisions, her reading library was voluminous and eclectic. For many years into my adulthood I

*All good writing comes out of aloneness. You have to do it on an open highway. You wouldn't want to do it in New York City. But on High-way 40 West or some of those big open highways, you can hold the wheel with one hand and write with the other.*

—SAM SHEPARD

spent thousands of dollars in psychotherapy, paying for an arena in which to express my quarantined anger, resentment, and self-pity at having been dealt this cruel blow in life. It wasn't until I was deeply engaged in my writing career that I realized just how fortuitous my childhood had been. Thanks to my particular set of circumstances and an inventive mother, I was a child who learned to keep her own company—and enjoy it.

Having said this, I do think it a myth that writers feel they must struggle all alone in a state of psychological misery and affliction, bereft of any stable human relationships. It is *because* of and *about* these relationships we write, even if we make them seem foreign. But on the other hand, often we surround ourselves with so many people and so much diversion as a means of preventing us from fulfilling our creative promises to ourselves. It was Chekhov who complained, "My country house is full of people, they never leave me alone; if only they would go away I could be a good writer." And Richard Ford expands on this observation when he said in an interview, "It's addictive to be out in the world, partly because it's a lot easier than staying home and doing your work. I'm a gregarious person and my work asks me to be the opposite. . . . It's not romantic, the isolation. It's kind of grueling."

### The Writer's Mentor Suggests . . .

It is most important to create a balance in your life between solitude and a social life. Having a regular change of scene is crucial to maintaining your creative fluency. If you are too social, then your writing life will suffer, but if you spend too much time away from loved ones, or even strangers, your emotional and creative well-being may suffer. If you are someone who has great difficulty in being alone, try writing in public spots for a while. That could be your local coffee house, book store, library, or park, or even at a writing partner's house. You probably don't want it to be too rousing of a joint; the point is to do your work, after all. You may discover that you produce very well under those circumstances and that it is unnecessary for you to be "locked away" in your study or office. This method can also work for a writer who becomes too insular and isolated. Ease yourself into writing in a public location for brief periods. You might find that the stimulation and activity galvanize your creative process all the more.

❖ ❖

# How can I stay motivated to write?

> I try to work every day, even when I'm not
> motivated. Ritual is very important to me.
> —*MEL RAMOS*

People often say they have difficulty in staying motivated to write. If this is the case for you, it would be helpful to take a period of time—sooner rather than later—to reexamine why you thought you wanted to write in the first place. If your reason revolves around a fantasy of living a romantic writer's life, à la Hemingway or Virginia Woolf, you're better off doing something—anything—else. (Remember, both Hemingway and Woolf committed suicide.) Writing, especially earning your livelihood as a writer, is a path fraught with loneliness, disappointment, depression, anger, jealousy, and anxiety. That's a lot to take on. Of course, when someone starts to write, she thinks all she needs to do is get a rough draft of a story, poem, or bit of narrative facts down on paper and agents and editors will be waiting in line to, respectively, represent and publish it. Every one of my Writer's Mentor clients is dismayed and not a little disgruntled to learn just how tough it is to stay with their writing long enough to actually see it in print.

However, if your reason for writing stems from a profound love of words and their infinite combinations, an enjoyment of solitude and self-exploration, a confidence in the originality of your viewpoint, or the unqualified need to share your ideas, you may have the stamina it takes to develop the daily habit of writing.

A prerequisite to a writing life is the ability to spend countless hours by yourself in deep contemplation. This doesn't mean thinking about yourself necessarily, but it does mean being focused on what you think about a particular subject or idea. It means training yourself to stay focused on the work at hand. It means building and sustaining a working momentum. And it means being willing to admit that you don't know something, are stuck, or need to scrap weeks of effort and begin anew.

Henry James wrote, "To live in the world of creation—to get into it and stay in it—to frequent it and haunt it—to think intensely and fruitfully—to woo combinations and inspirations into being by a depth and continuity of attention and meditation—this is the only thing." If this sums up your foundation for wanting to write, then you are well on your way.

I often joke that the reason I have chosen the writing life as my lifestyle is because it is a mental and emotional impossibility for me to work for anyone other than myself. Whenever I start feeling the slightest disenchantment with my work, I simply think of the alternative—working for wages on someone else's timeframe—and I notice that my motivation instantly improves. Writers do tend to be mavericks (if not downright eccentrics) of one kind or another. They have great difficulty with any external control or impositions, but they will work tirelessly—without any outer-imposed schedules, save deadlines—doing what they love (and sometimes hate), which is writing. Writing itself must be the ultimate motivator.

## The Writer's Mentor Suggests . . .

Aside from internal incentives, there are four primary methods for forging the necessary motivation for beginning writing and for conditioning and stimulating your ongoing writing practice.

1. Find a writing partner and/or a writing group. Having this type of support can do wonders for your motivation. Groups usually

*You write by sitting down and writing. There's no particular time or place—you suit yourself, your nature. How one works, assuming he's disciplined, doesn't matter.*
—BERNARD MALAMUD

*Don't work too hard. Fool around a bit. Be lazy. Don't worry, Life is—forever.*
—HENRY MILLER
IN A LETTER TO
LAWRENCE DURRELL

are formed by a recognized writer who facilitates writing exercises, sharing of responses, and outside assignments, but a group of peers can be equally helpful. The main imperative is consistency. Meet with a writing partner or with your group on a regular basis. Agree beforehand on what you will accomplish before the next time you meet and hold that agreement sacred. Mark your datebook with your scheduled meetings and honor them. There is something significant that happens when you are accountable to another human being—it's called commitment.

2. Writers' conferences can be stimulating and worthwhile experiences. Conferences are held throughout the year in countless locations. Here you will have opportunities to connect with other writers of every level and of every genre and to meet with published authors. You will also meet agents and editors. Many "deals" are made at such events. Look for local writers' conferences or make the investment in attending one outside your area. It is well worth the expenditure in time and money. The annual March issue of *Writer's Digest* magazine has a comprehensive listing of writers' conferences.

3. Share your writing with five kinds of readers who can advise you on how to improve it and offer an infusion of enthusiasm and support.

   - Friends and family
   - Potential readers of your work
   - Literate, objective readers
   - Experts who are knowledgeable about your subject
   - A devil's advocate

4. A writing consultant or professional editor may assist your process in a number of ways. She can help you in the development and formulation of your project as well as in the editing of it. A good editor is a collaborator. After the initial work is done by you, writing becomes a two-person effort. It is necessary to have another (or other) minds with which to wrestle and exchange ideas. And a writing consultant, like a writing com-

panion, can also be that stimulus you need to keep your efforts going. I recently received this lovely E-mail from one of my Writer's Mentor clients: "It is to your sense and sensibility that I anticipate submitting both the proposal and the pages: The companionship of the page is what draws me to this alliance, whatever the page is labeled." In a phrase, it is this "companionship of the page" that a writing consultant can offer you and your work.

⌁∴ ∴⌁

## Is it important to do other activities in addition to my writing?

> Writing requires huge amounts of solitude.
> What I've done to soften the harshness of
> that choice is that I don't write all the time. . . .
> I'm interested in many other things. . . .
> I like to go out—which includes traveling; I
> can't write when I travel. I like to talk. I like
> to listen. I like to look and to watch.
> —SUSAN SONTAG

"The twin activities of running and writing," wrote novelist Joyce Carol Oates, "keep the writer reasonably sane. . . ." Because writing is such a compulsive and obsessive activity, it is important to balance out your life as a writer with other means of occupying your time and relaxing and refueling your mind. Every experience finds its way—if only indirectly—back into the primary vocation of writing. If you write on a regular—even if not daily—basis, you will need to either continue with or discover alternative pursuits. It is natural to become so enamored with a new passion that you lose track of other side interests.

*Do painting, cycling, movies, friends after writing.*
—HENRY MILLER

The Pulitzer Prize–winning author of *The Shipping News,* Annie Proulx, writes about her mania for flea markets and yard sales and, especially, secondhand bookshops. Both the English Romantic poets and the New England Transcendentalists were tireless walkers. And Henry David Thoreau admitted that if he spent less than four hours a day walking, he felt "as if I had some sin to be atoned for."

For ten years I lived in a small seaside village, which is intoxicatingly beautiful but bereft of cultural stimulation. For quite a while I was making regular trips to New York City, where I would binge on the arts: theatre, films, museums, performance art, symphonies and operas, lectures, bookstores. I was in bliss when I returned home and eager to settle down to my daily ritual of writing and walking on the beach. As lovely a life as it was, it would have been intolerable for me to exist and work without those intermittent periods of creative nourishment that the arts afforded me.

During an agonizing six-year period of writing, novelist Mark Salzman returned to his first love, the cello. The period had seemed like a "vocational crisis" to him, and it was music that saw him through the writing. As a young man Salzman had had a devotion to the cello, as well as a consuming enthusiasm for kung fu, so having twin passions for music and writing seemed perfectly natural to him. His is a striking example of how a secondary source of activity or expression can stir your primary artistic form.

The novel Salzman wrote during that period is titled *Lying Awake;* it tells the story of a Carmelite nun, Sister John of the Cross, who has a crisis of belief after she is diagnosed with a brain tumor. She must decide whether to have the prescribed operation, but she fears that an operation will end the transcendent visions she has regularly experienced.

Salzman's two avocations, playing the cello and practicing kung fu, afforded him the "space" needed to fulfill his vocation, writing.

### The Writer's Mentor Suggests . . .

1. If you don't already have a secondary passion, like Mark Salzman and Joyce Carol Oates, take up either a musical instrument,

a new athletic endeavor, gardening, or volunteer work at the local SPCA or Marine Wildlife Refuge. Choose something that will sustain your interest, something that is a great recreation from writing. You will find, even though the activity isn't writing, that it is relaxing, often inspiring, and actually creative for your own work.

2. In *The Vein of Gold,* Julia Cameron proposes a weekly "Artist Date," which she describes as "an hour or longer weekly block of time spent on yourself and with yourself, doing something festive." This is a wise and most enjoyable "assignment." Museums of any type are obvious considerations, as are aquariums, local historic homes of writers or noteworthy persons, musical and theatre events, or, for nature lovers, a walk on the beach or in the woods, a day spent sailing or skiing. Make it a weekly custom. It will serve you well as a restorative respite. Design four—one month's worth—appointments with yourself, and keep them.

⁌ ⁍

# How do i deal with failure in and success with my writing?

> A writer's life is only ever acceptance or rejection, surfeit or famine, and nothing in between. The ones who [stay the course] aren't necessarily the most gifted but those who can focus well, discipline themselves, persevere through hard times, and spring back after rejections that would cripple others.
> —*DIANE ACKERMAN*

On December 24, 1990, my first manuscript was accepted by a publishing house. Two days later I met with that publisher personally and received the first of three installments of an advance on future sales of the book that would become *On Women Turning 40: Coming Into Our Fullness.* Before I cashed the check I stopped at Kinko's and made a copy of that check—which I still have to this day.

Later that day, at a boutique in the chic enclave of Berkeley's 4th Street marketplace, I bought a gift for myself. It was an antique Mexican silver and onyx brooch, in the form of a well-endowed female with wings, which measured 3-by-3 inches. Because her body swooped back into a U-shape, as if she were flying, I called her "The Soaring Woman." She looked how I felt. I didn't consider her a Christmas present—she was a reward, a prize, a way of celebrating my success. Even though I had been working on that book already for five years, the events of that day seemed like the beginning of my career.

But in truth, it was the first *public* success in my occupation as a full-time writer. For all along, during those previous five years of writing, I'd had countless personal successes, such as coming up with a good idea by being focused on and sensitive to what was happening in my own life and in the lives of those around me, deciding to explore the topic of women turning forty—and doing it, committing to the researching and writing of what I hoped would be a book, interviewing that first woman, calling up Natalie Goldberg on my birthday to invite her to be a participant in *On Women Turning 40,* Natalie saying yes, putting together my first book proposal—without the assistance of a "writer's mentor," finding an agent, and writing, writing, writing.

Of course, there were also plenty of experiences that might easily have been construed as failures, such as the decisions of those well-known women who declined to be interviewed for the book; the weeks, sometimes months, of dry spells when I succumbed to feelings of self-abnegation and defeat; the difficult circumstances of my personal life; and, worse yet, the "rejections" from fifteen or more publishers. Samuel Beckett had tacked to the wall beside his desk a card on which were written the words "Fail. Fail again. Fail better."

*Success is a finished book, a stack of pages each of which is filled with words. If you reach that point, you have won a victory over yourself no more impressive than sailing single-handed around the world.*

—TOM CLANCY

What remains important is that I survived the rejections and so-called failures to experience what was unanimously perceived as success. So it was all downhill from there, right? Not exactly. During the subsequent years, it has been quite dismaying—if not, indeed, a little traumatizing—to discover that the publishing world was *not* waiting with baited breath for each succeeding manuscript; that two of my treasured works were discontinued or rendered "out-of-print" before each had even reached the one-year mark; that although my advances had increased over time, at one point in my career they also boomeranged; and that the publishing industry itself was becoming an unwieldy dragon, swallowing whole and spitting out writers and books as if, like a spoiled child, it couldn't make up its mind for what it was really hungry.

Now, after more than a decade, my perception of success has altered. I consider myself successful because, foremost, I continue to write—and increasingly *love* to write, my work continues to be published by people who think it is worth publishing, and I have built and maintained strong and supportive professional relationships with my agent of ten years, Ellen Levine, and her staff, and, more recently, with my editor Leslie Berriman.

I have learned three important truths about the success/failure scale for a writer: (1) your definition of each changes over time; (2) selling a piece of writing should be considered a gift, not a given; and (3) success is never one-directional; there are inevitable backslides and disappointments. That's why it's imperative to love the process of writing. The work itself is the only absolute. One cannot force one's work to be successful. Fruition requires an element of grace.

Many currently praised and celebrated writers were fairly unknown and/or underappreciated during their day. It is nearly impossible to imagine that Charles Dickens was thought of as a penny-a-liner for his serially published novels such as *David Copperfield* and *Oliver Twist*, which now are considered literary masterpieces. And it is tragic to realize that both Virginia Woolf and Sylvia Plath took their own lives before their work later catapulted them into a cultdom and canonization of literary nobility. Zora Neale

*Failure: Is it a limitation? Bad timing? It's a lot of things. It's something you can't be afraid of, because you'll stop growing. The next step beyond failure could be your biggest success in life.*

—DEBBIE ALLEN

*My great fear has always been complete and utter failure. Hence, you see, the dispossessed people in my fiction, and why I try to earn as much money as I can.*

—PETER ACKROYD

Hurston, a graduate of Barnard, an anthropologist, a Guggenheim Fellow, and the author of four novels, an autobiography, and two folklore anthologies, as well as many stories, knew a modest literary success at a fairly young age. But before her death in 1960, at the age of fifty-seven, due to poverty, Hurston had been supporting herself as a domestic maid. After suffering a stroke in 1959, and because of her indigence, she was forced to move to a welfare home, where she died less than a year later. A service and burial were delayed for more than a week while friends raised money for the funeral. Now Hurston's work is on high school and university reading lists around the country. Her most well-known book, *Their Eyes Were Watching God,* sold fewer than 5,000 copies when it was first published in 1937; in the 1990s alone it sold more than a million. A contemporary writer, Robert M. Pirsig, had a happier outcome after receiving rejections from 121 publishers for his book *Zen and the Art of Motorcycle Maintenance,* which would eventually sell more than 3 million copies.

The publishing industry can be a harsh mistress. And because the publishing marketplace is fiercely competitive, it takes resiliency and savvy for a published writer to continually reinvent himself and continue to find favor with editors who seek to publish his work. So it is best to adhere to a personal, well-considered set of values and sense of what constitutes both failure and success. Believe in your vision and in yourself as a writer, and with considerable hard work and, again, grace, your vision may find its place into print.

### The Writer's Mentor Suggests . . .

1. The best way to deal with failure is to write. Today sit down and write in the third person a vignette about your fear of failure. Begin the first sentence with your first name, such as, "Cathleen was in a state of near-catatonia. Whenever she looked at the manuscript waiting on her desk her entire autonomic system responded with the flight reflex. She was terrified that. . . ." And continue writing in detail about those imagined fears. These

anxieties might include not having a topic, not knowing how to begin (continue, end, whatever) a project, recently discovering that a book already exists on the topic you wished to write about, worrying about an advancing deadline, a distressing mental block about what happens next, anger that your advance wasn't larger, despair that this may be your last opportunity to sell a short story (poem, article, essay, screenplay, book), worrying about how you will pay the rent in two weeks' time, or the gnawing suspicion that your boyfriend is seeing someone else. Of course, there are countless things to fear, and these are just a few. What are your "character's" fears? Do this exercise for as many days as it takes to exorcise these fears. And repeat it whenever they reemerge.

2. The best way to deal with success is to write. In the same manner as in exercise 1, write about your success. Allow yourself to feel the support you have received from family members and friends. Recall the unadulterated joy you felt when you learned of your first literary success. (This success can range from the time in fifth grade that your essay was honored by your teacher to the publication of a poem, story, book, essay, article.) Envision that moment and, through your writing, make it live.

3. Decide what is *your* definition of success. Remember to maintain your definition within the parameters of your present capabilities. For example, if you are writing your first short story, it is unlikely—although not impossible—that it would be accepted for publication by the *New Yorker,* but there are any number of other possibilities. Write down your definition(s). Do the same with your definition of failure. Do not set such high goals that because you are striving higher than your current ability you cannot appreciate what success does come your way.

4. For each success attained, let someone else know and, in some way, celebrate with them.

# The Writer's Mentor at the Movies
## *The Whole Wide World*

He is a pulp fiction writer. She says she is "working" on a novel titled *I Gave My Daughter Movie Fame.* He reads (and publishes in) *Weird Tales.* She reads *Smart Set, Cosmopolitan, Saturday Evening Post.*

He is a mama's boy, at once selfless in his care of his invalid mother and neurotically dependent. In her early twenties, she has already left home to teach high school in a neighboring town.

He has a reputation for being eccentric, morose, unpredictable, a misfit. She is conventional, socially attuned, proper, a bit of a snob.

He writes. She wants to be a writer.

They are an unlikely pair, but they find interest, intrigue, intelligence, and humor in each other and develop a turbulent emotional friendship.

He is Robert E. Howard, the creator of *Conan the Barbarian* and *Red Sonia,* who died tragically by his own hand at the age of thirty in 1935. She is Novalyne Price, who in 1985, at the age of seventy-six, wrote her first book, the memoir *One Who Walked Alone*— an account of her complicated relationship with Robert—from which this deeply moving film, *The Whole Wide World,* was adapted.

Although little known, *The Whole Wide World,* which takes place in West Texas during the mid-1930s and stars Vincent D'Onofrio and Renee Zellweger (it was released in late 1996, after her breakthrough role in *Jerry Maguire*), is a visceral, incisive examination of the loneliness and the obsessive nature of the writing life.

Robert's mental energy is dazzling to Novalyne, and his enthusiasm for his work exemplary. The first time she visits him at his home she is stunned to hear him bellow aloud the words to the storyline as he obsessively types them on paper. He is a man possessed—conjuring lurid yarns and erotic adventures, oblivious of anyone or anything other than his characters, who offer him an escape from a world in which he doesn't fit. The adrenaline rush in this creative moment is palpable. Later, when Novalyne questions Robert about his process—"Do you always tell the story as you're writing it?"—he responds, "It's a helluva noise, ain't it? I find if I talk them out, hear the words, the yarn goes a little bit smoother." His voice brings the words to life.

In a beautiful scene, Novalyne and Robert are leaning against Robert's Ford roadster convertible in a spent cornfield under a harvest moon, and she asks him to tell her about his work. She wants to know about Conan. He is clearly pleased at her interest and says that he writes about giant snakes, muscle men, big-busted naked women, and men struggling to survive. Novalyne doesn't quite know how to respond except with laughter and says that she wants to write about ordinary farm people. "You stick with me, girl, and I'll teach you about writin' and men!" he teases her. "Excitement's my specialty. Excitement and adventure."

But some months later, when Novalyne takes Robert home to meet her mother and grandmother, there is a tense moment when her mother thanks him for teaching her daughter about writing. He looks accusingly at Novalyne and says, "Well, your ears must be keepin' it secret, 'cause your hands ain't been typin' it out." Translation: Writers write.

It is shortly after this that an emotionally frightened Robert lets Novalyne know that he can't be tied down. "The road I walk, I walk alone. When you're young, you feel the lust for adventure buried in your subconscious." Novalyne sensibly realizes that Robert's inner conflicts will not allow him to find a sense of peace or even comfort with another human being, and the two drift apart. Soon she is accepted into a master's program at Louisiana State to complete an advanced teaching degree. Three weeks after she arrives, a telegram bears the news of Robert's suicide.

The writing life is lonely and difficult.

On a bus from Louisiana to Robert's funeral, a mournful Novalyne tells an inquiring fellow-passenger about the friend she has lost. "He was the greatest pulp writer in the whole wide world," she gushes. "He was a writer and he made his living writing stories."

Fifty years later, the same can finally be said of Novalyne.

# CHAPTER 12

# THE INNER LIFE
## *of the*
# WRITER

## *Writing as a Life Choice*

I want to be a writer, but I don't like to write. What should I do?

I've just turned fifty. Am I too old to start a career in writing?

Does a difficult childhood benefit or impede a writer's work?

When will I be able to quit my job and write full time?
Will I ever be able to make a living as a writer?

How can I make a contribution with my writing?

Why do writers write? What are the goals of writing?

The Writer's Mentor at the Movies: *My Brilliant Career*

THE INNER LIFE OF THE WRITER: WRITING AS A LIFE CHOICE probes the existential nature of the writing life and confronts issues faced by writers every day. This chapter offers questions to ask yourself if you find that the fantasy of being a writer takes precedence over your desire and commitment to actually write. It quells the uncertainties of those who begin to write only later in life. It takes an honest look at the dream of "making a living as a writer." It acknowledges that for many writers, writing becomes a way in which they can reclaim the sense of personal autonomy denied them as children. The final two questions in this chapter address the notion that writing is in the service of communication and the subjects of how to make a contribution with your writing and explore your goals as a writer. The film explored in this chapter is *My Brilliant Career*, from an autobiographical novel that is based on the true-life experiences of Australian writer Miles Franklin. Even at the age of sixteen Miles knew her own mind and made writing her life choice.

# I WANT TO BE A WRITER, BUT I DON'T LIKE TO WRITE. WHAT SHOULD I DO?

> If I write a page a day, I'm lucky. But if I
> write less . . . It's a very uncomfortable
> process; I don't like it at all.
> —EDMUND WHITE

These are some of the most accurate and unaffected words I've seen written about the ongoing wrestling match most writers suffer through in quest of their craft. During my years of mentoring would-be writers I have encountered this paradoxical dilemma more times than I care to count. And I've had to confront it in myself as well. Sometimes writing feels like pulling teeth, except the pain isn't localized in the mouth; it is much more pervasive. It's like pulling your soul out of your skin.

The trouble with the celebrity-driven times during which we live is that writers are more often valued for their popularity, like movie actors, than for intellectual discourse or influence. Think of the star appeal of a smart, charismatic Martin Amis or the famous wealth of a glamorous Danielle Steel. Yes, we want to know what our writers think about the important issues of politics, cultural identity, global economics, but what really piques our curiosity is to have a glimpse into their abusive childhood or hear a titillating tale about their extramarital affair. What we tend to forget is that most of the writers who endure don't think of themselves as "famous" but simply as writers doing their work. Harold Brodkey, the short story writer (almost as well known for a twenty-five-year spell of writer's block as he is for his fiction), illuminates this myth by his remark, "I'm not famous. My image is famous. It's a shadow I don't even cast."

When popular genre writers such as Stephen King, John Grisham, and Michael Crichton command seven-figure book advances, they are raised to the ranks of the consecrated in the average reader's imagination. In a culture dominated by pop commercialization, who wouldn't want the financial remuneration and security of that breed of author?

However, in order to join the ranks of the Writer, one must make the act, the process of writing, a (if not *the*) passion of both one's waking hours and dreamtime. Dorothea Brande, in her 1934 original version of *Becoming a Writer,* stated plain as day that if you fail repeatedly at holding to a writing schedule, "give up writing. Your resistance is actually greater than your desire to write, and you may as well find some other outlet for your energy early as late." This is serious stuff. I use this caveat on clients (and myself) on a regular basis. It usually sobers up each of them (and me) post haste.

Edmund White, in an interview for the *Paris Review,* says that he can go an entire year or two or even three without picking up a pen. But, of more interest to me, he says that he remains perfectly content during these seemingly fallow times. He wonders if all of the many writers who say, "I must write; I'm driven to write" are simply mouthing clichés because, in theory, writers are *supposed* to operate on compulsion, or if instead they are speaking merely from an economic perspective.

It is as if White, the prolific author of both fiction and nonfiction, through his own confession has given me permission to be in the love/hate relationship that I often have with my own writing. For so many years I wondered what was wrong with me. With each new project I would undergo an absolute dread, a near-debilitating battle with myself. To all around me I would be miserable. I was virtually incapacitated. But I could not enjoy anything else I was doing either because the demons of "should" were controlling me.

Perhaps you are a writer without that kind of inner combat. If so, consider yourself among the lucky ones: the process will be more immediately pleasurable for you. However, if you are not, just know you are not alone.

*Sometimes I can spend whole days doing nothing more than picking the lint off the carpet and talking to my mother on the phone.*

—BETH HENLEY

## The Writer's Mentor Suggests . . .

1. Have an extended heart-to-heart with yourself. Try to get to the core of why you think you want to be a writer. Is it for fame and

fortune? Was your father a journalist and you have been raised to see yourself as one, too, but your affinity lies with veterinary medicine or auto mechanics? Do you enjoy attending book signings and readings and think you'd love to go on a book tour touting your latest novel? Do you see yourself on *Oprah*? Perhaps you "know" you could have done a better job on those last three mystery novels you've read?

Or do you genuinely believe you have a message or something of value to share with the world? Just remember, it is the *rare* writer who achieves any semblance of prominence and/or financial security through writing. There are probably more animals or automobiles that could benefit from your service; most writers detest book tours; you must have a product *before* you get on *Oprah;* as poorly written as you may think those mystery novels were, the writers sat down every day like stone masons and laid down word after word.

2. Make a commitment to yourself to write every day, at the same time of day, if possible, for a preordained amount of time— thirty minutes is fine. Just focus on writing one day at a time. Choose a topic that is nonthreatening to you. Write. Then plan out another week of writing time. Think only in terms of baby steps. You aren't committing to write the Great American Novel—yet. If this doesn't work, try that heart-to-heart I mentioned earlier.

3. Enter into a dialogue with your subject matter. Ask it questions. What interests you about this topic? What does it have to teach you?

4. Don't think about what it is to *be* a writer; think about what it is to *write*. And write.

⋰ ⋱

# I'VE JUST TURNED FIFTY. AM I TOO OLD TO START A CAREER IN WRITING?

> As you get older, you want to pull things
> together—put all the fragments into
> something like a novel.
> —HARRIET DOERR

As everyone knows, writing is a vocation that can be a lifelong praxis lasting until one's latest, if not last, years. But is it a prerequisite to begin the practice of writing at an early age? "Let everyone take heart from Harriet Doerr, who, at the age of seventy-three, has published her first novel," read the December 7, 1983, review by Anatole Broyard of Harriet Doerr's first novel, *Stones for Ibarra,* in the *New York Times Book Review.* Take heart, indeed. If we imagine having a second, third, or fourth act to our lives, Harriet Doerr—also the author of a another novel, *Consider This, Senora,* published in 1993, ten years after *Stones for Ibarra,* and of *The Tiger in the Grass: Stories and Other Inventions,* a combination of memoir and short fiction published in 1996—has lived them. Perhaps the most heartening aspect of this true story is that Harriet Doerr not only started writing at the age of sixty-seven, but that she successfully *published* her work as well. Broyard continues to compliment the first work by writing, "It's a very good novel with echoes of Gabriel García Marquez, Katherine Anne Porter and even Graham Greene." We should all be so fortunate to be compared to such stellar literary names.

In the early 1970s, Ms. Doerr, a native Californian, decided to return to college. As a young ingenue she had attended Smith College in 1928 for one year and had progressed to Stanford University a year later, but she never completed her undergraduate work. When she became a widow at the age of sixty-five, after forty-two years of marriage, Ms. Doerr returned to Stanford to complete her B.A. in European History. And, then, she began taking classes with John L'Heureux, Director, at the time, of Stanford's Creative Writing Program.

*Stones for Ibarra* is based on three stories, first published in literary magazines, about an American couple living in a small Mexican village (not in Provence!). Although Ms. Doerr and her husband had been such a couple themselves, she insists that the novel is not autobiographical. After she won an award for these stories, a scout from Viking publishers brought them to the attention of a senior editor, who felt that because they all involved the same people in the same place, the stories could be assembled into a cohesive novel. Writing shorter fiction seemed easier to Ms. Doerr than a full-fledged novel, but she received encouragement and support from her long-distance editor, who had no idea of Ms. Doerr's age.

After careers in painting and cooking, including owning and running an eponymous restaurant, I began to write just as I was about to enter my forties. I wrote about what I was personally experiencing, what was emotionally true for me at the time: my fear of aging and the trepidation I felt at the possibility of coming to the end of my life without having fully lived it. As I began to discuss the forties dilemma with other women, the idea for my first book, *On Women Turning 40: Coming Into Our Fullness*, began to develop. At first I thought, How can I write? I have no training, and besides, I'm too old to *begin* learning a new craft and art form. But as the days and weeks passed and I became a bit more confident of my vision, I made a commitment to the project. That commitment changed my life, and I marvel now at how I could *ever* have felt "too old" to try anything (except, perhaps, a career as a ballet dancer). And shortly after I turned forty, when I first learned of Harriet Doerr's work and the literary journey that began in her mid-sixties, my resolve to live fully and to attempt, and perhaps succeed, at new endeavors has become part of who I am.

About beginning to write at a later age, Harriet Doerr, then nearing ninety, said in an interview after the publication of her third book, "I don't necessarily feel wiser now. I don't think you ever get wiser. But maybe your insights become deeper. As you grow older, you do accumulate an awful lot of ideas and have a lot more to fish out of the pool."

*I didn't start writing until I was fifty.*

—DOMINICK DUNNE

*It's funny to be fifty-nine and busier than I was ten years ago. Before now I have never felt that I was a writer from the moment I get up until the moment I get into bed. I have never filled the day and the night with so much writing.*

—JOHN IRVING

*The Writer's Mentor Suggests . . .*

1. What's in your "pool" of memories? Where have you lived? Whom have you loved? Hated? Why? Have you traveled extensively or spent your entire life in one community? Who were your parents? Your children? What animals have you loved? What are you most ashamed of having done in your life? What do you most regret not having done? Go fishing in your own "pool."

2. Read Harriet Doerr's *Stones for Ibarra* to see how she first wrote stories and then compiled them into a novel.

❖  ❖

# DOES A DIFFICULT CHILDHOOD BENEFIT OR IMPEDE A WRITER'S WORK?

> For Christ sake write and don't worry what
> the boys will say nor whether it will be a
> masterpiece nor what. I write one page of
> masterpiece to ninety one pages of shit. I try
> to put the shit in the wastebasket. . . . Forget
> your personal tragedy. We are all bitched
> from the start and you especially have to be
> hurt like hell before you can write seriously.
> —*ERNEST HEMINGWAY,*
> *IN A LETTER TO F. SCOTT FITZGERALD*

> The loss of childhood is the beginning of poetry.
> —*ANDREI TARKOVSKI*

Writing is a way of connecting—with ourselves and with others. It is often because we *haven't* connected as children that we are driven to concretize our thoughts and feelings on paper. We have to make them real to ourselves before we can make them real to anyone else. When a child lacks any healthy form of mirroring, either from a parent or another caring adult, that child's sense of emptiness can be devastating. In her essay *A Room of One's Own Is Not Enough,* Joan Bolker writes, "A childhood or an education that fails to provide us with the sense that we have truly been heard makes it nearly impossible to write." I would say that it is *because* we have never been heard that we extend ourselves through writing. According to many writers, loneliness was the only constant in their lives as children. For those who as children developed elaborate fantasy lives, it is a natural extension as an adult to call the imagination home. For many writers, childhood is the source of everything.

Russell Banks talks about voices buzzing around in an "aural memory bank," which can be tapped into, similar to forgotten visual memories. He doesn't think there is a sharp difference between children and adults. "Who is to say that the inner life of a child is less complex or intelligent than the inner life of an adult?"

"Okay, okay, lighten up already. We *all* have our little horror stories," reads the caption of a cartoon by the inimitably dark Callahan. The image is of an analyst sitting in a chair facing away from the patient, who bears an unmistakable resemblance to the Mary Shelley character Frankenstein. Graham Greene once remarked that childhood is the writer's bank balance. As writers we are graced with a store of experiential fecundity waiting to be applied to stories, poems, and essays. Even if you consider yourself one of the "lucky" ones who enjoyed a relatively unscathed childhood, writing about your individual experiences can be a source of self-reflection and a way to communicate your perspective to other members of your family, if not the world at large.

Intermittently, I am working on a novel about one year in my life, from the age of seven to eight. I consider this to be the last year my psyche belonged to a child. It's the before and after. Living alone with my remarkably eccentric mother, that year—1955—was a series

*The best gift a writer can have is a horrible childhood.*
—PAT CONROY

of bizarre, if primarily harmless, happenings. I remember spending Thanksgiving at the local rescue mission, serving bread and soup to the indigent; watching Marilyn Monroe's skirt blow up around her waist in *The Seven Year Itch;* grieving the loss of my pet turtle, Crabby; crying when, after a sudden stop, a quart glass bottle of milk fell from the back window ledge of my grandfather's gray two-door Ford coupe and broke on my head. I also remember going regularly to Starr's ice cream parlor and getting a double scoop of my favorite peach ice cream. And I'll never forget the night my mother and one of her boyfriends took me to a midget wrestling match. These memories were part of a childhood that ended soon thereafter. And these rather offbeat experiences developed, if not a misfit, at least a taste for the unconventional.

Perhaps being an outsider is mandatory to the writing life. Lonely children develop powers of observation and an exceptional capacity for empathy that serve them well in later life. And learning to entertain yourself at a young age is a habit that dies hard. Writing becomes a way in which one reclaims the sense of personal autonomy denied at a young age.

### The Writer's Mentor Suggests . . .

1. Make a list of some of your most memorable childhood experiences—a mixture of both the toxic and tranquil. Then from each memory write a 1–2 page detailed account.

2. Read a few memoirs or novels based on a child's life and compare and contrast in writing your own life as a child . Some considerations are *The Liar's Club,* by Mary Karr; *This Boy's Life,* by Tobias Wolff; *Affliction,* by Russell Banks; *Autobiography of a Face,* by Lucy Grealy; *Bastard Out of Carolina,* by Dorothy Allison; *Lives of Girls and Women,* by Alice Munro; and *The Great Santini,* by Pat Conroy.

3. Make a preliminary outline of chronological childhood experiences as if you were going to write a childhood memoir and see where that takes you.

# WHEN WILL I BE ABLE TO QUIT MY JOB AND WRITE FULL TIME? WILL I EVER BE ABLE TO MAKE A LIVING AS A WRITER?

> The first job of a writer is to get a job.
> —*TONI MORRISON*

"Don't quit your day job" is a rule that holds firm at just about every level of writing, unless you are or your mate is independently wealthy or you've just won the lottery. Remember, even to win the lottery you must first buy a ticket. In a sense, your "day job" *is* that ticket, and you buy it day after day. In a wild writing workshop I took with novelist Tom Robbins in 1994, he wisely said that when students and beginning writers come to him and ask what kind of work they can do that will allow them time to write, he points them in the direction of a nursing career. He went on to clarify that a nurse works in a hospital, a place where life and death are active teachers. Every day a nurse is witness to any number of emergencies, tragedies, and miracles. This kind of throbbing environment can feed any imagination, but it is particularly fertile for a writer. I would add to nursing the professions of psychotherapy, teaching—anything, really, that deals with people and their emotional lives.

When I began writing my first book, the fantasy of a future when I could quit my "day job" held me fast in its grip, too. At that time, while living in Los Angeles, I was a professional cook working as a personal chef to luminaries such as investment banker Michael Milken (pre–junk bond disclosure), actors Melanie Griffith and Don Johnson (during their second go-round), and the Eagles' band member Glenn Frey. The work was quite lucrative and creative in its own way, and, most important, I enjoyed it. Still, there was a voice that insidiously stewed and slowly fermented inside me, saying, Fine, but you won't be a *real* writer, you know, until you give up cooking and write full time. That reverie ensconced itself in my attitude and flattened everything I did, cooking or otherwise. Eventually, the day came when, after my father's sudden death from a massive coronary and with a modest inheritance, I finally realized my dream to write full-time and quit my "day job". It's true, I was able to proudly say to whomever might inquire, "Yes, I do, I make my living as a writer." But during the following twelve years I struggled with the depression and stress caused at least partially by economic strain. My credit cards were charged to the max, and I needed a new car that I couldn't afford, and I had no savings or retirement, and I rented the house in which I lived. My father's money had been spent supplementing my dwindling advances and royalties "just until my ship comes in," I assured myself. Well, my ship was a ghostly galleon. Need I say it never arrived? What I did have, though, was plenty of hubris and debt. I slowly began to take my financial responsibility seriously, and along with it the sobering reality that I simply was no Amy Tan, or even Tom Clancy. The six-figure advances just weren't rolling in as I had planned.

In those early days, when I first began fantasizing about becoming a full-time writer, I arrogantly declared to a published friend and mentor that within five years I would be supporting myself as a writer. She looked at me with a mixture of pity and amusement and with an unforgettable laugh said, "*I* don't make my living from writing and I've been writing for *twenty-five* years." I was stunned, hurt, and, at the time, more than ever determined to prove her wrong. Five years came and went. I did prove her wrong, but unfortunately it came at an extreme cost to my peace of mind, body, and soul.

Most often people are eager to leave their jobs not because they want to *write* eight hours a day but because they wish to *stop* doing whatever type of work they have been doing. The important thing is to find some form of long-term employment, whether it be self-employment or work within a business or organization, that you enjoy doing—or at least don't loathe doing—and will continue to enjoy so that it will support your writing. It is also important to be mindful of a work schedule that will afford you the time to write. It serves a writer well to think in terms of her writing as a growing entity that cannot survive on its own.

*Chase your passion, not your pension.*

—EDWARD JAMES OLMOS

Even the exceedingly prolific Joyce Carol Oates and the Nobel Laureate Toni Morrison teach. I don't know for sure, but I suspect that, for them, it has less to do with financial remuneration than with doing something *other* than writing, something that gets them into the world among people and around ideas.

Support your art; don't expect it to support you.

## The Writer's Mentor Suggests . . .

Buy a book on careers such as *What Color Is Your Parachute?* or visit a career counselor to get advice on what variety of careers are available in your geographic area, and brainstorm about which ones best suit your interests and needs. You may want a position that offers health insurance and/or a retirement plan. (Don't laugh about the retirement plan. Now, past fifty, I fully expect, or at least hope, to die at the typewriter, so to speak. But taking stock of my financial "portfolio" now will determine whether, in older age, I continue to work so hard out of desire or out of economic necessity.)

❖   ❖

# How can i make a contribution with my writing?

It is the deepest desire of every writer, the
one we never admit or even dare to speak of:
to write a book we can leave as a legacy.
And although it is sometimes easy to
forget, wanting to be a writer is not
about reviews or advances or how many
copies are printed or sold.
—ALICE HOFFMAN

When I began writing *On Women Turning 40*, the notion of having it make some contribution to other women's lives was an unarticulated yet integral part of my overall motivation: to befriend forty, itself and everything it represents, and to cultivate a circle of intimate relationships with women of diverse backgrounds and experiences, all of whom have at least one thing in common—their age.

As the years sped by and my number of published books accumulated, reassuring friends, generous colleagues, and appreciative readers validated that the aggregate of the decade series—*On Women Turning 30: Making Choices, Finding Meaning; On Women Turning 40: Coming Into Our Fullness; On Women Turning 50: Celebrating Midlife Discoveries; On Women Turning 60: Embracing the Age of Fulfillment;* and *On Women Turning 70: Honoring the Voices of Wisdom*—had, indeed, made something of a contribution to the field of women's studies.

On reflection, however, making a contribution with my writing was not my primary purpose for writing. No, it was the doing—equally pleasure-filled and tormenting—the process of researching and writing and all that it reciprocated to me. But it is also quite wonderful to know that thousands of woman (and men) have read and benefited from my work. Both the passion for the work and a sense of contribution go hand in hand.

Don DeLillo says that during periods of writing he has no thoughts about his audience, but when he does think of his work out in the world in published form, he imagines it being read by "some stranger somewhere who doesn't have anyone around him to talk to about books and writing—maybe a would-be writer, maybe a little lonely, who depends on a certain kind of writing to make him feel more comfortable in the world."

In the end, it would seem, writing is in the service of communication. It is a way that humans have of connecting with one another, of communicating the ideas that are difficult or even impossible for most of us to say.

*You don't write because you want to say something; you write because you have something to say.*

—F. SCOTT FITZGERALD

### *The Writer's Mentor Suggests . . .*

What project are you currently working on? A series of poems?

A nonfiction book on self-help or history or cultural studies? A short story or a novel? Whatever it may be, ask yourself the following questions:

- Why am I writing this poem, story, study?
- Where do I want my work to go?
- Who is my audience?
- Does the content of my work have influential or lasting power?
- Will it add something of value to the world?

⁓ ⁓

# WHY DO WRITERS WRITE? WHAT ARE THE GOALS OF WRITING?

> Why do I write? The truth, the unvarnished
> truth, is that I haven't a clue. The answer to
> that question lies hidden in the same box
> that holds the origin of human creativity,
> our imperative need as a species to commu-
> nicate, and to be touched.
>
> —*GLORIA NAYLOR*

Writing is a form of thinking. If you listen to yourself and put your thoughts on paper, you will have a strong sense about how your mind works and organizes ideas. Thinking and writing are themselves matters of taking things apart and putting them together in new ways. When asked why he writes, Don DeLillo said that maybe he wanted to learn how to think. He claims not to know what he thinks about any given subject until he sits down and writes about it. The memory can only hold so many concepts or images until it surrenders to forgetfulness by way of overwhelm. Ideas accumulate and are too complex to be held in the mind all at once; it makes sense that

*Each of us is like a desert, and a literary work is like a cry from the desert, or like a pigeon let loose with a message in its claws, or like a bottle thrown into the sea. The point is: to be heard—even if by one single person.*

—FRANCOIS MAURIAC

*The role of the writer is not to say what we can all say, but what we are unable to say.*

—ANAÏS NIN

you can only get to those ideas through and by way of writing. Flannery O'Connor, too, said, "I write because I don't know what I think until I read what I say."

Writing is a method of self-definition, a way of placing yourself more clearly in the world, of separating yourself from other people, their feelings and desires, their perceptions and expectations. Through writing you find and define your own. Writing makes what you think and feel distinct from the thoughts and feelings of others.

Writing allows us to explore, comprehend, and integrate a previous experience, to relive it with the depth of mature understanding. In this way, writing is a form of self-therapy: the telling and retelling, the verbalization satisfies the compulsion to share our story with others. As in psychotherapy, the healing is in the telling. For Tennessee Williams, writing was his way of staving off his eventual "destruction." "I work hard these days. For me there is either success or destruction sooner or not so sooner and so I work."

Diane Ackerman called writing her "form of celebration and prayer [and] inquiry." Observing or commemorating experiences through your writing can bring deep satisfaction. Writing as a form of meditation, of mindfully being present in the moment, places you in a timeless reality; it connects you to the unseen forces that truly inhabit and guide your life. Probing, researching, and learning about new areas of interest is essential to most writers.

In an interview, Doris Lessing said, "I think a writer's job is to provoke questions. . . . Something that would start [people] thinking in a slightly different way." She believes that writers are "more sensitive to what's going on" because they spend their time thinking about "how things work, why things happen."

Aloneness in life is an existential given. Writing is a way of coping with and rationalizing the world. It also teaches you to be comfortable with solitude and to, if not enjoy, at least tolerate your own company and to be grateful for the deep emotional states that writing can induce.

In *Letters to a Young Poet*, Rainer Maria Rilke writes, "Ask yourself in the silent hours of your night: Must I write?" If you cannot *not* write, you have your answer.

*So why do I write, torturing myself to put it down? Because in spite of myself I've learned some things. Without the possibility of action, all knowledge comes to one labeled "file and forget," and I can neither file nor forget.*

—RALPH ELLISON

*Writing a book is always the fruit of, and testimony to, a possession. When we really write, we write to free ourselves from a matter at once explicit and obscure that began to possess us long before we noticed it.*

—ANTONIO MUÑOZ
MOLINA
(TRANSLATED BY
MICHAEL MCGAHA)

*The Writer's Mentor Suggests . . .*

1. Sit down with a pen and paper and ask yourself why you write. You probably write for a variety of reasons. There may be over-arching reasons as well as a specific rationale for every piece of writing or project you do. List those reasons.

   Do you write to

   - organize your thoughts for yourself?
   - share your story with others?
   - satisfy a compulsion?
   - earn a living as a writer?
   - fulfill a passion for putting words and ideas on paper?
   - generate a product to represent you in your profession?
   - dispense your expertise to a wider audience?
   - explore your psyche and foster contact with a form of inner guidance?
   - save your life?
   - explain yourself to others?
   - preserve an historic record?
   - clarify misunderstandings?
   - learn about new subjects?
   - give voice to inspiration?
   - create art?
   - connect with others?
   - stave off boredom?
   - experience pleasure?
   - find meaning in your life?

2. For each reason that you list, write a brief essay on how you previously have, presently do, or possibly can actualize this motive through your writing.

# The Writer's Mentor at the Movies
## My Brilliant Career

"This story is going to be all about me. Here is the story about my brilliant career," writes Sybylla Melvyn, a headstrong young woman, at the beginning of *My Brilliant Career*. The film was adapted from an autobiographical novel by Australian writer Miles Franklin and takes place in 1897 in the Australian Outback. In a voice-over we hear Sybylla's thoughts when she says she has always known that she belongs to the world of art and literature and music. We feel her longing to broaden her intellect and to develop her fledgling artistic capacity.

However, her dreams seem incongruous with her lot in life as the eldest of five or six siblings on a small impoverished farm. One of the characteristics needed by a writer is an ability to internalize and, when necessary, disregard the rest of the world. Sybylla does this superbly, especially when her family seems most in need of her physical assistance as they struggle against the elements—literally holding down the fort—during a drought-induced dust storm. She wants no part of the daily chores—cleaning the house, milking the cow, cooking the food, darning the socks—and while every other family member is attuned to their duty, she obliviously plays the piano.

Just when it seems that Sybylla will be turned over as a general servant to a wealthy family because her own parents can no longer afford to room and board her, she is rescued by a letter from her wealthy maternal grandmother inviting her to come and live with her. "Your family always had illusions of grandeur," Sybylla's father says rather accusingly to her mother. And once we see the refined environment in which she was brought up, we realize that long ago her mother, too, must have had a few exalted dreams of her own.

In her first starring role, a fresh Judy Davis is the epitome of a headstrong young woman who spurns the social expectations of turn-of-the-century Australia. Her broad, freckled face and unruly Gibson Girl–styled, tangerine-colored hair are a perfect metaphor for unconventionality and irreverence. Sybylla is a giant sunflower, loudly exclaiming her presence. And Davis' elemental energy and charisma ensure a remarkable performance.

Another characteristic necessary to the writer's life is a belief in one's own strengths and abilities. As if she had already been guaranteed of her future literary success, a skittish but confident Sybylla equally negotiates life's opportunities and reversals. Even when a nearly irresistible, wealthy, aristocratic bachelor, Harry Beecham (played by Sam Neill), enters her life and proposes marriage, this feisty could-be Cinderella cleaves ever more vigorously to her literary aspirations. She is determined to put passion on paper. "Give me a chance to find out what's wrong with the world . . . and me," Sybylla tells a disappointed but patient Harry. "Find out who I am. Then I'll marry you."

Instead of marriage, as a result of her parents' financial plight, Sybylla finds herself in conscription as a governess to another family whose living conditions are far worse than those at her own home. Tutoring a randy batch of offspring in an open-air, dilapidated shack, pigs and chickens wandering freely, Sybylla is beginning to see what's wrong with the world—and herself. After two years pass, Harry once again pursues this intelligent, independent, outspoken young woman. But as before, Sybylla declares passionately, "I want to be a writer. And I've got to do it now. And I've got to do it alone."

In the end, sometimes the most powerful ally a writer has is his or her own commitment to be a writer and, against severe odds, to continually make writing a life choice. The final scene of *My Brilliant Career* has Sybylla writing throughout the night to complete her first novel. Alone, she carries the wrapped manuscript—her only copy— to her postbox, and as she lets the first rays of the early morning sun graze her euphoric face, an endnote on the screen reads:

*My Brilliant Career* was published in 1901 in Edinburgh, Scotland.

# POSTSCRIPT

Words which are flowers become fruits
which are deeds. . . .
—OCTAVIO PAZ,
FROM "HYMN AMONG THE RUINS"

The highlight of the evening's events at the March 2001 Academy Awards ceremony was Stephen Soderbergh's acceptance speech for the Best Director Award for the film *Traffic*. But his words became less of a speech when he steered attention away from himself and graciously projected it back to the nearly one billion viewers that night, saying that he shared the Oscar with artists, writers, actors, dancers, and "anyone who spends part of their day creating," because "without art this world would be unlivable." When I heard those words a powerful emotion welled up in my throat. And even as I write them here, the feeling repeats itself and I realize that it has now become a memory in my body.

Later that year, in my graduate program, I took a course titled "Cultural Mythologies II," which was taught by Dr. Dennis Slattery. Our assigned reading was Dante's *Divina Commedia,* and my school's three-month-long quarter system offered a natural division of parts for the reading of the *Inferno, Purgatorio,* and *Paradiso.* On September 10, we spent six hours—a luxury afforded programs with daylong classes such as those at Pacifica Graduate Institute—discussing the *Inferno.*

When that membrane between art and life, fiction and reality, evaporates, as it seemingly did for many of us on September 11, one is stunned by the unexpected power of this psychological crossover. It has infinite dimension and feels something like opening the door to a room in your home and stepping into an M. C. Escher drawing in which hands draw themselves, stairways lead nowhere, and fish transmute into birds. I had spent much of the preceding day reflecting on an imagined Inferno, but on that morning I awakened to a living inferno.

My friend Madeleine, with whom I was staying in Ventura, bounded into my room at around 5:55 A.M. and, for an imperturbable Swedish national, conveyed an uncommon urgency. Even if one did not witness the carnage and destruction on television as it happened, the subsequent relentless replaying of the images—the airliners lunging into the mesh and glass belly of the World Trade Center, the violence of the incendiary eruption, the unthinkable avalanche of 110 floors, twice—have emblazoned them onto the world psyche. Oddly, or perhaps not so odd, on that unforgettable Tuesday my sense of reality shifted between Dante's thirteenth-century Inferno and our own twenty-first century inferno. And I was stunned by the relevance of this more-than-seven-hundred-year-old literary work of art.

Like most people I know, for weeks I was unable to work. After the unimaginable loss of life and the level of human suffering on the 11th, my attitude about pretty much everything, including being a writer, was, "So what . . . ? Who cares . . . ? What's the point?" In a writing class I taught at the UCLA Extension Writer's Program in mid-October, one of my students perfectly articulated this state when she said to the other students and me, "As a novice it's hard enough to keep my momentum up for writing, but now I feel totally incapacitated." Around that time, a stricken Joan Didion on the *Charlie Rose* show said, "I don't think any writer in America didn't feel the day it happened that everything they were working on was in some way irrelevant. And then you start finding ways in which to deepen your understanding of what you were doing—it's a new level."

On September 11, Steven Soderbergh's words, "Without art this world would be unlivable," took on an entirely new significance. At first I began to write in my journal—my thoughts, fears, anxieties—finding words to express each emotion I felt. It was through this process that I began to understand the true purpose for writing. It is—above all else—to develop a form of communion with our inner life. A way in which we know ourselves. What we think. What we feel. And by extension, it is how we communicate these thoughts and feelings to others. I began to see that there is more of an imperative for writing, indeed, for all the arts, than ever before. So I have moved from the "so what" stance to an "as if" perspective. I want to live as if—even with the horror we have known and continue to be threatened with—writing is worthwhile because it gives us to ourselves, and then to each other.

CATHLEEN ROUNTREE

APTOS, CALIFORNIA

NOVEMBER 11, 2001

# Acknowledgments

During the process of writing any book there are many circles of family, friends, colleagues, and, in this case, students who make countless contributions to the author. I wish here to express my deepest appreciation to all those who have been a part of my life during the writing of this book.

Ellen Levine, my literary agent and friend, goes beyond the call of duty in her Jack Russell persistence and tenacity in placing her clients' manuscripts. Her sense of fairness and loyalty to those she loves and represents is astounding and unfailing. Having Ellen stand before me as an advocate (and often behind me as a one-woman cheerleading squad) during my entire writing career has been a considerable gift and the one constant in an industry of continual upheavals and inevitable disappointments. Words can only suggest my profound appreciation for her. I often think that Ellen embodies the spirit of the legendary agent, Audrey Wood. I also thank the entire staff of the Ellen Levine Literary Agency, especially Louise Quayle and Diana Finch.

A special debt of gratitude goes to my editor at Conari, Leslie Berriman, who, in a spark of ingenuity, saw that my many years of mentoring and teaching writing had already laid the groundwork for *The Writer's Mentor*. During a personally trying year and a half of laboring this book into existence, her continued willingness to provide a galvanizing encouragement has truly made the completion of this book possible. After producing three books together and benefiting from her fine editing skills, perennial patience, and generous collaborative spirit, I have come to appreciate Leslie as a contemporary Maxwell Perkins.

A pleasure of working with a smaller publisher is getting to know everyone who puts so much effort into making your book fly. I, therefore, wish to acknowledge the entire staff at Conari Press, especially Brenda Knight, the "queen of sales," and her associates, Brian Reed and Don McIlraith; the book designer, Lisa Buckley, and the designer of the beautiful and original cover, Stephanie Dalton Cowan; the superb copy editor, Pam Suwinsky; the publicity manager, Leah Russell; publicist, Rosie Levy; events coordinator, Julie Kessler; production manager, Jenny Collins; and managing editor, Heather McArthur.

For more than ten years I have taught courses at the University of California-Santa Cruz, Extension. Throughout those years I have been fortunate to work with Judy Rose, the Director of Humanities and the Writing Program. Judy has always been eager for every new course I've designed—whether it be in writing, art, film studies, or women's studies—as well as for the tried and true courses. My gratitude for her trust in my judgment is beyond words. I also thank her generous and efficient co-workers at UCSC, Extension; Marlene Aza, Elizabeth Coble, and Kat Meads.

To Dr. Linda Venis, Program Director of the esteemed Writers' Program at the University of California-Los Angeles, Extension, I offer many thanks for her enthusiasm for my work and for hiring me to teach courses at UCLA, Extension. I also wish to acknowledge her attentive and professional staff, Kristin Petersen, Alyssa Pera, Cindy Lieberman, and Sabrina Sztain.

For four years the Pacifica Graduate Institute community—composed of its administration, staff, distinguished faculty, and fellow graduate students—has provided a rich environment for an unparalleled combination of academic study and personal development. I am grateful to everyone who has made this possible for me. In addition to each of my classmates in the Mythological Studies

Program, I especially wish to thank Edie Barrett, Dr. Patrick Mahaffey, Dr. Ginette Paris, Dr. Dennis Slattery, Dr. Christine Downing, Dr. Randi Gray-Kristensen, Dr. Daniel Noel, Dr. David Miller, Hendrika de Vries, Dr. Kathleen Jenks, Dr. Dawn George, Dr. Richard Tarnas, and the entire staff of the library and the bookstore.

I have been privileged to work with such interesting and intelligent clients in my Writer's Mentor business and students in both my university teaching and private writing groups. I have learned as much from them as, I hope, they have learned from me. I thank each of them.

Everyone needs a Computer God, and mine was Douglas Broyales, who performed miracles with the cyber-ignorant.

Several people have offered their support in a variety of ways; they are John Beebe, Alec Cast, Mark Chimsky, Kevin Connelley, Daniel Cook, Christiane Corbat, Mike De Boer, Nancy B. Frank, Ronnie Georges, Manuel and Laura Gomes, Janice Gordon, Fran and Kendall Larsen, Lisa Leeman, Marsea Marcus, Pat and Kate McAnaney, Leana and Carl Melat, Kate Minor, Pilar Montero, Ruth Morgan, Vicki Noble, Michael Park, Hope Rhode, Vicki Schot, Susanne and Ann Short, MaryAnn Soule, Dennis St. Peter, Karen St. Pierre, John Velcamp, Madeleine and Sandy Waddell, Nancy Wells, Char and Greg Wolf, and Michael and Diane Wright.

As this is a book about mentoring and writing, I feel compelled to mention some of the exceptional people I have been most fortunate to meet and, in many cases, been blessed to call friends. The following have been role models in living a life of integrity and/or mentors of creativity: Isabel Allende, Ruth Asawa, Nancy Ashley, Clair Braz-Valentine, Judy Chicago, Colette Dowling, Sylvia Earle, Riane Eisler, Leah Friedman, Natalie Goldberg, Lee Grant, Jane Goodall, Anna Halprin, Vijali Hamilton, Molly Haskell, Carolyn Heilbrun, Judith Hennessee, Amy Hertz, Bronwyn Jones, Coeleen Kiebert, Gwen Knight, Jacob Lawrence, Ursula LeGuin, Madeleine L'Engle, Linda Leonard, Doris Lessing, Mary Mackey, Mary Ellen Mark, Deena Metzger, Inge Morath, Ann Richards, Betye Saar, Terry Sendgraff, June Singer, Liz Smith, Gloria Steinem, Rose Styron, Hal and

Sidra Stone, Mary Travers, Fay Weldon, Terry Tempest Williams, Marion Woodman.

Dios Rountree is my round-the-clock companion, entertainer, and Muse. I am grateful for his infectious joy and for being the personification of devotion. Life would be much less interesting and eventful without him. During periods of travel, he is cared for by my friend Cathy Meehan, her children Christina and Danny, and their clan of Springer Spaniels: Harley, Lady, Tiana, Cocoa Puff, Sadie, and Amber. I thank all of them for providing an enjoyable and safe environment for "Don Dios."

There are five dear friends whose profound love and support deserve my deepest gratitude. My love and thanks go to Deanne Burke, Maurine Doerken, and Katherine Spilde for seeing me through the dark times; to Pat Zimmerman for her invariable good humor and rare generosity; and to Christian Wright for being my son, the sun.

# Books on Writing

*ANTHOLOGIES*

*Advice to Writers*, compiled by Jon Winokur

*Asian American Women Writers (Women Writers of English and Their Works)*, edited by Harold Bloom

*Black-Eyed Susans/Midnight Birds: Stories by and about Black Women*, edited by Mary Helen Washington

*Black Women Writers at Work*, edited by Claudia Tate

*Latina Self-Portraits: Interviews with Contemporary Women Writers*, edited by Juanita Heredia and Bridget A. Kevane

*To Live and Write: Selections by Japanese Women Writers*, edited by Yukiko Tanaka

*Walking on Alligators*, Susan Shaughnessy

*The Writer's Home Companion*, edited by Joan Bolker

*Writing Women's Worlds: Bedouin Stories*, Lila Abu-Lughod

*THE CREATIVE PROCESS AND IMAGINATION*

*Creative Characters*, Elisabeth Young-Bruehl

*Creators on Creating*, edited by Frank Barron, Alfonso Montuori, and Anthea Barron

*Narrative Design*, Madison Smart Bell

*The Poet at the Piano*, Michiko Kakutani

*Thinking Through Writing*, Susan R. Horton

*EDITING AND REWRITING*

*The First Five Pages*, Noah Lukeman

*A Piece of Work*, edited by Jay Woodruff

*Self-Editing for Fiction Writers*, Renni Browne and Dave King

*The New Journalism,* edited by Tom Wolfe and E. W. Johnson
*New Yorker's Life Stories,* edited by David Remnick
*On Writing Well,* William Zinsser
*Writing Creative Nonfiction,* edited by Philip Gerard and Carolyn Forche

### PHILOSOPHIZING ABOUT WRITING

*Becoming a Writer,* Dorothea Brande
*The Forest for the Trees,* Betsy Lerner
*If You Want to Write,* Brenda Ueland
*The Right to Write,* Julia Cameron
*Writing Down the Bones* and *Wild Mind,* Natalie Goldberg

### POETRY

*How to Read a Poem . . . and Start a Poetry Circle,* Molly Peacock
*Metaphors We Live By* and *More Than Cool Reason,* George Lakoff and Mark Johnson
*Poem Crazy,* Susan G. Wooldridge
*The Poet's Companion,* Kim Addonizio and Dorianne Laux
*The Rule of Metaphor,* Paul Ricoeur

### STYLE AND CRAFT

*The Art of Styling Sentences,* Marie L. Waddell, et al.
*The Deluxe Transitive Vampire,* Karen Elizabeth Gordon
*The Elements of Style,* Strunk and White
*Sin and Syntax,* Constance Hale

### WRITERS ON WRITING

*The Art of Writing,* Lu Chi
*Compared to What?,* Thomas Farber
*Henry Miller: On Writing,* Henry Miller
*Steering the Craft* and *Dancing at the Edge of the World,* Ursula K. LeGuin
*Working Days* and *Journal of a Novel,* John Steinbeck
*Writing a Woman's Life,* Carolyn Heilbrun
*The Writing Life* and *Living by Fiction,* Annie Dillard

### THE WRITING PROCESS

*The Courage to Write,* Ralph Keyes
*Finding Your Writer's Voice,* Thaisa Frank and Dorothy Wall
*On Writer's Block,* Victoria Nelson
*Word Painting,* Rebecca McClanahan
*Writing in Flow,* Susan K. Perry
*Writing with Power,* Peter Elbow

*The New Yorker Book of Literary Cartoons,* edited by Bob Mankoff
*Ways of Seeing* and *About Looking,* John Berger
*The Writer's Desk,* Jill Krementz

# Reference Works

*BOOKS*

*Acronyms, Initialisms, and Abbreviations Dictionary.* Ed. Pamela Dear. Detroit: Gale Group. Annual.

*The American Desk Encyclopedia.* Ed. Steve Luck. New York: Oxford University Press, 1998.

*The American Heritage Book of English Usage.* Boston: Houghton Mifflin, 1996.

Baker, Sheridan Warner. *The Practical Stylist with Readings and Handbook.* 8th ed. New York: Longman, 1997.

Bailey, Edward P., and Philip A. Powell. *The Practical Writer.* 7th ed. Stamford, Connecticut: Harcourt Brace, 1998.

*Bartlett's Familiar Quotations.* 16th ed. Ed. John Bartlett, Justin Kaplan. Boston: Little, Brown, 2001.

*Benet's Reader's Encyclopedia.* 4th ed. Ed. Bruce Murphy. New York: HarperCollins, 1996.

Bernstein, Theodore M. *The Careful Writer: A Modern Guide to English Usage.* New York: Athenaeum, 1977.

Carroll, David. *The Dictionary of Foreign Terms in the English Language.* New York: Dutton/Plume, 1973.

*The Chicago Manual of Style.* 14th ed. Chicago: University of Chicago Press, 1993.

*Companion to Literary Myths, Heroes and Archetypes.* Ed. Pierre Brunel. New York: Routledge, 1996.

*The Concise Columbia Encyclopedia.* 3rd ed. Ed. Paul Lagasse. New York: Columbia University Press, 1995.

*Dorland's Illustrated Medical Dictionary.* 29th ed. Philadelphia: Saunders, 2000.

*Facts in a Flash: A Research Guide for Writers.* Ed. Ellen Metter. Cincinnati: Writer's Digest Books, 1999.

Follett, Wilson. *Modern American Usage.* New York: Hill and Wang, 1998.

Fowler, H. W. *The New Fowler's Modern Usage.* 3rd ed. Ed. R. W. Burchfield. New York: Oxford University Press, 2000.

*Funk & Wagnalls Standard Dictionary of Folklore, Mythology, and Legend.* Ed. Maria Leach. New York: HarperCollins, 1984.

Glazier, Stephen. *Random House Webster's Word Menu.* Rev. ed. New York: Random House, 1998.

Graves, Robert, and Alan Hodge. *The Use and Abuse of the English Language.* 2nd ed. New York: Marlowe, 1995.

Greenbaum, Sidney. *The Oxford English Grammar.* New York: Oxford University Press, 1996.

Hirsch, E. D., Jr., Joseph F. Kett, James Trefil. *The Dictionary of Cultural Literacy.* 2nd ed. Boston: Houghton Mifflin, 1993.

*International Who's Who.* London: Europa Publications. Annual.

*McGraw-Hill Dictionary of Scientific and Technical Terms.* 5th ed. Ed. Sybil P. Parker. New York: McGraw-Hill, 1994.

*Merriam-Webster's Biographical Dictionary.* Rev. ed. Springfield, Mass.: Merriam-Webster, 1995.

*Merriam-Webster's Dictionary of English Usage.* Rev. ed. Springfield, Mass.: Merriam-Webster, 1993.

*Merriam-Webster's Encyclopedia of Literature.* Springfield, Mass.: Merriam-Webster, 1995.

*Merriam-Webster's Geographical Dictionary.* 3rd ed. Springfield, Mass.: Merriam-Webster, 1997.

*The New Encyclopedia Britannica.* 32 vols. Chicago: Encyclopedia Britannica. Updated annually.

*The New York Public Library Desk Reference.* 2nd ed. New York: Hungry Minds, 1993.

*The Original Roget's International Thesaurus.* 5th ed. Ed. Robert L. Chapman. New York: HarperCollins, 1992.

*The Oxford Companion to English Literature.* 6th ed. Ed. Margaret Drabble. New York: Oxford University Press, 2000.

*The Oxford Companion to Philosophy.* Ed. Ted Honderich. New York: Oxford University Press, 1995.

*The Oxford Dictionary of English Etymology.* Ed. C. T. Onions. New York: Oxford University Press, 1972.

*The Oxford Illustrated Encyclopedia.* Ed. Harry Dudge. New York: Oxford University Press, 1993.

*The Oxford Thesaurus.* American ed. Ed. Laurence Urdang. New York: Oxford University Press, 1992.

*The Random House Dictionary of the English Language.* 2nd ed. unabridged. New York: Random House, 1987.

*The Random House Encyclopedia.* Rev. 3rd ed. New York: Random House, 1990.

Strunk, William, Jr., and E. B. White. *The Elements of Style.* 4th ed. Boston: Allyn & Bacon, 1999.

*Webster's Third New International Dictionary.* Springfield, Mass.: Merriam-Webster, 2000.

*Who's Who in America.* Chicago: Marquis. Annual.

*World Almanac and Book of Facts.* New York: World Almanac Education. Annual.

## ONLINE REFERENCE SOURCES

*Bartlett's Familiar Quotations*
    www.bartleby.com/99

Cliche finder
    www.westegg.com/cliche

*Oxford English Dictionary*
    www.oed.com

The Quotations Page
    www.starlingtech.com/quotes

*Roget's Online Thesaurus*
    www.thesaurus.com

Rhyming dictionary
    www.WriteExpress.com/online.html

Webster's hypertext dictionary
    http://m-w.com/netdict.htm

Wilton's Etymology Page
    www.wilton.net/etymo.htm

Word play
    www.wordwithyou.com

# Web Sites

A+ Research & Writing Tips
   www.aci-plus.com/tips
Academy of American Poets
   www.tmn.com/Artswire/poets/page.html
All-in-One Search Page
   www.allonesearch.com
Amazon
   www.amazon.com
American Booksellers Association
   www.ambook.org
American Society of Journalists and Authors, Inc.
   E-mail: 75227.1650@compuserve.com
Articles about Writing
   www.sfwa.org/writing/writing.htm
Asian American Writer's Workshop
   www.panix.com/~aaww
Association of Authors Representatives, Inc.
   www.aar-online.org
The Authors Guild, Inc.
   E-mail: staff@authorsguild.org
Author Web Sites
   www.geocities.com/~bookbug/home.html
Biography Resource Center
   www.galegroup.com

Bookwire
    Links to author Web sites and author appearances
    www.bookwire.com
Book Zone
    Home pages of more than 600 publishers
    www.bookzone.com
bricolage writer's e-zine
    http://bel.avonibp.co.uk/bricolage/bricolage.html
California Writers Club
    E-mail: studio@crl.com
Canadian Authors Association
    www.islandnet.com/~caa/national.html
Castle Aphrodesia
    Resources for writers of medieval romantic fiction
    www.ceridwyn.com/aphrodesia
Chapter One
    First chapters of hundreds of books
    www.psi.com/ChapterOne/#ChapterOne
Children's Literature Web Guide
    www.ucalgary.ca/~dkbrown/index.html
The Children's Writing Resource Center
    For writers of juvenile topics
    www.mindspring.com/~cbi
Copywriters Council of America, Freelance
    E-mail: CCA4DMCOPY@aol.com
Crimewriters.com
    www.hollywoodnetwork.com/Crime
Cyberink Press Resource Center
    References and resources for self-publishers
    www.cyberinkpress.com/link1.htm
Editor & Publisher
    Links to major online newspapers and research information
    www.mediainfo.com
Editorial Freelance Association
    www.the-efa.org
Education Writers Association
    E-mail: ewaoffice@aol.com
E-mail Discussion Lists
    www.delphi.com/navnet/faq/mlistsq.html

Facts for Fiction
    www.factsforfiction.com
Fiction Links
    www.writerspage.com/write/masterlink
Finding Expert
    www.askanexpert.com
Freelance Online
    www.FreelanceOnline.com/faqs.html
Guide to Writers Conferences
    www.Shawguides.com
Historic Events and Birth-Dates
    www.scopesys.com/today
Hollywood Writers Network
    http://screenwriters.com
Horror Writers Association
    www.horror.org/hwa
Information Please
    Capsule biographies
    www.infoplease.com
Inkspot Writer's Forum
    www.inkspot.com/~ohi/inkspot/home.html
Inscriptions
    Extensive listing of contests for writers
    www.come.to/Inscriptions
International Association of Business Communicators
    www.iabc.com
International Association of Crime Writers, Inc., North American Branch
    E-mail: mfrisque@igc.apc.org
International Women's Writing Guild
    www.iwwg.com
Internet Sleuth
    www.isleuth.com
Internet Tools for the Advanced Searcher
    www.philib.com/adint.htm
Internet Writing Journal
    www.writerswrite.com/journal
InterZone
    Science fiction
    www.clark.net/pub/iz/Books/books.html

Journalist's One-Stop
  http://ksgwww.harvard.edu./~ksgpress/ksgnews.htm
Learn 2
  www.learn2.com
Library of Congress
  www.loc.gov
Literary Market Place
  www.literarymarketplace.com
Lyrics World
  www.summer.com.br/~pfilho
Media List
  www.webcom.com/~leavitt/medialist.html
Mystery Writers of America, Inc.
  www.mysterywriters.net
Mystery Writer's Resources
  www.zott.com/mysforum/default.html
My Virtual Reference Desk
  www.refdesk.com/facts.html
National Writer's Monthly
  www.writersmarket.com
National Writers Union
  www.nwu.org/nwu
New Dramatists
  www.itp.tsoa.nyu.edu/~diana/ndintro.html
Newspapers.com
  www.newspapers.com
NovelAdvice
  www.noveladvice.com
Novice Writer's Guide to Rights
  www.writerswrite.com/journal/dec97/cew3.htm
Online Learning
  www.onlinelearning.net/w99 (UCLA)
Overbooked
  Genre resources, including book links, author links, writing links, etc.
  www.overbooked.org/bklink.html
The Poetry Resource
  www.pmpoetry.com
Poets & Writers Inc.
  E-mail: PWSubs@aol.com

*Publishers Weekly*
    www.publishersweekly.com
Publishing Law
    http://publaw.com/articles.html
Publishing: Statistics and Research
    http://publishing.miningco.com/msub21.htm
The Reporters Network
    www.reporters.net
Romance Novel Database
    www.personal.sl.umich.edu/~sooty/romance
Romance Writers of America
    www.rwanational.com
Say It Better
    Writers' newsletter
    www.sayitbetter.com
Science Fiction and Fantasy Writers of America, Inc.
    www.sfwa.org
Society for Technical Communication
    http://stc.org
Society of American Business Editors and Writers
    www.missouri.edu/~sabew
Society of Children's Book Writers and Illustrators
    www.scbwi.org
Society of Professional Journalists
    www.spj.org
Tips for Writers
    www.tipsforwriters.com
TitleNet
    Search for title information
    www.titlenet.com
UCLA, Writing Classes
    www.onlinelearning.net/w99
University of Kansas, History Page
    http://history.cc.ukans.edu/history/WWW_history_main.html
U.S. Copyright Office
    http://lcweb.loc.gov/copyright
The Virtual Press
    Writers can promote their work here
    http://tvp.com

Western Writers of America
    www.imt.net/~gedison/wwa.html
Word Play
    www.wordwithyou.com
Write Express
    Rhyming dictionary for poetry
    www.WriteExpress.com/online.html
The Write Page
    Newsletter for genre fiction
    www.writepage.com
Writer
    http://web.mit.edu/mbarker/www/writers.html
*Writer's Digest* Books
*Writer's Digest* Magazine
    www.writersdigest.com
The Writer's Edge
    Information on the writing industry
    www.nashville.net/~edge
Writers' Groups and Organizations
    www.forwriters.com/groups.html
Writers Guild of America West
    www.wga.org
Writer's Internet Exchange
    www.writelinks.com/write/index.html
Writers Net
    Directory of literary agents and published writers
    www.writers.net
Writers On Line
    www.novalearn.com/wol
Writers On the Net
    www.writers.com
The Writer's Place
    www.awoc.com/AWOC-Home.cfm
Writer's Resources
    www.inkspot.com
The Writer's Resources
    www.interlog.com/~ohi/www/writesource.html
The Writers' Union of Canada
    www.swifty.com/twuc

Writing Contest Tips
www.ult-media.com/tips1.htm
Writing for the Web
www.electric-pages.com/articles/wftw1.htm
WritingSchool.com
www.WritingSchool.com
Xlibris
"Books on demand"
www.xlibris.com/html/publishing_your_book.html
Zeno's Forensic Page
users.bart.nl/~geradts/forensic.html

# Index

demographics, audience, 105
Deneuve, Catherine, 42
descriptive writing
    exercises for improving, 186–188
desk(s)
    and other writing receptacles, 46
    writing hours at, 66
despair, 209
dialogue, 218
diaries. *See also* journals
    as best friend, 136
    books on, 50, 84, 242
    of Nin, Anaïs, 74
Dickens, Charles, 207
Dickinson, Emily, 176
dictionaries, 183, 184
Didion, Joan, 234
Dietrich, Marlene, 24
Dillard, Annie, 30, 120
discouragement
    overcoming, 152–154
dissertations
    books about writing, 71
*Divine Comedy* (Dante), 16
Doerr, Harriet, 219–221
D'Onofrio, Vincent, 210
Dostoyevsky, Fyodor, 151
Dove, Rita, 46
Dowling, Colette, 4
drafts, 189, 191, 200
dream(s), 31–33
    as creative nourishment, 32
    Styron, William on, 32
    writing problems and, 33
driving
    brainstorming and, 17, 19
Dunne, Dominick, 161
Duvall, Shelley, 155

Eagles, The, 224
Eastwood, Clint, 17
editing, 64–65, 105, 130, 189
    books on, 50, 190, 241
    of ideas, 86
    step-by-step process for, 190–191

editors, 6, 7, 85, 200, 202, 207, 220
    professional, 202–203
Einstein, Albert, 17
Eisler, Riane, 4
Ellison, Ralph, 107
    on dreams, 33
e-mail. *See also* computers
    vocabulary-building lists, 184
    writing and, 95, 111–114
emotion(s), 197
    art and, 25
    journals and, 136
    relaxation in, 132–133
emulation
    of writers, 29–30
*Encyclopedia Britannica*, 183, 184
*English Patient, The* (Ondaatje), 100
environment, 9. *See also* rooms
    desks, 46
    rooms and sanctuaries, 39, 41–44
Escher, M. C., 234
*Esquire*, 4
essays, 99, 102, 104
    books on, 53, 242
    nonfiction, 100–101
excuses, 127
experience
    connection between imagination and, 25

failure
    in writing, 205–208
fame, 216, 217–218
Faulkner, William, 179
fear, 135, 146, 209, 235
    of bad writing, 181
    critic's and, 163
    in writing, 9, 128, 139, 141
    writing and overcoming, 142–144
feelings, 8, 222, 229
fiction, 24, 66, 101
    books on writing, 51, 242
    descriptive writing and, 185
    different genres in, 102
    exercises for descriptive writing, 186–
        188

instincts, 5, 83, 163, 185
intention, 133, 177
internal wrestling, 7
Internet. *See also* computers; Web sites
    writing and, 111–114
interruptions
    writing and, 125–128
interview(s)
    books on, 53, 242
    yourself, 89
intuition, 83, 163, 185
*Invisible Man, The* (Ellison), 33
Irving, John, 19, 97

Jackson, Holbrook
James, Henry, 99, 201
*Jerry Maquire,* 210
Johnson, Don, 224
Jones, James, 4
journal(s), 66, 105, 124, 148, 235
    benefits of keeping, 154
    best books on, 50, 242
    implement for self-reflection, 136
    memories in, 27
    Nin, Anaïs, 73
    writer's block and, 161, 162
*Joy Luck Club, The* (Tan), 32
Joyce, James, 42, 178
judgment, 164
Jung, Carl
    on "the collective unconscious," 21, 22
*Justine* (de Sade), 91

*Kansas City Star,* 178
Kaufman, Philip, 90
Keaton, Buston, 42
Kennedy, John F., Jr., 24
Keyes, Ralph, 143
*Killshot* (Leonard), 29
King, Stephen, 19, 97, 141, 148, 154, 155, 216
Kingston, Maxine Hong, 4
Korda, Michael, 80
Kramer, Jane, 100
Krementz, Jill, 41, 46

Kubrick, Stanley, 141, 154
Kusturica, Emir, 23

language, 27, 31, 100, 109, 177, 190, 193
    importance of words and, 181–184
    of text and time, 71
*Latcho Drom,* 23
Laughlin, James, 153
Lawrence, D. H., 73
Le Carré, John
    on formation of novels, 26
LeGuin, Ursula, 4, 42, 53
Lehman-Haupt, Christopher, 4
L'Engle, Madeleine, 4, 148, 161
Leonard, Elmore, 15
    on imitating/emulating, 29–30
Lerner, Betsy, 80
Lessing, Doris, 4, 42, 176–177, 229
*Letters to a Young Poet* (Rilke), 229
Levin, Arnie, 22
*Liar's Club, The* (Karr), 223
libraries, 48, 55, 99, 198
    proving out topics at, 105–106
life
    complications and interruptions of, 125–128
    importance of other activities in, 203–205
    inner, 235
    optimism in, 168
    as a writer, 215, 224–226
    writing, 11
    writing as saving, 135
*Light in August* (Faulkner), 179
listener
    becoming a good, 20, 27
    and inner self, 163
listmaking, 184
*Lives of Girls and Women* (Munro), 223
London, Jack, 21, 23
loneliness, 197, 229
    childhood, 222–223
    of writing, 10, 197, 198–200
Lowry, Beverly, 95, 108
*Lying Awake* (Salzman), 204

# About the Author

Cathleen Rountree, a seventh-generation Californian, is a writer, visual artist and photographer, educator and lecturer, cultural mythologist, film historian and scholar, and writing consultant and mentor. She is the author of eight books, including the celebrated decade series *On Women Turning 30: Making Choices, Finding Meaning; On Women Turning 40: Coming Into Our Fullness; On Women Turning 50: Celebrating Midlife Discoveries; On Women Turning 60: Embracing the Age of Fulfillment;* and *On Women Turning 70: Honoring the Voices of Wisdom.* She is also the author of *The Heart of Marriage: Discovering the Secrets of Enduring Love,* and *50 Ways to Meet Your Lover.* Currently she is writing a book about the transformative nature of movies and how to use them in your daily life.

Rountree lectures widely on a broad range of topics, from creative writing to film studies and appreciation, from visual arts to mythological studies, from women's studies to personal development. She has taught for more than ten years at the University of California, Santa Cruz, Extension, and teaches at the esteemed Writers' Program at the University of California-Los Angeles, Extension. She is also Adjunct Professor at John F. Kennedy University.

At the University of California, Berkeley, she initially studied Comparative Literature and Psychology; received a B.F.A. in Practice of Fine Art, Painting, and Art History; and became a candidate in Berkeley's M.F.A. program. In 1999 she received an M.A. in Mythological Studies and Depth Psychology at Pacifica Graduate Institute, where she is currently a Ph.D.

candidate. Her dissertation is on the confluence of cinema and psychology in the twentieth century.

She lives in a seaside village in Northern California with Dios, her Springer Spaniel companion and Muse.

She may be contacted at *www.cathleenrountree.com.*

# Contacting Cathleen Rountree, the Writer's Mentor

Cathleen Rountree has served as coach, consultant, teacher, and mentor to thousands of aspiring and established writers. Her Writer's Mentor service offers professional guidance and support at every level of craft and in most modes of expression.

The Writer's Mentor service will help you:

- Rewrite and Develop Projects
- Find Your Voice
- Organize Material
- Develop Clarity and Focus
- Make Writing a Practice
- Learn the Business of Being a Writer
- Explore Metaphor, Detail, and Specificity
- Write for Publication
- Tame the Inner Critic
- Release Writer's Block
- Write Proposals and Outlines
- Tap into a Flow of Creativity
- Structure Time and Meet Deadlines
- Enhance Memoirs and Family Oral Histories

Rountree lectures widely and presents seminars and workshops based on the material in this book at universities, writers' conferences, and writers' groups. To learn more about her Writer's Mentor coaching and consulting service, ongoing writing groups, and upcoming teaching and lecturing schedule, or to subscribe to her free E-mail monthly newsletter, *The Writer's Mentor Suggests . . .* , please visit her Web site at *www.cathleenrountree.com*.

# To Our Readers

Conari Press publishes books on topics ranging from spirituality, personal growth, and relationships to women's issues, parenting, and social issues. Our mission is to publish quality books that will make a difference in people's lives—how we feel about ourselves and how we relate to one another. We value integrity, compassion, and receptivity, both in the books we publish and in the way we do business.

As a member of the community, we donate our damaged books to nonprofit organizations, dedicate a portion of our proceeds from certain books to charitable causes, and continually look for new ways to use natural resources as wisely as possible.

Our readers are our most important resource, and we value your input, suggestions, and ideas about what you would like to see published. Please feel free to contact us, to request our latest book catalog, or to be added to our mailing list.

2550 Ninth Street, Suite 101
Berkeley, California 94710-2551
800-685-9595 • 510-649-7175
fax: 510-649-7190 • e-mail: conari@conari.com
http://www.conari.com